Education for
Upward Mobility

Education for Upward Mobility

Edited by Michael J. Petrilli

ROWMAN & LITTLEFIELD
Lanham • Boulder • New York • London

Published by Rowman & Littlefield
A wholly owned subsidiary of The Rowman & Littlefield Publishing Group, Inc.
4501 Forbes Boulevard, Suite 200, Lanham, Maryland 20706
www.rowman.com

Unit A, Whitacre Mews, 26-34 Stannary Street, London SE11 4AB

British Library Cataloguing in Publication Information Available

Library of Congress Cataloging-in-Publication Data Available

ISBN 978-1-4758-1975-5 (hardcover)
ISBN 978-1-4758-1976-2 (paperback)
ISBN 978-1-4758-1977-9 (e-book)

♾™ The paper used in this publication meets the minimum requirements of American National Standard for Information Sciences—Permanence of Paper for Printed Library Materials, ANSI/NISO Z39.48-1992.

Printed in the United States of America

Contents

Introduction

Michael J. Petrilli

This book seeks answers to a fundamental question, perhaps one of the most important questions in America today: How can we help children born into poverty transcend their disadvantages and enter the middle class as adults? And in particular, what role can our schools play?

Its animating idea—that excellent schools can be engines of upward mobility—is nothing new. When President Lyndon B. Johnson signed the Elementary and Secondary Education Act in 1965, he remarked, "As a son of a tenant farmer, I know that education is the only valid passport from poverty."

What *is* new is the nagging concern that social mobility in the United States has stalled. As conservative scholar Peter Wehner wrote recently, "Two-thirds of Americans believe that it will be harder for them to achieve the American Dream than it was for their parents, and three-quarters believe that it will be harder still for their children and grandchildren to do the same." And sure enough, the numbers are sobering, particularly for the poorest among us. Richard Reeves of the Brookings Institution explains, "Children born on the bottom rung have a four-in-ten chance of remaining stuck there in adulthood."

There's little doubt that education and opportunity are tightly joined in the twenty-first-century economy. Almost every week brings a new study demonstrating that highly skilled workers are rewarded with stronger pay and excellent working conditions, while Americans with few skills are struggling to keep work.

Expanding educational achievement, then, appears to be a clear route to expanding economic opportunity. Yet much of our public discourse ends there. Of course more young Americans need better education in order to succeed. But what kind of education, and to what end? Is the goal "college for all"? What do we mean by "college"? Is that too narrow an objective? How realistic is it? Do our young people mostly need a strong foundation in academics? What about so-called "noncognitive" skills? Should technical education make a comeback? How about apprenticeships? Can we learn from the military's success in working with disadvantaged youth?

Finding better answers to these questions is critically important if we want to make headway in interrupting intergenerational poverty. Particularly for the education reform movement, it's not enough to commit ourselves to "improving schools for the poor" or, in the anodyne language popular in some corners, "increasing the number of quality seats" in our cities. What kinds of schools? What kind of "seats"? With which destinations in mind?

Finding better answers to those questions is the purpose of this book. It is meant to provide fresh perspectives and concrete ideas for policymakers at every level of government: for leaders and policy analysts in education reform organizations in the states and in Washington, for philanthropists and membership associations, and for local superintendents and school board members.

RETHINKING EDUCATION REFORM'S "THEORY OF ACTION"

The genesis of this book was a nagging, suspicious feeling that we in the education reform movement might be overly focused on college as *the* pathway to the middle class and not focused enough on all of the other possible on-ramps (or off-ramps, for that matter).

We can be forgiven for doing so. We all see the widening gap between the highly educated and the poorly educated—gaps mirrored in income inequality, but also in family formation, civic participation, health, and even happiness.

So we conclude that we need to get dramatically more young people—and especially low-income young people—into and through higher education. That gets us off and running on today's reform agenda, starting with rigorous preschools; higher standards for grades K–12; effective teachers; no excuses, college-prep charter schools; and intensive efforts to help first-generation college students succeed. Most of the focus is on academics—especially reading and math—though we share a growing interest in "noncognitive skills," particularly the traits that will help students persist in high school and in postsecondary education.

Some of us will acknowledge that other supports along the way are helpful—from health clinics in schools to classes for parents to wage supports and more. But the goal remains the same: upward mobility via excellent education, from pre-K through college.

But what if, by putting all of our focus on preparing students for college, we're overlooking other issues that matter just as much, like decisions around parenting and a strong work ethic, or the acquisition of useful workplace skills while in high school? What if, by spending all of our efforts trying to boost the proportion of low-income students who are making it to and through four-year degrees from 10 or 15 percent to 20 or 25 percent, we're ignoring the needs of everyone else?

The purpose of this book is to start an honest conversation about these issues and more, one that finds a middle ground between the utopianism that characterizes so much of the reform movement (let's get every child college- and career-ready!) and the defeatism that emanates from too many corners of the education system (there's nothing we can do until we end poverty!).

CAN SCHOOLS DO IT ALONE?

It's worth pausing on that last point—*can* schools do anything in the face of poverty? Many reform critics on the left argue that it's unfair and naïve to expect schools to do much to address intergenerational mobility unless we're willing to adopt a "broader and bolder" strategy that includes lots of out-of-school antipoverty strategies too. And certainly many education and antipoverty scholars, such as Richard Murnane and Greg Duncan, co-authors of *Restoring Opportunity: The Crisis of Inequality and the Challenge for American Education,* embrace a more comprehensive approach.

Nobody denies that poverty is strongly correlated to low student achievement and high dropout rates; reformers, though, believe that great schools can weaken the relationship between students' socioeconomic status and outcomes; they can also point to examples (like the Knowledge Is Power Program network of charter schools) where this has been done.

Nor do many people disagree that factors outside of schools' control can impact how students perform. There's little doubt that our schools would achieve better results if fewer students grew up poor or in fragile, single-parent homes.

Poverty and fragmented families create enormous challenges for our schools. First, poor students tend to enter school (even preschool) with severe disadvantages. They tend to have very small vocabularies compared with their middle-class peers; they tend to struggle with so-called noncognitive skills such as "executive function"; and they tend to bring greater health issues, such as asthma or lead poisoning.

Once in school, their difficult home environments create continuing challenges. Their parents, who tend to be poorly educated and stretched thin, are not as capable of helping them with homework; they don't enjoy the same enrichment and tutoring opportunities as their more affluent peers; and they tend to lack calm, appropriate spaces to study.

So it's easy to empathize with high-poverty schools and the challenges they face. But a separate question is whether most such schools are doing all they can to help children succeed despite these challenges. This is the question that lies at the heart of the school reform debate now raging nationwide.

Personally, I find parts of the "broader/bolder" agenda compelling. We can't ignore, for instance, the fact that many low-income children bring mental health challenges to school with them, thanks to the extreme stress and frequent trauma they experience in their daily lives. Ensuring that they have access to high-quality mental health services is essential if we want to alleviate their suffering and help them focus on their schoolwork. Similar arguments can be made for programs dealing with nutrition, dental care, and other social services.

And no, schools can't "fix" poverty by themselves. Many other efforts are needed, including prison reform, more generous tax credits for the poor, and regulatory reform to eliminate the red tape keeping many low-income individuals from starting new businesses.

Still, this book is going to focus on what schools *can* do. Partly that's because of its audience: people like me, who spend their days thinking about how to improve our education system or, better yet, who are actually *doing* it. We all have our views on broader antipoverty efforts, but we generally don't have much sway over them. So we need to focus on what's within our locus of control.

And partly it's because, as we will see, most schools could be doing much more than they are doing today to encourage upward mobility. Maybe someday we will declare that schools are doing all they can to help poor children climb the ladder to the middle class, and we'll move on to out-of-school issues. But that day is far away.

OUTLINE

With inspiration from Steven Covey, this volume starts with the end in mind—a clear understanding of what it takes for young people to escape poverty and climb the ladder to the middle class. The book begins with the critical years between the ages of eighteen and twenty-four—when young people are finishing their educations, starting their careers, serving in the military, or, in the words of MacArthur Genius Roland Fryer, "doing stupid shit." Preparing students to take advantage of opportunities and avoid damaging detours during those formative years is a core mission for our education system. It's important, then, to understand the common pathways out of poverty, the role of higher education of various stripes, and the significance of the "success sequence."

Then, once our destination is clear, we can turn to the question of the journey. Taking a life-cycle approach, our chapters will examine best practices in poverty-fighting schools from pre-K to twelfth grade—including a "multiple pathways" approach at the high school level.

Part I: Transcending Poverty through Education, Work, and Personal Responsibility

Part I looks at the tenets of upward mobility, as well as the social and economic forces that complicate and inform educational interventions. These chapters are particularly enlightening for educators and education policy analysts who may be unfamiliar with the antipoverty and higher education literature.

• Chapter 1: Education and the "Success Sequence" (Ron Haskins, Brookings Institution)

Several years ago, using Census Bureau data representative of the US population, Haskins and his colleagues analyzed the probability that individuals would live in poverty or have a middle-class income given how many of three norms of personal responsibility they had followed. Those three behavioral norms were whether the person obtained a high school degree, whether the person worked full time that year, and whether the person had waited until the age of twenty-one and was married before having children. They then calculated the probabilities of being in poverty and being in the middle class for various groups as defined by the number of norms that the groups followed in their personal lives.

The results showed that those who violated all three norms had a 76 percent chance of living in poverty and a 7 percent chance of being in the middle class in a given year. By contrast, those who followed all three norms had a 2 percent chance of living in poverty and a 74 percent chance of reaching the middle class. Thus, those who followed what might be called the "success sequence" of finishing at least high school, working, and waiting until turning twenty-one and marrying before having children were highly unlikely to live in poverty and had a very good chance of entering the middle class.

While these correlations do not prove causation, there is abundant evidence—much of it from studies whose designs do permit causal conclusions—that increasing education, work, and marriage would reduce poverty rates and increase income. In this chapter, Haskins contemplates what schools can do to increase years of education, increase work rates, and prepare adolescents for responsible behavior regarding their choices on family formation. Areas explored include high-quality career and technical education (especially career academies), teenage pregnancy prevention programs, and the question of whether low-skilled, low-wage work really is a dead-end proposition. Haskins concludes that college need not be the only pathway to the middle class—work and personal responsibility can be, too.

- **Chapter 2: Big Payoff, Low Probability: Postsecondary Education and Economic Mobility in America (Andrew Kelly, American Enterprise Institute)**

How is it that rising educational attainment and increased access to college have not made a dent in economic mobility? In this chapter, Kelly argues that the problem lies in the disconnect between the payoff to a college degree—which is big, on average—and the number of disadvantaged Americans who actually make it that far—which is small. College does have a large effect on one's chances of moving up, but those benefits only accrue to those who actually finish a degree. The most recent data suggest that, on average, college dropouts are no better off than those who never go at all. Moreover, the big payoff we hear so much about is only an average; a nontrivial proportion of graduates actually do no better than their peers who were educated only through high school.

Put simply, for far too many disadvantaged high school graduates, access to college is a dead end rather than an on-ramp to the middle class. Low-income students are underrepresented at every stage of the college-going process, from aspirations and college readiness to enrollment and completion. Many disadvantaged students who graduate high school are not ready for college, yet all of them are eligible to enroll in college and access federal financial aid. But the vast majority wind up in remedial courses they are unlikely to pass. Most of those on the margin ship off to low-quality institutions that graduate few students and leave them with little but debt and regret.

Given these realities, Kelly concludes that many individuals would be better off pursuing something other than a four-year or a two-year degree, such as a short-term vocational certificate or an apprenticeship that provides access to skills and a job. But such alternatives are often treated as a last resort instead of a worthwhile option. Consequently, they are underdeveloped and underfunded. Kelly ends by proposing policy changes to fix that, as well as policies and practices that will help more low-income children climb the mountain to two-year and four-year degrees.

- **Chapter 3: The Certification Revolution (Tamar Jacoby, Opportunity America)**

In this chapter, Jacoby discusses the exciting potential of industry-certified credentials that are transforming training in many technical fields and providing new pathways to upward mobility.

Already, according to the Census Bureau, 25 percent of US adults—or more than 50 million people—hold a nondegree credential, defined as a professional certification, license, or educational certificate. Business leaders from the National Association of Manufacturers to the Business Roundtable are changing how they do business to accommodate the new approach. Ferment and enthusiasm stretch across the political spectrum. And the nation's leading education foundations are pouring millions of dollars into refining and advancing what they see as a transformative idea with ramifications for both secondary and postsecondary education.

Through journalistic reporting and a review of the research literature, Jacoby unpacks this new development, highlights best practices, and points to policy barriers that are keeping it from taking root in more places. She concludes that industry-certified credentials can transform high schools and higher education—if their advocates can address skeptics' major reservations. One of the most significant concerns that must be overcome is the fear that, much like old-fashioned vocational education, nondegree credentials will give rise to a parallel, alternative track with less prestige, inferior teaching, and lower expectations for students.

Jacoby acknowledges that there's clearly a danger of that. Change, however, could also go the other way. Today, the gold standard is a college degree, but this preference could shift as nondegree credentials evolve. If and when they prove they can open the same doors, earn the same or better returns in the labor market, and point the way to a potentially more flexible, rewarding future of lifelong learning, why couldn't alternative credentials earn as much respect as degrees? Nondegree credentialing is already starting to take the stigma out of practical, job-oriented training. What's wrong, after all, with learning a skill that gets you a job? Surely that's why most people go to college in the first place.

- **Chapter 4: How Apprenticeship Approaches Can Spur Upward Mobility in the United States (Robert Lerman, Urban Institute)**

Apprenticeship is an approach that combines classroom-based vocational education; structured, work-based learning; and paid work and production aimed at helping novices master an occupation. Apprenticeships are subject to externally imposed training standards, particularly for their workplace component. They usually last between two and four years and lead to a recognized credential certifying the apprentice's ability to perform the required tasks of a fully qualified worker in the occupation. Unlike internships, apprenticeships require far more in-depth training, involve paid work, and lead to a recognized occupational credential. Unlike paid work experience, apprenticeships allow their participants to learn skills in formal classes and absorb their workplace learning in a highly structured setting.

Overall, the evidence demonstrates that apprenticeships (1) increase earnings of participants; (2) increase productivity and yield positive returns to firms; (3) enhance the quality and pay in jobs not requiring a bachelor's degree; (4) can expand substantially with modest government funding; (5) yield long-run savings in public money by lessening the need for high-cost, postsecondary education; (6) rely on learning by engaging in real production and earning while learning; (7) offer routes to rewarding careers not tied to an academic-only approach; (8) avoid the pitfalls of other training programs that are a poor fit for employer needs; (9) improve the transition from school to career; and (10) provide a sense of occupational pride and identity in apprentice graduates.

In this chapter, Lerman provides evidence of these benefits of apprenticeships, particularly as they relate to helping low-income individuals escape poverty; explains how they work in the United States and elsewhere; points to specific programs here and abroad that show promise, including apprenticeship programs at the high school, postsecondary, and even "college-plus" levels; and discusses the policy changes needed to bring the approach to scale and put it on an even playing field with traditional higher education.

Part II: Multiple Pathways in High School: Tracking Revisited?

Next, we'll dive deep into the adolescent years, when many students are making critical choices that impact the rest of their lives. A key question is whether we should move away from comprehensive high schools and today's widespread focus on "college prep for all" and toward a "multiple pathways" approach, including high-quality career and technical education and youth apprenticeships. (The conclusion from part I is clear: Yes, we should.) But how might we do so without the downsides of old-fashioned tracking? And what can we do for the students who arrive in high school vastly unprepared?

• Chapter 5: Small High Schools of Choice (Peter Meyer, *Education Next*)

In this chapter 5, Meyer examines the lessons from New York City's successful small schools movement in the 2000s. He argues that breaking up large, comprehensive high schools and turning them into smaller, mission-focused schools of choice (some of which were focused on "college prep," while others embodied high-quality career and technical education) has been demonstrated to improve student outcomes, especially in terms of high school graduation rates and postsecondary completion.

But Meyer also tackles the toughest dilemma of the high school years: how best to serve students who arrive many years below grade level in reading, writing, and math. After all, both college-prep and career and technical education programs work best for students who enter ninth grade with strong basic skills; what do we do for the kids whose basic academic skills are sorely lacking? Meyer describes Gotham's imaginative use of "recuperative education," including "transfer schools" that work to quickly remediate students who are one or two years behind grade level and get them back on the college-prep or career-tech path. And he contemplates what needs to happen for this approach to high school reform to spread far beyond New York City.

- **Chapter 6: College-Prep High Schools for the Poor (Joanne Jacobs, freelance writer and blogger)**

In chapter 6, Jacobs profiles three college-prep high schools that are beating the odds and explores what they are doing that is so successful. One is a comprehensive high school along the Rio Grande that embraced an "early college" model; a second is an inner-city private high school in Chicago; and the third is an urban charter school in San Jose.

So what are these schools doing right? Jacobs finds that they start early, establishing feeder schools; create a safe, supportive, college-going culture with high expectations; use a longer school day, summer school, or both; and introduce students to the larger world they hope to enter. Some also provide support services to their graduates to help them persist through college and complete their degrees.

Jacobs concludes by considering what policymakers and philanthropists might do to bring such schools to their communities.

- **Chapter 7: High-Quality Career and Technical Education (Robert Schwartz, Harvard University, and Nancy Hoffman, Jobs for the Future)**

Chapter 7 starts by restating the case made in Harvard's 2011 report, *Pathways to Prosperity*. First, if fewer than one young person in three is successfully completing a four-year college degree by the age of twenty-five, does it really make sense to organize high schools as if a college degree should be the goal for all students? Second, respected economists are now telling us that at least 30 percent of the jobs projected over the next decade will be in the "middle skills" category (technician-level jobs requiring some education beyond high school, but not necessarily a four-year degree); shouldn't we start building more pathways from high school to community college to prepare students to fill the best of those jobs, especially in high-growth, high-demand fields like information technology and health care? And third, if countries like Austria, Germany, the Netherlands, Norway, and Switzerland have built vocational systems that prepare between 40 and 70 percent of young people to enter the workforce by the age of twenty with skills and credentials valued by employers—and if these countries have healthy economies, stronger upward mobility, and much lower youth unemployment rates than the United States—shouldn't we study their policies and practices to see if there are lessons we can adapt to our own setting?

Schwartz and Hoffman then profile five models of high-quality career and technical education (CTE): Worcester Technical High School in Massachusetts (a stand-alone urban CTE high school); the Center for Advanced Research and Technology in Clovis, California (a regional CTE center); Wake Early College of Health and Sciences in Raleigh, North Carolina (a technically focused early college high school); Southwire 12 for Life in Carrollton, Georgia (an employer-sponsored school in a workplace); and District-Wide Career Academies in Long Beach, California (wall-to-wall career academies). They find much to like in each of these models, but propose a sixth that would represent the best of all worlds: a combination of career academies and early college high schools.

They conclude that a four-year degree, especially for low-income youth and students of color, absolutely pays off, and given the abysmally low attainment rates among those groups, we should be focused on increasing their access, retention, and completion at four-year institutions. But two-year degrees and one-year postsecondary certificates also pay off, and the pathways leading to these options need to be greatly strengthened and expanded as well if more young people are going to get launched on careers that can propel them into the middle class.

Part III: The Early Years

We'll finish with an examination of the foundational years. What are the best practices of poverty-fighting preschools, elementary schools, and middle schools? How can the years between pre-K and eighth grade get as many low-income children as possible ready for success across the multiple pathways discussed in part II? Should we embrace ability grouping and tracking? Should we place a heavy focus on noncognitive skills like drive and prudence? What does it mean to prepare little kids to follow the "success sequence" discussed in part I, rather than just "college and career readiness"?

- **Chapter 8: Starting at Five Is Too Late: Early Childhood Education and Upward Mobility (Elliot, Bryce Marable, and Jelene Britten, Ounce of Prevention Fund)**

The education kids need to break the cycle of poverty doesn't start with kindergarten entry. Upward mobility begins before birth, with critical support services such as effective prenatal care for pregnant mothers. Once children are born, however, it is up to the key adult figures in their life to respond to their natural curiosity and help them learn. Parents are the essential heart of this development, but many low-income families can benefit from having the right supports around them—including, but not limited to, educational supports.

So argue Regenstein and his colleagues as they discuss how families and professionals can work together to help poor children get off to a great start in the years from birth through kindergarten entry. This work has no simple solutions or silver bullets because it requires numerous connections that traditional education systems have not always fostered: between "academic" and "nonacademic" skills, between families and professionals, and between early learning providers and the public schools. Best practices in the early years can put kids on a positive trajectory heading into kindergarten and, ideally, inform best practices in kindergarten and beyond.

Regenstein et. al. review the evidence base supporting early childhood initiatives, especially for poor children, and profiles programs that have proven to be particularly effective.

- **Chapter 9: Poverty-Fighting Elementary Schools: Knowledge Acquisition Is Job One (Robert Pondiscio, Thomas B. Fordham Institute and Democracy Prep)**

Any discussion of the best way to prepare low-income children for upward mobility must begin by attending to their verbal proficiency and growth, argues Pondiscio. An education is a complex, multifaceted thing. There are no magic bullets. But if you were to wish for one positive outcome—and one only—that would set a low-income child on the path to upward mobility, you would almost certainly wish for that child to have a big vocabulary. That one tool is, as E. D. Hirsch Jr. observed, "a convenient proxy for a whole range of educational attainments and abilities." A wealth of words signals competence in reading and writing; vocabulary size also correlates with SAT success, which in turn predicts the likelihood of college-going and graduation.

There's just one problem: You don't increase verbal proficiency by "practicing" reading and writing. To a daunting degree, language is a cultural construct hemmed in by social and economic class. This places an extraordinarily daunting task before schools that commit themselves to raising the verbal proficiency—and therefore the life chances—of disadvantaged children.

What's needed is a distinctly old-fashioned kind of education, one focused on knowledge and vocabulary acquisition. Pondiscio explains how schools can teach these things well, both by laying out the evidence base and taking readers into schools that are getting it done.

- **Chapter 10: Tracking in Middle School (Tom Loveless, Brookings Institution)**

Chapter 10 argues something unthinkable to a large number of analysts who consider themselves equity minded: that tracking, the assignment of students to different classes on the basis of ability or achievement, may be a means of better preparing disadvantaged students for success in high school and beyond. This will require a mind-shift from policies emphasizing equal access to advanced courses for all or most youngsters to policies emphasizing talent development for high-achieving students. Middle schools prepare students for high school. By adequately preparing more impoverished middle school students for the academic demands of college-prep high school, including Advanced Placement courses, tracking can serve as a tool for greater fairness.

The chapter's objective is to convince readers that this is a plausible hypothesis—and to do so empirically, based on the evidence supporting three propositions:

1. Poor, Hispanic, and black middle school students are less likely to be enrolled in tracked classes than students who are socioeconomically better off, white, and Asian.
2. Middle schools serving predominantly disadvantaged students are less likely to offer tracked classes than schools serving advantaged populations.
3. Research on tracking is mixed, but studies focusing on its distributional properties—that is, how tracking differentially affects different kinds of students—generally show a positive effect for high-achieving students. That is particularly true for classes that group academically talented students together and offer an enriched or accelerated curriculum.

The upshot of these propositions is that high-achieving eighth graders in socioeconomically disadvantaged communities are denied an opportunity that their counterparts in advantaged communities enjoy. Kids from middle or upper-middle-class families are more likely to attend schools with tracked, high-achieving classes that prepare them for AP classes in high schools. They are more likely to have access to middle school classes that challenge them and allow them to excel. That's not fair.

I'll return in the Conclusion to tally the answers to our original questions: How can we help children born into poverty to transcend their disadvantages and enter the middle class as adults? And in particular, what role can our schools play? Do we need to rethink our approach to education policy? If so, what does that mean for the major reforms underway today, from implementing the Common Core State Standards to expanding parental choice to developing more effective teachers?

ACKNOWLEDGMENTS

Many people helped this volume come to life. Thanks go first to the trustees of the Thomas B. Fordham Foundation, who gave me the time and resources to pursue this project. Similar appreciations go to Kim Dennis and Courtney Myers at the Searle Freedom Trust, whose support will allow us to share this book far and wide. Many thanks, too, to the authors of this volume's ten excellent chapters, all of which exceeded expectations in terms of quality, focus, and persuasiveness. This book tackles a critically important topic, and all of our authors treated it as such. I also appreciate our authors for participating in a December 2014 symposium, "Education for Upward Mobility," which featured a fantastic keynote address by Hugh Price, former president of the National Urban League, and spot-on comments from Reihan Salam of the National Review Institute, Marc Sternberg of the Walton Family Foundation, Dacia Toll of Achievement First, Sheldon Danziger of the Russell Sage Foundation, Howard Fuller of the Black Alliance for Educational Options, Rick Hess of the American Enterprise Institute, and Andy Rotherham of Bellwether Education Partners.

At Fordham, Kevin Mahnken shepherded the papers through the copyedit process, which was ably tackled by Shannon Last and Pamela Tatz. And many thanks to Tom Koerner and Carlie Wall at Rowman and Littlefield, who were a joy to work with. Special thanks go to my mentor, Chester E. "Checker" Finn, Jr., who provided penetrating feedback on the entire volume at various stages of its development.

Success has many parents; any errors in this volume are mine alone.

Part I

TRANSCENDING POVERTY THROUGH EDUCATION, WORK, AND PERSONAL RESPONSIBILITY

Chapter One

Education and the "Success Sequence"

Ron Haskins

State and federal governments in the United States devote a considerable portion of their budgets to fighting poverty and promoting opportunity. Between the two levels of government, the nation now spends around $1 trillion annually on programs for poor and low-income individuals and families.[1] Yet progress against poverty has been modest and economic mobility has been stagnant for decades, while other nations have less poverty and more economic mobility than the United States.[2] Why has progress been so slow?

Several years ago, using Census Bureau data representative of the US population, my Brookings colleagues and I analyzed the probability that individuals would live in poverty or have a middle-class income[3] given how many of three norms of personal responsibility they had followed.[4] The three behavioral norms are whether the person obtained a high school degree, whether the person worked full time that year, and whether the person had waited until age twenty-one to marry and married before having children.

The results showed that those who violated all three norms had a 76 percent chance of living in poverty and a 7 percent chance of being in the middle class in a given year (figure 1.1). By contrast, those who followed all three norms had a 2 percent chance of living in poverty and a 74 percent chance of reaching the middle class. Thus, those who followed what might be called the "success sequence" of finishing at least high school, working, and waiting until age twenty-one to marry and marrying before having children were highly unlikely to live in poverty and had a very good chance of entering the middle class.

Now consider a second statistical exercise based on the population of US adults, again using Census Bureau data. Suppose we wanted to know whether behavioral changes would have an impact on the poverty rate. For example, would there be an impact on the poverty rate if all adults worked full time at

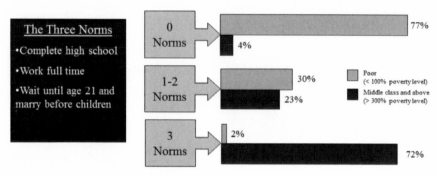

Figure 1.1.   What accounts for success?

whatever wage they actually earn for part-time work or, if they don't work at all, worked full time at the average wage earned by other Americans with their level of education? Similarly, would there be an impact on poverty if couples married at the same rate as they had in 1970?

To find out, we simulated an increase in the marriage rate to its level in 1970 by randomly matching single mothers and unmarried men who were similar in age, education, and race. We also performed separate simulations based on assuming that everyone had at least a high school degree and earned the same wage as other high school graduates, that no family had more than two children, and that cash welfare benefits were doubled.[5]

The results are summarized in figure 1.2. Our simulations suggest that the most effective way to reduce poverty would be for everyone to work full time. Full-time work, under our assumptions, would reduce the poverty rate by 40 percent. Increasing the rate of marriage to its 1970 level would be associated with a reduction in the poverty rate of a little more than 25 percent. Increasing education to the level it would be if everyone had at least a high school degree and reducing family size so that no parents had more than two children would be associated with a reduction in poverty of around 15 percent and 13 percent, respectively.

Some idea of the magnitude of these impacts can be obtained by comparing them with the impact of doubling the level of cash welfare. All are superior to the modest 8 percent reduction associated with doubling cash welfare. Thus, increasing full-time work would reduce the poverty rate by about five times as much as doubling cash welfare.

It will not escape notice that the factors shown in this exercise to be most effective in reducing poverty are similar to the behavioral norms shown in figure 1.1 to be closely associated with avoiding poverty and achieving

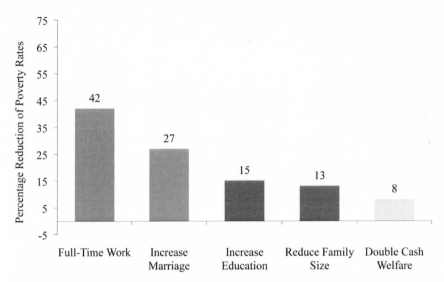

Figure 1.2.   **Five pathways to reduce poverty.**

a middle-class income. Both exercises suggest that increasing work rates, marriage rates, and education would substantially reduce poverty rates and increase the odds of earning a middle-class income.

Both of these statistical exercises are, in the jargon of social scientists, correlational in nature—meaning that the levels of two factors tend to be related in the sense that as the value of one increases or declines, so does the other. Both analyses show that education, work, and marriage are correlated with poverty and income. But under the rules of social science, showing that two factors are correlated does not permit the conclusion that one causes the other. The major concern here is that some unobserved and unmeasured characteristic of the individuals could be responsible for the observed correlations. For example, motivation or intelligence could be associated with both high levels of education, work, and marriage as well as lower poverty rates and higher income.

But there is abundant evidence, much of it from studies whose design permits causal conclusions, that increasing education, work, and marriage would reduce poverty rates and increase income. In the following separate sections on what schools can do to increase work rates, increase educational attainment, and prepare adolescents for responsible behavior regarding their choices on family formation, I will review some of the literature that supports the claim that these three factors are causally related to poverty and income.

An important, if somewhat obvious, point to make about the review of evidence on helping young people make better choices about work, education, and the kind of family they want to create is that the choices many of them now make—often without good advice or good examples in their families and neighborhood to follow and with little understanding of the long-term consequences of their choices—do not promote their economic well-being.

The major implication of the two statistical exercises reviewed previously is that if these choices could be improved so that adolescents and young adults could get a job that allowed them to work full time at a reasonable wage, get more education, and wait until age twenty-one to get married and have a baby, their economic status would be greatly improved. There are no grounds to think that without some intervention, the life-course choices made by young people will improve anytime soon. So the question before us is whether intervention programs that schools conduct can help young people improve these life-shaping choices.

PRELIMINARY CONSIDERATIONS

Before examining the role of schools in helping children make better life-course choices, three nonschool issues should be addressed. First, work, education, and marriage hinge on choices made by individuals. Although individuals can (at least partially) overcome bad choices made early in life with better choices made later, it is an unfortunate fact about the chronology of modern life in advanced economies that choices made during childhood, especially during adolescence, often have long-term consequences.[6]

This generalization applies especially to decisions about education, sex, and delinquent behavior. If a sixteen-year-old drops out of school, her odds of marriage, employment, and earnings shift in a negative direction. Further, in the case of teen births, research shows that the decisions of two sixteen-year-olds have important consequences for themselves, the child they create, and society, not least by increasing the odds that both the teen parents and their child will impose costs on government.

In fact, these costs begin within months of conception because most teens who give birth are eligible for Medicaid, which pays for prenatal care, delivery, and postnatal care. Medicaid pays for around 75 percent of teen births at a cost of around $2.3 billion annually. The National Campaign to Prevent Teen and Unplanned Pregnancy estimates that the total national cost that teen births impose on all levels of government for health care, child welfare, and (later) incarceration is $9.4 billion.[7] The point is that the life-course decisions being examined here have immediate consequences and can alter the remainder of a person's life—all the more reason schools should attempt to help adolescents learn to avoid bad choices.

A second issue that should be a major part of the discussion about improv-ing the life choices made by young people is that parents play an important role in guiding their children to make good choices. Parents can be models for the advantages of good choices; parents can directly intervene when children make a mistake, to put them back on the right path; and parents' involvement with their children from birth until they leave home for college or work con-tributes mightily to children's development, including the life-course deci-sions being examined here. Greg Duncan and Richard Murnane have shown that there are vast differences between how much wealthy parents and poor parents spend on enrichment experiences for their children such as sports, high-quality child care, home learning materials, trips to museums and simi-lar educational facilities, summer camps, music lessons, and private tutoring.[8]

But beyond parenting differences related to money, studies show that highly educated parents spend more time with their children than less-edu-cated parents; that they use this time productively in activities that stimulate language and cognitive development; that they speak more to their children during the preschool years so that by the time the children reach public schools, they have superior vocabulary skills; and that their parenting style (maternal sensitivity and responsiveness to the child during the preschool years) is more conducive to child development than the parenting style of low-income families.[9]

Thus, even though parents can have an immensely positive impact on their children's development, behavior, and life choices, research makes it all too clear that poor children, minority children, and children from single-parent families have parents who are less likely to stimulate their development when they are young and who are less likely to give them guidance throughout their childhood years.[10] These findings underscore the importance of the dramatic changes in family composition that have taken place among American fami-lies over the last four decades.

Figure 1.3 shows the rapid decline of marriage rates for women of all ages; the historic increase in nonmarital births that are, in part, a result of declining marriage rates; and the impact of these two changes on family composition since 1970. The upshot is that more children are living with a single parent and fewer are living with married parents. It follows that an increasing por-tion of the nation's children lives in the family form in which they are about four times more likely to be in poverty and less likely to experience parenting that supports their development and positive behavior—including the life-shaping choices they make.

As so often happens with the nation's social problems, society must fall back on the schools to help young people, especially the disadvantaged ones, make better life choices.

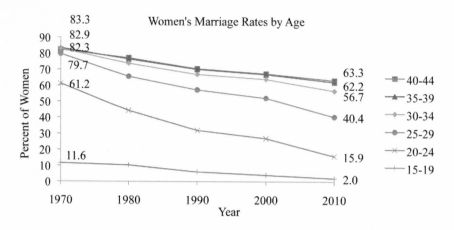

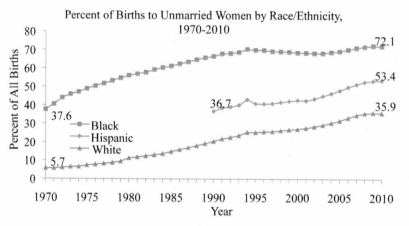

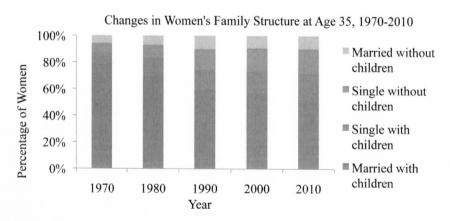

Figure 1.3 (Parts A, B, and C). Changes in family composition.

WHAT THE SCHOOLS CAN DO

In this chapter, I explore the proposition that schools should focus more attention on how to get students, especially those from poor and single-parent families, to accept more personal responsibility for their decisions about work, education, and family composition. More specifically, I examine what the schools can do to help children and adolescents improve the quality of their life-course decisions and acquire the knowledge and experiences that will support these improved choices.

Work

For young adults from low-income families, the key to financial well-being is work. If work rates could be improved—especially for males, whose work rates have been falling for decades—the nation's poverty rate would fall and kids from low-income families could escape poverty and improve their future incomes, with possible impacts on their marital prospects.

Unfortunately, historical trends in the work rates of American adults are decidedly a mixed bag. Figure 1.4 shows the employment-to-population (E/P) ratio for all men, never-married mothers, and black males between the ages

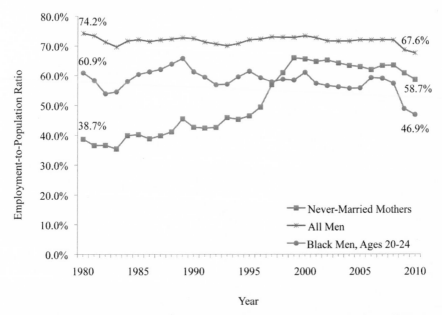

Figure 1.4. Employment/population ratios. Note: People who are in the military or who are incarcerated are not included in the data. (Brookings tabulations of data from the CPS Annual Social and Economic Supplement, 1980–2010.)

of twenty and twenty-four. The E/P ratio is the broadest measure of employment because everyone in the demographic group under examination is in the denominator and the number of people in that group who have a job is in the numerator. Unlike the unemployment rate, the E/P ratio includes people in the group who have dropped out of the labor force (but not those who are in the military or incarcerated; see the source note to figure 1.4).

The picture for never-married mothers, the group most likely to live in poverty, is encouraging. Their work rates skyrocketed between roughly the mid-1990s and the recession year of 2001. Since then, their work rates have diminished somewhat, but they were still about 25 percent higher in 2010 than in 1995, before welfare reform provided both positive and negative incentives for mothers on welfare or eligible for welfare to work.

During the period of increased employment among these mothers over the second half of the 1990s, poverty rates among children in female-headed families and black children (who are disproportionately in female-headed families) fell steadily and both reached their lowest level ever. These population-wide results are consistent with the claim from our two statistical exercises above that increased employment will lead to reductions in poverty.

But the picture is not as encouraging for males. Work rates among males have been declining for more than three decades for reasons that are not altogether clear. If work rates among all men are worrisome, work rates among young black men are alarming. The E/P ratios of young black men were less than 60 percent in only nine of the last thirty-one years and are now under 50 percent. Self-sufficient communities and healthy marriages cannot be sustained when fewer than half the young men living there are working.

Can the schools play a role in helping all young people, especially young minority males, increase their work rates? Most schools focus their efforts on helping students learn basic skills and prepare themselves for education at two- or four-year colleges. For those concerned primarily with students from poor and low-income families, as I am here, the focus should be on placing a greater emphasis on the work and career goals of students who seem unlikely to attend a postsecondary institution. In addition, schools should make a special effort to help disadvantaged students who would have difficulty in four-year institutions because of their poor academic preparation.

Of course, there are students from poor families who are highly qualified, not just for four-year colleges but also, in some cases, for elite colleges.[11] Those students should be identified early and helped with their college selection and with obtaining scholarships, both issues about which most low-income parents would have difficulty giving good advice. If these superior students from poor families can be directed toward four-year schools, as we will see (see figures 1.5 and 1.6), their economic futures have a very high probability of boosting them well above the economic levels of their parents and even above that of the average US household. But schools should also provide an intense focus on two-year colleges, including or especially the certificate programs most of them offer, for disadvantaged students who are not well qualified for four-year institutions.

It follows that an important strategy the schools should employ to augment the career choices of the mediocre students from poor families in order to help them secure their financial future is education that includes acquiring skills that are of practical use in the market place. At least two strategies are supported by rigorous evidence of success.

The first is the career academy.[12] Few education programs have stronger evidence of success. The academies usually enroll around two hundred students in grades nine through twelve in order to create small learning communities, often as a school within a school. Students take classes in both academic and technical subjects that are often organized around career themes.

Importantly, the programs emphasize practical experience in the work world by forming partnerships with local employers. Academy students have the opportunity to work directly with employers in their community and engage in activities such as job shadowing, career fairs, and hearing from guest speakers from local businesses. Employers also teach students how to locate potential jobs and how to apply. This instruction includes help with preparing resumes and tips for participating in job interviews.

The research firm MDRC evaluated career academies using a gold standard design implemented at eight sites and involving a total of nearly 1,400 students, 85 percent of whom were Hispanic or black. The study followed students from all eight sites for eight years after their expected graduation date. Perhaps the most notable impacts during the school years were on increased attendance and school credits earned, as well as—based on interviews with students—a sense of attending a school with a "family-like" atmosphere.

But the most notable impacts occurred at the eight-year follow-up point. Program participants earned a total of $16,704 more in 2006 dollars (approximately $19,300 in 2013 dollars) over the eight years of follow up than did students in the control group. This effect, which was concentrated mainly among young men, is due to increased wages, more hours worked, and greater employment stability, all signs of greater labor-force attachment among male students who participated in the program.

Perhaps most surprisingly, at the eight-year follow up when participants were in their mid-twenties, there were several impacts on marital status and parental status, both for the full sample and especially for young men who participated in the academy program. More specifically, a young man in the academy program was 33 percent more likely to be married and living with his wife and more than 45 percent more likely to be a custodial parent than a young man in the control group.

Of course, it is not clear that all the nation's approximately 2,500 career academies produce similar impacts on the education, work, and family composition choices of young people. Nonetheless, this trifecta of impacts shows that well-implemented school programs can have major impacts on the decisions that young people, many or even mostly from poor families, make about all three elements of the success sequence.

Happily, it should be possible to augment the work impacts of career academies by combining them with youth apprenticeship programs. Consider an apprenticeship program that the Georgia state legislature established in 1992 legislation. Students learn about the program during their freshmen and sophomore years and can join the program as juniors or seniors. The program features around 2,000 hours of work-based training and another nearly 150 hours of related coursework.

The outcome of the program is that students not only earn their high school diploma but also earn a certificate of industry-recognized competencies relevant to occupations that require at least a moderate level of skill (and often more), such as electrician, plumber, and welder. This certificate can be of great value when high school graduates are looking for their first job. Surveys of employers indicate that they are highly satisfied with the program and with the program graduates they hire. In fact, more than 95 percent of employers say that the program is beneficial to their company and that they would recommend the program to other employers.

I end this section on work by putting in a good word for the often-demeaned value of low-wage jobs. Schools should aim to help young people qualify for skill-based employment or move on to two-year or four-year colleges, but they should do so while emphasizing that the first step to financial success is often a low-wage job.

One of the most important aspects of American social policy is the stream of work support benefits that Congress created over the past several decades to provide assistance to low-income workers, particularly those with children. These work supports include the Earned Income Tax Credit, the Child Tax Credit, food stamps, school lunches, Medicaid, and child care assistance. It is not unusual for a single mother with two children to receive $7,000 or even more from this package (not counting the Medicaid coverage) of work supports, most of it in cash. The work support system greatly increases the incentive for low-wage work by ensuring both that work pays and that even unskilled workers are almost always better off working than on welfare. Equally important, many workers begin in low-wage jobs and, by accumulating work experience and perhaps some formal training, move on to better jobs, often with better employers.[13]

Education

Figure 1.5 captures the relationship between years of schooling and family income for people during their prime earning years, between the ages of thirty and thirty-nine. Three points about the figure are notable.

First, for every year since 1963, as a group, people with more education made more money than people with less education. In fact, as improbable as it might seem, the lines representing the relationship between education and family income never touch. That's more than four decades over which none of the data points violate the conclusion that the average income of Americans with more education is greater than the average income of Americans with less education. Second, the line graphs portraying the average income of people with different levels of education are getting farther and farther apart over time. In 1963, the difference in family income between those without a high school education and those with an advanced degree was about $32,650. In 2011, the difference was a little over $77,000, well over twice as much as in 1963 (all in constant 2011 dollars). The payoff to education is growing over time. Third, for more than two decades, only those with a four-year degree or an advanced degree have, on average, experienced increased annual income.

An important part of the story about education and income implied by figure 1.6 is that in order to earn a decent income, most people will need some education beyond high school. For kids from poor families, getting a college

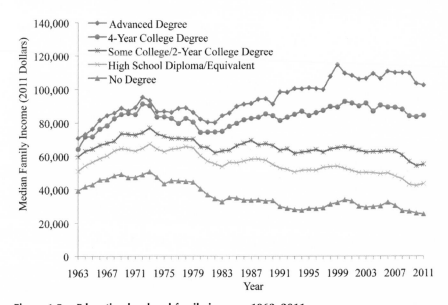

Figure 1.5.   Education level and family income, 1963–2011.

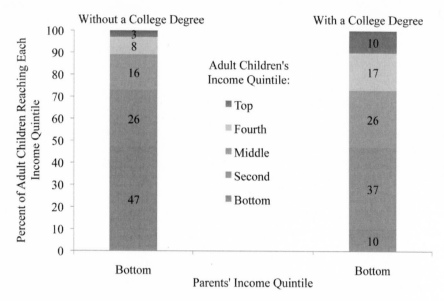

Figure 1.6.   Income for adult children with and without college degrees by parents' income.

degree is associated with an enormous positive impact on their adult income. Figure 1.6, based on the Panel Study of Income Dynamics (PSID), shows the income of adult children whose parents were in the bottom income quintile.

The bar graph on the left is for adult children who did not earn a four-year college degree, while the bar graph on the right is for adult children who did earn a four-year college degree. Obtaining a college degree noticeably shifts the entire distribution of income in the second generation. For example, 47 percent of those without a college degree themselves wound up in the bottom income quintile as adults, compared to 10 percent of those with a college degree.

Similarly, without a college degree, only 3 percent of adult children whose parents were in the bottom income quintile made it all the way to the top quintile, compared with 10 percent of those with a college degree. The point is that even children from families in the bottom quintile can dramatically alter their economic future by obtaining a four-year college degree.

Many studies demonstrate that a large number of children from low-income families are not prepared for college. The PSID shows that whereas 53 percent of children from the top quintile obtain a four-year degree, only 11 percent of children from the bottom quintile achieve a college degree.[14] There are many reasons for the low rate of college completion by children from poor families, but among the most important is their lack of academic preparation for college.[15]

The National Assessment of Educational Progress rates the preparation of high school students for college work as *basic, proficient,* or *advanced.* Of students eligible for the National School Lunch Program, only 21 percent were proficient or advanced in reading and only 10 percent were proficient or advanced in math. By contrast, among children from families with incomes above the cutoff for school lunch, 44 percent were proficient or advanced in reading and 32 percent were proficient or advanced in math.[16] Children at the basic level are considered to be poorly prepared for college work.

This lack of academic preparation prevents many children from low-income families from entering quality four-year institutions—but what about community colleges? What if these marginal students knew that they needed education beyond high school and, after being honest with themselves about their lack of preparation for a four-year college (perhaps with advice from teachers or counselors), decided to continue their education at a community college?

For many students, even the academic requirements of a community college calls for serious and sustained effort if the student is to be success-ful. Unfortunately, experience with the remedial English and math courses required of many students who lack basic skills when they enroll in a com-munity college shows that these programs usually fail.[17]

Despite these problems with students who enter community colleges with academic deficits, recent programs developed at community colleges around the nation are beginning to show that these deficits can be overcome.[18] Two approaches to helping these students have been tested by random-assignment designs.

In one approach, MDRC tested a strategy called "Learning Communities" at Kingsborough Community College in Brooklyn. The basic intent of the program was "to build social cohesion among students and faculty" and to help students develop better study skills. The study assigned incoming fresh-men participating in the program to groups of fifteen to twenty-five students. These small groups of students took three courses together: an English course pitched at their level of performance; a regular college course, such as psy-chology or sociology; and a "student success course" that taught effective study habits and other skills related to academic success in college.

The faculty members in the program coordinated their assignments and met together periodically to review the progress of participating students. The study randomly assigned nearly 1,500 students participating in the experi-ment, mostly from low-income and minority families, to the program group or the control group. At the end of two years, students participating in the

Learning Communities said in an interview they felt "integrated" into the school community and felt more engaged in their courses, as compared with students in the control group. They also passed more courses and earned more credits during their first semester, moved more quickly through their remedial English course, and were more likely to pass a required English skills assessment test. All these effects were modest but nonetheless demonstrate that marginal students can be helped to be more successful at community college. The key now is to build on the success of the Kingsborough approach.[19]

A second approach, tested at Delgado Community College in New Orleans, examined the impact of giving students a $1,000 scholarship for two semesters if they attended college at least half time and maintained a C average. The program randomly assigned students, most of whom were single mothers in their twenties, to an experimental or control group. There was an array of effects of the scholarship, including an increased likelihood of attending school full time, greater persistence in staying in college, and completing more credit hours. Evidently, for students trying to balance family responsibilities, work, and a community college education, a little cash can go a long way toward clearing time to concentrate on schoolwork.

Thus, there is ample evidence that if students from disadvantaged backgrounds participate in career academies during high school, their work rates, income, and marriage rates can be enhanced. Similarly, if disadvantaged students can be helped to enroll in two- or four-year colleges, there are programs that can help them succeed—which, in turn, will give them an advantage in the job market. The key to success is developing programs tailored to the special needs of students from poor families that aim to help them make better decisions about work and college. If more high schools and colleges offered the types of programs reviewed here and paid attention to implementing them aggressively with good teachers, more students from poor families could boost their prospects.

In this section, I have emphasized efforts to help young people from poor families enroll in and complete a bachelor's degree at a four-year college or complete an associate's degree or professional certificate at a community college. But I would also emphasize that obtaining a high school degree is still the basic requirement for avoiding poverty and pursuing economic mobility. One of the three basic norms in the success sequence that helps people avoid poverty and enter the middle class is obtaining a high school degree.

Equally important, a high school degree is the gateway to subsequent education at community colleges and four-year colleges and thus, in all likelihood, to earning a middle-class wage. Based on everything we know (see figure 1.5 for a good example), it is better to have a high school degree than to not have a high school degree. In raising the sights of the schools to help more kids prepare for two- and four-year colleges, we should not lose sight of the vital importance of a "mere" high school degree.

Marriage and Family Composition

Family background has major impacts on children's development as well as their school performance.[20] In general, research shows that the best rearing environment for children is a married-couple family.[21] Yet, as portrayed so vividly in figure 1.3, it would be difficult to exaggerate the extent to which family composition has changed in America over the last four decades, with the result that more and more children are being reared by single parents.

There is only modest evidence that schools can do much to boost marriage rates,[22] but there is good evidence that delaying the age of first childbirth until young women and men are in their twenties can promote education and subsequent employment.[23] An important way that schools can help teens be responsible and take an important step toward fulfilling one element of the success sequence is to teach them about responsible sexual behavior.

The federal government, under both Republican and Democratic administrations, has made a major commitment to providing funds for communities, including schools, to establish programs that teach teens to avoid early sex and pregnancy. Republicans and Democrats often differ sharply about whether programs should focus exclusively on teaching abstinence or also include instruction about methods of birth control.[24] Even so, most programs do both.[25]

Preventing teen births is one of the rare social issues about which evidence demonstrates unequivocally that great progress has been made. The teen birth rate has been cut by 36 percent since 2007 and by an impressive 57 percent since 1991. In 1991, 61.5 of every 1,000 female teens gave birth. By 2013, the number giving birth had declined to 26.6 per 1,000.[26] One reason may be that a number of programs that meet high standards of program evaluation have been shown to be effective in reducing teen pregnancy, sexually transmitted infections, or some aspect of teen sexual activity.

The Department of Health and Human Services (HHS), implementing legislation enacted by Congress in 2009, reviewed over one thousand studies of teen pregnancy prevention programs and found that thirty-five model programs had evidence of success on one or more of these measures.[27] HHS is now funding more than one hundred local programs with the new money that Congress provided in the same 2009 legislation—most are being conducted in the public schools, most use one or more of the thirty-five model programs, and nearly all are being carefully evaluated (largely by random-assignment designs) to ensure that they continue having impacts.[28]

The HHS systematic review of pregnancy prevention programs is part of a major initiative by the Obama administration to reduce the teen pregnancy rate by expanding what is now widely referred to as *evidence-based policy.* Although definitions vary, the two primary characteristics of the Obama definition of evidence-based policy are (1) directing the highest possible proportion of federal grant funds to programs that have been shown by rigorous evaluations to produce positive impacts and (2) requiring all programs receiving federal funds to conduct high-quality evaluations and use the results to improve the programs. The administration's vision is that following evidence-based policy over many years will gradually increase the share of federal dollars being spent on programs known to produce significant benefits and simultaneously develop additional programs and practices supported by rigorous evidence.[29]

An important characteristic of the federal teen pregnancy prevention programs is that communities have a great deal of flexibility in picking the kind of programs they favor. And the fact that they can select from a list of thirty-five programs, including several that are abstinence-based (see table 1.1 for examples), means they have a wide range of program characteristics from which to choose. Moreover, the Obama administration allows about 25 percent of the 2009 funding (which now totals over $200 million a year for the major evidence-based programs) to be spent on innovative programs, so communities have even more choices.

Table 1.1. Overview of Selected Teen Pregnancy Prevention Program Models Eligible for Tier I Funding, Including Impacts

Name of Program	Brief Description	Impact
Aban Aya Youth Project	Middle schools; African American students in grades 5–8; Afro-centric social development curriculum; four-year period (risky sexual behaviors)	Male participants reported having had less sexual intercourse; no program impact for female participants
Adult Identity Mentoring (Project AIM)	Middle schools; low-income youth ages 11–14; group-level youth development intervention; twelve sessions over six weeks (risky sexual behaviors)	*Three months later:* participants were less likely to report having had sexual intercourse *A year later:* males were less likely to report having had sexual intercourse; no program impact for females, sexually inexperienced youth, or the full sample

Name of Program	Brief Description	Impact
Children's Aid Society (CAS)— Carrera Programs	After-school programs or community-based organizations; youth ages 11–12; holistic approach; seven years (pregnancy prevention)	Female participants were less likely to get pregnant or to become sexually active; no program impact for male participants
FOCUS	Specialized settings; female Marine Corp recruits ages 17+; curriculum-based intervention; four two-hour sessions (pregnancy and STD* prevention)	*Eleven months later:* sexually inexperienced were less likely to report having had multiple partners since graduating; no program impact on number of partners for sexually experienced; no program impact on condom use
It's Your Game: Keep it Real	Middle schools; students in grades 7–8; classroom and computer-based program; twelve fifty-minute lessons over two years (HIV*, STI*, and pregnancy prevention)	*A year later:* less sexually experienced were less likely to report having initiated sexual activity
Project TALC	After-school programs or community-based organizations; adolescent children with HIV-positive parents; intervention based on social learning theory; twenty-four sessions over four to six years (HIV and pregnancy prevention)	*Four years later:* participants were less likely to report being teenage parents
Rikers Health Advocacy Program (RHAP)	Specialized settings; incarcerated inner-city adolescent males ages 16–19; problem-solving therapy approach; four, one-hour sessions over two weeks (HIV prevention)	*Ten months later:* heterosexual participants with prejail sexual experience reported higher frequency of condom use during vaginal, oral, or anal sex; no program impact on number of sexual partners or frequency of anal sex
Teen Outreach Program	High schools; disadvantaged and high-risk youth in grades 9–12; youth development framework; nine months of programming including twenty-five sessions of curriculum and twenty hours of community service (youth development)	*At end of school year:* female participants were less likely to report a pregnancy

*HIV, Human immunodeficiency virus; STI, sexually transmitted infection; STD, sexually transmitted disease.

There is no doubt that many schools are interested in either having their own pregnancy prevention program or teaming with other community-based organizations to support such programs. I know of no definitive evidence on the overall quality of these programs or even a representative sample of the programs, but based on reading many documents and talking with people in the field in recent years, I would not be surprised to find that many of the programs produce modest results, more or less like most other intervention programs run in the schools. However, the research reviewed by HHS in its evidence review shows that there are thirty-five program models with strong evidence of success. HHS is now three years into working with over one hundred local sponsors to determine whether these evidence-based model programs can be scaled up to more and more sites.

Thus, there is solid evidence that if schools implemented evidence-based teen pregnancy prevention programs that fit local values, especially regarding abstinence-only approaches and so-called comprehensive approaches that feature both instruction in abstinence and in use of effective means of birth control, they could help teens make better decisions about whether to remain abstinent—and, if the teens decide to engage in sexual intercourse, to use effective forms of birth control.[30]

Moreover, there are a variety of sources of federal and, in many states, state and local funding to pay for these programs. This funding includes programs like those outlined previously that are specifically devoted to reducing teen pregnancy, as well as more general sources of funding that can be used for teen pregnancy prevention like Medicaid, the Maternal and Child Health Block Grant, and the Temporary Assistance for Needy Families program.[31] In short, we have programs that have proven to be effective in limiting both teen sexual activity and pregnancy, and we have multiple sources of funding for these programs.

If more schools followed the evidence-based path and mounted good programs while evaluating their impacts and using the results to improve their programs, more teens would avoid the long-term barriers to a productive life imposed on them by a teen birth or would not have to decide whether to have an abortion, which may also have long-term effects.[32] Again, helping teens make responsible choices will pay off for them, for the children they bear later in life, and for society.

CONCLUSION

The argument of this chapter is that schools can play an important role in helping children and adolescents make good choices about education, work, and marriage. This is in no way to suggest that the traditional goals of education—to give students a solid footing in English, math, history, and the sciences—should be diminished. However, students—especially those from poor and minority families—should be constantly exposed to teachers, coursework, and programs that emphasize the importance of personal responsibility. Several programs that rigorous evaluations have shown help students make responsible choices in work, education, and marriage are available for schools and communities to use. Students should know that educational attainment (years of schooling) is the most direct determinant of adult income, and they should know that sexual activity carries grave consequences. In addition, the schools, working with parents and community organizations, should ensure that adolescents are encouraged to participate in community-based programs that teach healthy behavior and encourage sexual abstinence—and, where abstinence fails, use of effective forms of birth control. Students from poor and minority families in particular should be given the opportunity to take courses that give them marketable skills and direct exposure to the world of work. Schools can and must balance the goals of preparing students for four-year colleges, two-year colleges, and employment, and to take seriously the proposition that learning about and accepting personal responsibility for life-course choices regarding work, education, and family are vital to their success.

NOTES

1. "Spending for Federal Benefits and Services for People with Low Income, FY2008–FY2011: An update of Table B-1 from CRS Report R41625, Modified to Remove Programs for Veterans," Congressional Research Service, Memorandum to the Senate Budget Committee, October 16, 2012, http://www.budget.senate. gov/republican/public/index.cfm/files/serve/?File_id=0f87b42d-f182-4b3d-8ae2-fa8ac8a8edad; Ron Haskins, Testimony to the Budget Committee on Federal Spending, US House of Representatives, April 17, 2012; Nicholas Eberstadt, *A Nation of Takers: America's Entitlement Epidemic* (Washington, DC: American Enterprise Institute, 2012).

2. Miles Corak, "Income Inequality, Equality of Opportunity, and Intergenerational Mobility," *Journal of Economic Perspectives*, forthcoming.

3. Defined as at least three times the poverty level or about $56,000 for a family of three in 2013.

4. Ron Haskins and Isabel Sawhill, *Creating an Opportunity Society* (Washington, DC: Brookings Institution Press, 2009).

5. These simulations were originally reported in Ron Haskins and Isabel Sawhill, *Work and Marriage: The Way to End Poverty and Welfare,* Welfare Reform and Beyond Policy Brief #28 (Washington, DC: Brookings Institution, 2003).

6. Isabel Sawhill, Quentin Karpilow, and Joanna Venator, *The Impact of Unintended Childbearing on Future Generations* (Washington, DC: Brookings Institution,

2014), http://www.brookings.edu/~/media/research/files/papers/2014/09/12%20im-pact%20unintended%20childbearing%20future%20sawhill/12_impact_unintended_childbearing_future_sawhill.pdf; Martha J. Bailey, *Fifty Years of Family Planning: New Evidence on the Long-Run Effects of Increasing Access to Contraception*, Working Paper 19493, NBER Working Paper Series (Cambridge, MA: National Bureau of Economic Research, 2013), http://www.nber.org/papers/w19493.pdf.

7. *Counting It Up: The Public Costs of Teen Childbearing: Key Data* (Washington, DC: National Campaign to Prevent Teen and Unplanned Pregnancy, 2013), http://thenationalcampaign.org/sites/default/files/resource-primary-download/count-ing-it-up-key-data-2013-update.pdf.

8. Greg J. Duncan and Richard J. Murnane, *Restoring Opportunity: The Crisis of Inequality and the Challenge for American Education* (Cambridge, MA: Harvard Education Press, 2014).

9. Ariel Kalil, "Inequality Begins at Home: The Role of Parenting in the Diverging Destinies of Rich and Poor Children," in *Families in an Era of Increasing Inequality: Diverging Destinies*, ed. Paul R. Amato, et al. (New York: Springer, 2014); Betty Hart and Todd R. Risley, *Meaningful Differences in the Everyday Experience of Young American Children* (Baltimore, MD: Paul H. Brookes, 1995); Jane Waldfogel and Elizabeth Washbrook, "Early Years Policy," *Child Development Research* (2011): 1–12.

10. Annette Lareau, *Unequal Childhoods: Class, Race, and Family Life* (Berkeley: University of California Press, 2003).

11. Caroline Hoxby and Christopher Avery, "The Missing 'One-Offs': The Hidden Supply of High-Achieving, Low-Income Students," in *Brookings Papers on Economic Activity*, ed. David H. Romer and Justin Wolfers (Washington, DC: Brookings Institution, Spring 2013), http://www.brookings.edu/~/media/projects/bpea/spring%202013/2013a_hoxby.pdf.

12. James J. Kemple, *Long-Term Impacts on Labor Market Outcomes, Educational Attainment, and Transitions to Adulthood* (New York: MDRC, 2008).

13. John Karl Scholz and Carolyn Heinrich, eds., *Making the Work-Based Safety Net Work Better* (New York: Russell Sage, 2009).

14. Julia Isaacs, Isabel Sawhill, and Ron Haskins, *Getting Ahead or Losing Ground? Economic Mobility in America* (Washington, DC: Brookings Institution and the Pew Charitable Trusts Economic Mobility Project, 2008), 96.

15. Ron Haskins, Harry Holzer, and Robert Lerman, *Promoting Economic Mobility by Increasing Postsecondary Education* (Washington, DC: Economic Mobility Project, Pew Charitable Trusts, 2009).

16. Andrea Venezia and Laura Jaeger, "Transitions from High School to College," *Future of Children* 23 (2013): 117–36.

17. Thomas Brock, *Evaluating Programs for Community College Students: How Do We Know What Works?* (New York: MDRC, 2010).

18. See chapter 4 in this volume by Robert Lerman.

19. Michael J. Weiss, et al., *A Random Assignment Evaluation of Learning Communities at Kingsborough Community College: Seven Years Later* (New York: MDRC, 2014).

20. James S. Coleman, et al., *Equality of Educational Opportunity* (Washington, DC: National Center for Educational Statistics, 1966).

21. Sara McLanahan and Gary Sandefur, *Growing Up with a Single Parent: What Hurts, What Helps* (Cambridge, MA: Harvard University Press, 1994).

22. Daniel T. Lichter and Deborah Roempke Graefe, *Finding a Mate? The Marital and Cohabitation Histories* (New York: Russell Sage Foundation, 1999).

23. Jane Leber Herr, *Does it Pay to Delay? Decomposing the Effect of First Birth Timing on Women's Wage Growth* (Cambridge, MA: National Bureau of Economic Research, 2008), http://users.nber.org/~herrj/Herr_PayToDelay_May08.pdf; Jennifer B. Kane, et al., "The Educational Consequences of Teen Childbearing," *Demography* 50 (2013): 2129–50.

24. Ron Haskins, *Show Me the Evidence: Obama's Fight for Rigor and Evidence in Federal Social Policy* (Washington, DC: Brookings Institution Press, 2015), chapter 3.

25. Douglas Kirby, *Emerging Answers: Research Findings on Programs to Reduce Teen Pregnancy* (Washington, DC: National Campaign to Prevent Teen Pregnancy, 2001).

26. Brady E. Hamilton, et al., "Births: Preliminary Data for 2013," *National Vital Statistics Reports* 63, no. 2 (2014).

27. Haskins, *Show Me the Evidence,* chapter 3.

28. For details of how the evidence review was conducted, see *Identifying Programs That Impact Teen Pregnancy, Sexually Transmitted Infections, and Associated Sexual Risk Behaviors, Review Protocol: Review Protocol, Version 2.0* (Princeton, NJ: Mathematica Policy Research, 2010), http://www.hhs.gov/ash/oah/oah-initiatives/teen_pregnancy/db/eb-programs-review-v2.pdf; for a list and characteristics of the 35 programs and a searchable database, see "Evidence-Based Programs," last updated on August 21, 2014, Office of Adolescent Health, http://www.hhs.gov/ash/oah/oah-initiatives/teen_pregnancy/db/tpp-searchable.html.

29. Ron Haskins, *Show Me the Evidence.*

30. M. Antonia Biggs, et al., "Did Increasing Use of Highly Effective Contraception Contribute to Declining Abortions in Iowa?," *Contraception,* forthcoming; Gina M. Secura, et al., "Provision of No-Cost, Long-Acting Contraception and Teenage Pregnancy," *New England Journal of Medicine* 371 (2014): 1316–23.

31. For a list and overview of most of these sources of funding, see Federal Funding Streams for Teen Pregnancy Prevention (Washington, DC: National Campaign to Prevent Teen and Unplanned Pregnancy, 2014), http://thenationalcampaign.org/resource/federal-funding-streams-teen-pregnancy-prevention.

32. Studies on the long-term mental health effects of young women having an abortion is a matter of contention among psychologists; see American Psychological Association Task Force on Mental Health and Abortion, *Report of the APA Task Force on Mental Health and Abortion* (Washington, DC: American Psychological Association, 2008), http://www.apa.org/pi/wpo/mental-health-abortion-report.pdf.

Chapter Two

Big Payoff, Low Probability: Postsecondary Education and Upward Mobility in America

Andrew P. Kelly

Since the earliest days of the Republic, it has been an article of faith that higher education is one of America's primary engines of economic mobility. In 1786, John Adams wrote,

> But before any great things are accomplished, a memorable change must be made in the system of Education and knowledge must become so general as to raise the lower ranks of Society nearer to the higher. The Education of a Nation, instead of being confined to a few schools & Universities, for the instruction of the few, must become the National Care and expence, for the information of the Many.[1]

Twenty-five years later, shortly after founding the University of Virginia, Thomas Jefferson described the leavening effect of public universities:

> [In] establishing an institution of wisdom for them we secure it to all our future generations; that in fulfilling this duty we bring home to our own bosoms the sweet consolation of seeing our sons rising, under a luminous tuition, to destinies of high promise; these are considerations which will occur to all.[2]

After signing the Higher Education Act in 1965 at his alma mater, Southwest Texas State College, Lyndon Johnson told the audience, "This legislation will swing open a new door for the young people of America. . . . It means a way to deeper personal fulfillment, greater personal productivity, and increased personal reward."[3]

This faith in higher education as a social leveler has driven America's steady march toward mass higher education. In the mid-nineteenth century, federal policymakers laid the groundwork for publicly funded state university systems. In the twentieth century, they created a generous system of loans and grants for low-income students. States built and rapidly expanded four-year institutions, followed by community colleges, in the process redefining what college looks like and whom it was meant to serve.

By many measures, this faith in higher education has been rewarded. High school graduation and college enrollment rates have increased, especially among minorities and low-income students.[4] Meanwhile, the proportion of recent high school graduates enrolling in college grew from just under half in 1979 to more than two-thirds in 2010.[5] Among children born in the bottom income quartile in the 1960s, less than 20 percent enrolled in a four-year college; twenty years later, nearly 30 percent of the bottom quartile did.[6]

Meanwhile, since the dawn of mass higher education, the payoff to a college degree has grown and the fortunes of those with just a high school diploma have dimmed. The benefits are particularly large for low-income students who earn a degree.[7] Not surprisingly, research on mobility has found that children born into disadvantaged families who earn a degree are much more likely to climb the economic ladder than those who do not complete college.[8]

These increases in college access should be great news for mobility, right? Not exactly. While mobility has not declined, a comprehensive longitudinal study of millions of families found that mobility rates have remained largely stagnant over the past two decades.[9]

How is it that rising educational attainment and increased access to college have not made a dent in economic mobility? The problem lies in the disconnect between the payoff to a college degree—which is big, on average—and the number of disadvantaged Americans who actually make it that far—which is small. College does have a large effect on one's chances of moving up, but that effect only accrues to those who actually finish a degree. The most recent data suggest that, on average, recent college dropouts are no better off than those who never go to college at all.[10] And if nearly everyone at the top of the economic ladder gets a college degree, it will be that much harder for those without one at the bottom to move up.

For far too many disadvantaged high school graduates, access to college is a dead end rather than an on-ramp to the middle class. Low-income students often graduate high school unprepared for college-level work, yet all of them are eligible to enroll in college and access federal financial aid.

The majority of those who do enroll wind up in remedial courses that they are unlikely to pass, and many of them wind up with little but debt and regret. Many of these individuals would be better off pursuing something other than a four-year or a two-year degree—a short-term vocational certificate or an apprenticeship that provides access to skills and a job. But such alternatives are often treated as a last resort instead of a worthwhile option and are underdeveloped and underfunded.

At the other end of the spectrum, low-income students who are academically ready face their own set of obstacles. College costs have skyrocketed over the past three decades, but family incomes have not kept pace. First-generation college students often lack the information necessary to make good decisions about where to attend. As a result, far too many of these students ship off to low-quality institutions that have every incentive to take their tuition dollars and less incentive to worry about how they fare on campus. Even our highest achieving low-income students are less likely to earn a college degree than our lowest-achieving high-income students.[11]

In short, the existing system is not narrowing gaps between high- and low-income families; rather, it is widening them. But all is not lost. Researchers and innovators are learning how to help more low-income Americans—both the high achieving and those with academic needs—find postsecondary options that will provide the skills and knowledge necessary for economic success. New approaches to developmental education, financial aid, college guidance, and vocational education have shown what is possible when we think beyond the traditional model.

In this chapter, I provide an overview of the impact of two-year and four-year degrees on economic mobility and the status quo in college attainment among low-income students. Using data from national surveys, I highlight the disconnect described previously: while a college degree can act as a catapult for those born in the bottom, very few actually make it that far. I go on to examine the major "chokepoints" on the road to postsecondary education. I conclude by discussing potential reforms that can help jumpstart postsecondary education as an engine of mobility.

WHAT WE KNOW: ON AVERAGE, A COLLEGE DEGREE ENHANCES MOBILITY

Recent studies of economic mobility capture what many American families already know: it is becoming increasingly difficult to get ahead in this country with no more than a high school diploma.[12] Using data from the Panel Study of Income Dynamics (PSID), the Pew Project on Economic Mobility found that completing a four-year degree improves both absolute mobility (you are better off than your parents) and relative mobility (your position on the economic ladder is higher than your parents'). Figure 2.1 reproduces Pew's findings on the relative mobility of children born into the bottom income quintile who earned a college degree.

Fully 47 percent of those who did not complete a four-year degree remained stuck in the lowest income quintile as adults; just 10 percent of those

Adult Income Quintiles of Children
Born in Bottom Quintile (Pew, 2012)

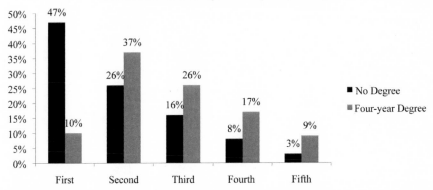

Figure 2.1. The effect of a college degree on economic mobility (reproduced from Pew's *Pursuing the American Dream* study)

who earned a four-year degree faced the same fate. Of the most disadvantaged college graduates, 37 percent wound up in the second quintile, while more than half (53 percent) reached the middle quintile or above as adults. Just 27 percent of non-degree-holders made it to the middle.

In a 2009 study, the Brookings Institution's Ron Haskins found similar effects. Whereas 16 percent of four-year college grads born in the bottom quintile remained there, 45 percent of nongraduates did. Among disadvantaged college grads, 62 percent wound up in the middle or above. In fact, this group exhibited almost perfect mobility: their chances of falling into any one quintile as an adult were roughly equal (approximately 20 percent).[13]

Earning a college degree has a substantial effect on mobility for two reasons. First, the college wage premium is larger than ever before. Second, disadvantaged students seem to benefit the most from postsecondary education.

Economic Returns Remain Robust

Despite all of the popular hand wringing over "boomerang kids" (college grads who return home to live with their parents) and crippling student debt, the wage premium attached to a college degree is as large as ever. But it is important to distinguish between trends in absolute returns (that is, what college completers earn) and trends in the wage premium (that is, the gap between the earnings of college graduates and those of high school diploma holders).

On the one hand, the earnings of recent college graduates have actually declined over the past decade, as the proportion of grads working in low-wage jobs that do not require a college degree has grown.[14] On the other, because the wages of high school graduates have essentially remained flat since the 1970s, the college wage premium has remained robust, peaking in 2001 and holding steady throughout the first decade of the 2000s.[15] Some analysts have found that the premium is larger than ever; in 2013, workers with a four-year degree earned 98 percent more per hour than those with just a high school diploma, up from 85 percent in 2003.[16] Thus while the costs of going to college have grown, so has the opportunity cost of *not* going.

Selection effects explain some of these patterns: college graduates are very different people, in terms of skills, work ethic, and intelligence, than high school graduates. But a voluminous scholarly literature on the returns to schooling has found that college attendance and completion have sizable positive effects on labor-market success even after accounting for these differences.[17] This is true for associate degrees and bachelor's degrees, as well as vocational certificates.[18] Evidence also suggests that there is a "sheepskin" effect, where those who complete a credential earn more than those who finish the same number of credits.[19]

It is beyond the scope of this chapter to survey this literature in detail, but summarizing it is simple enough: *on average,* completing college pays.

Disadvantaged Students Benefit the Most

Averages can cover up important differences across groups. From the perspective of those interested in social mobility, the question of who benefits most from earning a college degree is important. If those born in the upper end of the income distribution benefit more than those born at the bottom, higher education may make it harder to move up, and vice versa.

Recent research has shown that disadvantaged students benefit the most. In their 2010 study, Brand and Xie found that the returns to college were not uniform across different groups but were largest for those low-income students that were on the margin of attending college at all.[20] Likewise, Dale and Krueger found that the payoff to earning a degree from an elite college was larger for students from disadvantaged families.[21] Finally, a study of community college outcomes found that older, dislocated workers reaped significant benefits from taking community college courses in technical fields.[22] In other words, a college education pays more for those with less.

Caveat: On Average ≠ Always

There are important caveats to keep in mind. First and foremost, a positive average return does not mean everybody benefits. A recent analysis by the

Federal Reserve Bank of New York found that the bottom 25 percent of bachelor's degree recipients earn little more than a high school graduate and have not earned more since the 1970s.[23] This finding jibes with Arum and Roksa's follow-up study to *Academically Adrift*, which found that only a quarter of graduates had found jobs paying more than $40,000 a year. More than half were unemployed, working part time, or earning less than $30,000 a year.[24]

Relying on average returns also ignores significant differences across fields of study, particularly at the sub-baccalaureate level. In their analysis of the returns to different bachelor's degrees, Carnevale, Strohl, and Melton found that the median computer science and engineering major earned 60 to 70 percent more than those who majored in the humanities, education, or psychology and social work.[25]

In a study of the returns to sub-baccalaureate credentials in Washington State, Dadgar and Trimble found that while associate degrees were valuable overall, men with associate degrees in business, humanities, and allied health did not realize a significant payoff, while those with associate degrees in science and mathematics, nursing, and construction earned significantly more.[26] They also found that most short-term certificates (less than one year in length) were not worthwhile. In other words, some programs are worth the investment, but some plainly are not.

Finally, a positive wage premium does not necessarily translate to greater relative or absolute mobility. Graduating from college can be better than not, but if nearly everyone born in the top also earns a degree, then it will be more difficult for low-income graduates to improve their relative position on the economic ladder. Meanwhile, declining absolute wages may also mean that while degree holders are better off than their contemporaries who are high school grads, they may not actually be faring better than their parents.[27]

Caveat: Going to College ≠ Finishing College

It is most important to distinguish between going to college and finishing college, because the two have very different effects. This elementary point is often missed in the debate, as analyses of whether going to college is "worth it" almost always compare degree completers to those who finished high school. This, despite the fact that somewhere between 40 and 45 percent of those students who start a degree never finish one and that the dropout rate is much higher among disadvantaged students.[28] To determine the costs and benefits of going to college, any estimate of the returns must be weighted by the probability of finishing.

It is true that some analyses have found that earning credits, especially in technical coursework, can pay off.[29] But the latest data show that the wage premium attached to "some college, no degree" is "virtually zero, averaging −3 percent for median earners and 5 percent for 90th percentile earners."[30] As I show in the next section, this distinction is crucial to understanding how college access affects upward mobility. Because so many low-income students start but never finish a college credential, access to college alone often fails to catapult them up the economic ladder.

WHAT WE KNOW: VERY FEW
LOW-INCOME STUDENTS EARN A CREDENTIAL

The mobility-enhancing effect of a four-year college degree is substantial for those children born at or near the bottom, but very few actually make it that far. In this section, I use data from the Education Longitudinal Study (ELS) to show how low-income students are underrepresented at every stage of the college-going process, particularly when it comes to college attainment. The ELS provides a recent snapshot of the gaps in college aspirations, readiness, application, and completion between students born in the bottom income groups and those born in the top.

Table 2.1 reports attainment rates from the final round of ELS data collection, disaggregated by students' socioeconomic status (SES) in the base year. The ELS data include a derived variable that measures a student's SES—an amalgam of income, parents' education, and parents' occupation—and divides respondents up into quartiles based on that measure. For simplicity's sake, I collapse the second and third quartiles into a "middle" category.

Nearly two-thirds of students from the lowest SES quartile reported no college credential eight years after graduating high school. The modal category was some college but no credential. When it comes to the big payoff reported in studies of economic mobility—the one attached to a four-year degree—a paltry 14 percent of students from the bottom actually experience

Table 2.1.   Attainment by Base-Year Socioeconomic Status, ELS Cohort

Highest Education Level	Base-Year Socioeconomic Status		
	Lowest	Middle	Highest
High school or below	29.0	15.1	3.7
Some college, no credential	35.9	35.1	23.8
Undergraduate certificate	12.6	11.2	5.8
Associate's degree	8.1	9.8	6.7
Bachelor's degree or above	14.3	29.0	60.0

Note: Author's calculations from public-use ELS data, base year (SES, 2002), and third follow up (attainment, 2012).

it. An additional 21 percent earned either an associate's degree (8 percent) or a certificate (12.6 percent), bringing the overall attainment rate (degrees and certificates) to just over one-third.

Contrast that pattern with that for the highest SES group—the very people that students from the bottom are trying to catch. Nearly three-fourths of them earned some kind of postsecondary credential over that period (72.5 percent), and almost none failed to make it to at least "some college." Among those in the highest SES group, 60 percent went on to earn bachelor's degrees or above—an insurance policy against falling from the top of the heap. The Pew analysis of college and mobility found that only 9 percent of those born in the top quintile who earned a four-year degree fell below the middle quintile as adults.[31]

Among those who start college, the results for students from the lowest SES quartile are equally discouraging. More than half have some college but no credential, double the proportion of dropouts from the highest SES quartile. Of those who enroll, 20 percent go on to earn a bachelor's degree; the proportion of BA earners is three times as large in the high-SES group (Table 2.2).

There are plenty of explanations as to why low-SES students would lag behind their peers, some of which are to be expected. We would not expect students who do not aspire to college or are not college-ready to wind up there (though many in both groups still do). The next sections detail the major choke points in the college pipeline. For now, it is worth pointing out that the lower-income lag is evident at each stage of the college-going process. Table 2.3 displays four of those important phases: college aspirations as sophomores, taking an entrance exam, college-application behavior, and college enrollment within two years of graduating high school.

Two-thirds of students aspire to a credential, but only 40 percent take an entrance exam and about half enroll by the time they are two years out of

Table 2.2. Attainment among Those Who Enrolled in College by Base-Year SES, ELS Cohort

	Base-Year Socioeconomic Status		
Highest Education Level	*Lowest*	*Middle*	*Highest*
Some college, no credential	50.6	41.3	24.7
Undergraduate certificate	17.8	13.1	6.0
Associate's degree	11.4	11.5	7.0
Bachelor's degree	20.2	34.1	62.3

Note: The authors' calculations were made using public-use ELS data and were restricted to subsample of only enrollees: those who were enrolled in a postsecondary institution and those who were not enrolled but were previously enrolled in a postsecondary institution (third follow up, 2012).

Table 2.3.   Stages of College-Going Process by Base Year SES, ELS Cohort

Stages of the College-Going process	Base-Year Socioeconomic Status		
	Lowest	Middle	Highest
Aspired to graduate from two- or four-year college or above[1]	66.4	77.9	89.9
Took a college entrance exam	41.6	62.0	87.0
Applied to at least one college in senior year	62.1	70.4	86.3
Enrolled in college within two years of high school graduation	50.8	71.5	90.7

Note: The author's calculations were made using public-use ELS data, base year (SES, aspirations, 2002), first follow up (took a placement exam, applied to college, 2004), and second follow up (enrollment, 2006).

1. Technically, one of the response categories corresponded to whether students planned to "attend or complete" two-year or vocational school. I include that as an indicator of aspiration to a credential in Table 3.

high school. For those at the top, they aim higher and their aspirations more readily translate to behavior: 90 percent aspire to a postsecondary credential, 87 percent take an entrance exam, and 91 percent enroll in a program by the time they are two years out of high school.

These patterns help explain why the expansion of college access has failed to markedly boost mobility and may, in fact, increase inequality. Very few children born to affluent families miss out on the college wage premium, while two-thirds of poor children enter the workforce without it. Because a degree is also an insurance policy against falling out of the top, high attainment rates among the higher income group make relative mobility even less likely for disadvantaged students.

Other evidence suggests that low-income students made only small gains in four-year college attainment over the past two decades. Bailey and Dynarski find that the bachelor's degree attainment rate among those born in the lowest income quartile in the 1960s was just 5 percent; by the 1980s cohort, that rate had increased to 9 percent (the dataset used in their analysis also sampled students in the eighth grade). These gains paled in comparison to those made by the highest quartile, where attainment rose from 36 percent to 54 percent across those two cohorts.[32]

So, to reiterate once again: Earning a four-year degree certainly enhances mobility, but only a very select group of low-income students make it that far. Put another way, in assessing the impact of college-going on mobility, we have to weight that big payoff by a low probability. True, the picture is somewhat rosier when you include associate degrees and vocational certificates. But the point remains: while our postsecondary system can act as an engine of social mobility for those who complete a degree, only a small segment of low-income Americans cross the finish line.

THE DILEMMA OF COLLEGE
READINESS (OR THE LACK THEREOF)

What explains lackluster college-completion rates among our most needy students? In diagnosing the problem, it is helpful to distinguish between two groups: those who are not college-ready when they graduate high school and those who are. Though students in the latter group have enough trouble running the gauntlet to a degree or certificate, those who are not academically prepared face extremely long odds.

Unfortunately, far too many low-income students fall into the unprepared group, and few of them are successful in college. Under federal law, anybody with a high school diploma can access federal student aid and can use it to pay for up to two semesters of remedial coursework. States allow high school graduates to enroll whether they are college-ready or not and spend billions on remedial coursework at four-year and community colleges.[33]

Just how bad is it? A recent report by the college admissions testing service ACT found that among the 1.8 million students who took a college-readiness assessment in 2014, just 26 percent met college-ready benchmarks in all four subjects (English, reading, math, and science).[34] College-readiness rates were higher on individual assessments—64 percent were deemed ready in English—but just 44 and 43 percent met the standard in reading and math, respectively.

National estimates of college-remediation rates echo these findings. A study by Complete College America found that more than half of all students enrolling in two-year colleges were placed into remedial courses. At four-year colleges, the remediation rate among first-time students was 20 percent.[35] The Beginning Postsecondary Students (BPS) survey, administered to students starting college in 2004, found that 68 percent of public community college students took at least one remedial course and that those students were required to take an average of 2.9 remedial courses. Readiness is particularly low among disadvantaged students, who often attend low-performing high schools. BPS data show that 58 percent of students from the lowest income group (in both two- and four-year colleges) took at least one remedial course and were required to take, on average, 3.1 remedial courses.[36]

Students who are not college-ready are much less likely to be successful on the path to a credential, and remediation does little to improve their chances. The relationship between remedial classes and student success is a hotly debated topic and one that is difficult to parse due to selection effects. Are students enrolled in remediation less successful because they are not college-ready or because the remedial courses cause them to drop out? The research on this question is mixed, with some finding sizable benefits for those who actually finish remedial courses but low completion rates across all those who test into remediation in the first place.[37]

Setting aside these debates, the descriptive data tell a discouraging story: Complete College America found that just over 60 percent of community college students who are placed into remediation actually pass those courses, and only 22 percent of them go on to pass credit-bearing college courses. They estimated that just 9.5 percent of those remedial students would go on to finish a degree within three years, as compared to 13.9 percent of their college-ready peers.[38]

Solutions for Non-College-Ready Students

What, then, do we do about college readiness? It is a difficult problem to solve at the higher-education policy level, given how much responsibility is borne by high schools, which are governed by the K–12 system. That being said, some promising ideas have emerged.

One is to adopt the logic of prevention in helping low-income students avoid remediation completely. Some students test into a semester or more of remedial coursework because they are unprepared for the placement test. Providing students with low-cost opportunities to diagnose their academic needs and address them prior to taking the placement tests would lower remediation rates.

In California, for instance, the California State University System's Early Assessment Program tests high school students between their junior and senior years to diagnose their likelihood of placing into remediation at a CSU campus. Students are then provided with a menu of options, including an online tutorial, designed to help them achieve college readiness. Evaluations of the program have found that it reduces the likelihood of placing into remediation.[39] Students who avoid remediation amass more credits and are more likely to graduate.

Of course, many students will still fail to reach college-ready benchmarks before they graduate from high school. However, the diagnostic assessment enables students and counselors to recognize this before they matriculate, and the results can then be used to refer students to career and technical programs for which college-ready proficiency in math and English may not be a prerequisite. Informational interventions—where third parties provide students with personalized guides to their options—could then guide these students toward worthwhile options.

It may also be possible to reform remedial coursework such that the courses are more effective in teaching the basic skills students need. Some campuses have found success using a "corequisite" or integrated remedial model, where students receive additional academic support at the same time that they take substantive, credit-bearing coursework. Washington State's Integrated Basic Education and Skills Training pairs basic-skills teachers with occupational faculty to design and teach courses that cover both basic and career skills. Though corequisite programs have yet to be evaluated by random-assignment study, early evaluations are promising.[40]

But it's also naïve to think we can reverse years of subpar math and English instruction in a couple of semesters. Needed is a much more coherent pre-K–12 reform agenda—like the one spelled out in this book—that helps prepare more low-income students for the rigors of college and holds K–12 schools accountable when they fail to do so. Playing catch-up after students graduate from high school is clearly not working.

Even with significant gains, though, many low-income students will not be ready for the rigors of a four-year bachelor's degree. Therefore, improving mobility will also require providing multiple pathways to the middle class, including via nondegree credentials, as Tamar Jacoby argues in her chapter. The country's focus on college readiness (reinforced by the Common Core State Standards) has often cast these occupational options as a last resort, the domain of the most difficult-to-educate students.

The truth, however, is that some occupational certificates pay sizable returns that are comparable to the payoff for associate or bachelor's degrees.[41] Returns vary considerably across fields, and not all certificates are worth the investment (cosmetology and culinary arts pay low returns, while nursing and information technology pay off well). Overall, though, research suggests that certificate holders earn 20 percent more than high school graduates, and some earn more than those with a bachelor's or associate's degree.[42] In other words, these programs can be "trajectory-changing" for low-income students and should not be treated as a last resort for students who are not college-ready.[43]

CHOKE POINTS TO COLLEGE COMPLETION FOR COLLEGE-READY, LOW-INCOME STUDENTS

Low-income students who graduate high school ready for college-level work have one strike fewer against them. But academic preparation does not entirely explain why low-income students lag behind their peers. One National Center for Education Statistics (NCES) analysis found that low-income students who scored in the top 25 percent in math and reading as high school seniors had a lower probability of earning a bachelor's degree than high-income students who scored in the bottom 25 percent academically.[44] Thus even high-achieving low-income students fail to reach the finish line. What gives? I highlight three major "choke points" here: college affordability, information problems, and low-performing colleges.

College Affordability

College costs have increased at two to three times the rate of inflation, pricing many low-income families out of the market and forcing others to take on significant debt. The sticker price of tuition has grown precipitously since the 1980s, and increases have been particularly steep since the mid-2000s; at both two-year and four-year public institutions, tuition and fees have increased by nearly 30 percent since 2008.[45]

When the latest recession ravaged most state budgets, legislatures cut the amount of public subsidy per student that their public colleges received. Public institutions made up the gap by increasing their tuition.[46] The steady increase at private nonprofits began earlier and has been somewhat less steep of late, partly because tuition prices are so high to begin with.

What does this mean for low-income students? Higher-education advocates are fond of pointing out that net prices—what students actually pay after accounting for grants and scholarships—have not risen as fast as sticker prices. But family incomes have declined over the last six years, meaning that even slow-growing net prices have taken an increasingly large chunk of their income. Moreover, to the extent that families fail to realize the distinction between sticker prices and net prices (and, as the next section points out, many do), high sticker prices might deter them from applying in the first place.

Historically, the federal government has tried to keep college affordable through grants and loans. However, this approach is no longer keeping pace with soaring tuition, raising questions about the sustainability of federal aid programs. Despite record increases in the size of the Pell Grant over the course of President Obama's first term, its purchasing power has never been lower, washed out by increases in tuition.[47] In fact, data suggest that the moderation in net prices during the recession was due to the unprecedented boost in Pell Grant spending over that period. That boost has now been eaten up by subsequent increases in tuition, and net prices are growing again.[48]

Long story short, everybody is paying more for college these days, and poor students with college aspirations are forced to take on jobs, attend part time, and/or take on large loans. Students who must work to cover expenses have less time to focus on their studies, putting their academic standing in jeopardy. Those who attend part time—80 percent of whom work while enrolled—are far less likely to finish college than those who enroll full time. According to one NCES analysis, 85 percent of students enrolled exclusively part time did not finish a degree within six years after starting school, compared to 35 percent of full-time enrollees.[49] For some students, the prohibitive costs of attendance may put college out of reach entirely.

Information Problems

For a half-century, federal policy has focused on ensuring that low-income students can pay for college. This approach assumes that they are aware of their financial aid options and have enough information to choose the college that best fits their needs. If students have imperfect information on college costs, financial aid, or institutional quality, then they may enroll in college that is unlikely to provide a return on their investment.

Unfortunately, prospective students in all income groups lack basic information on costs, financial aid, likely returns, and differences in institutional quality. A national study of perceptions of college costs found that just 31 percent of parents were able to provide an accurate estimate of the cost of two- or four-year college.[50] Low-income and first-generation students and their families are particularly underinformed. Studies have found that low-income parents overestimate the cost of college by two to three times and are often unable to identify existing sources of financial aid.[51]

When it comes to choosing a college or program, a nontrivial number of high-achieving, low-income students enroll in colleges that are less selective than they are academically qualified to attend.[52] Research has shown that this decision—dubbed "undermatching"—actually reduces a student's chances of graduating.[53] When it comes to choosing programs at the sub-baccalaureate level, Jacobson and LaLonde found that just 6 percent of community college students in Florida earned a two-year degree in a moderate- or high-return field, while 12 percent earned a degree in a low-return field.[54]

There is a fair amount of "overmatching" going on, as well, where students choose to enroll in institutions that are significantly more demanding than their academic ability. In a national study of college choices, Dillon and Smith found that the majority of students were "mismatched" to their college—25 percent overmatched, 28 percent undermatched—and that mismatches resulted from student choices rather than admissions decisions.[55]

Though some amount of overmatching is evident among low-income students, Dillon and Smith find that it is much more prevalent among low-achieving wealthy students. Among students with high school GPAs lower than 2.5 in the ELS cohort, nearly a quarter from the lowest SES quartile attended a four-year college (7.7 percent attended a selective or moderately selective campus), as compared with the 61.6 percent of low-achieving, high SES students who went to a four-year campus.

In addition to "mismatching," some students on the verge of enrolling just never show up, falling victim to what researchers call "summer melt." In their study of summer melt, Castleman and Page found that somewhere around 20 percent of students experience summer melt, and in some school districts the rate was as high as 40 percent among low-income, first-generation students.[56] In the absence of school counselors to help answer questions and nudge them along over the summer, low-income students can fall out of the pipeline.

Some of these information problems reflect a failure to capitalize on existing resources. But it is also true that some questions are either not answerable with existing data or not answerable until after the student has applied and been accepted. For instance, students only learn what they will actually pay after they apply, are accepted, and receive a financial aid award.

This sequencing can lead students to eliminate institutions on the basis of their sticker price, even though their net prices may be far lower. Meanwhile, other information that may be especially critical to low-income students is simply not systematically available—the rate at which recipients of federal-grant financial aid graduate from different institutions, for instance, or the earnings of graduates from particular programs.

All of this leads to a scenario where low-income students—from the most qualified to those on the margin—make enrollment decisions that decrease their chances of success. The lack of data on earnings also makes it more difficult to illustrate to families that there are paths to the middle class other than a four-year degree. Without these data, families cling to the belief that a BA is the only route to success.

Colleges and Policies Are Not Designed to Support Student Success

To be sure, many low-income students make suboptimal choices about where to go to college. But not all of them have access to a quality option in the first place. The average graduation rate among four-year colleges is less than 60 percent and is about half that at two-year colleges.[57] Colleges are typically funded on the basis of enrollments, not student outcomes; whether they prepare their students for success after school or not, colleges are paid in full. Federal loan and grant programs subsidize attendance at any program and at any price, so long as the program is accredited. In other words, most colleges have every incentive to enroll students but fewer to ensure they are successful.

Take, for instance, the way postsecondary programs are typically structured. Students are given wide latitude in choosing what courses and what major they would like to enroll in. Although it is a deeply ingrained value in American higher education, this freedom to choose and lack of structure can lead students—particularly first-generation ones—to swirl, taking courses here and there but not making much progress toward a degree. This lack of structure is at least partly to blame for the fact that most graduates finish with excess credits.[58] And when it comes time to trim and balance the budget, colleges often make choices that hurt student success, reducing course offerings and raising tuition.[59]

Meanwhile, within classrooms, most PhD-trained professors were never taught how to teach students or assess learning. Despite its ubiquity, the standard college lecture is proving inferior to new methods of teaching like hybrid courses.[60] Likewise, student support systems are usually passive; students get help with academic support or career advising only if they walk into the office that houses those services on campus. Students who are at risk of dropping out often simply stop showing up to class and are unlikely to take it upon themselves to get the help they need.

The system itself often feels tilted in favor of institutions and against the interests of students. Credit transfer is a case in point. Even though a third of students transfer from one college to another, they are often unable to bring all of the credits they earned at the first institution to the second.[61] Colleges claim this is a question of ensuring academic standards. But the truth is, they have zero incentive to accept transfer credits; each credit accepted is one fewer that an incoming student would have to pay for. The lack of credit portability is effectively a tax on students who transfer, extending their time to degree, raising the cost of completing, and potentially dissuading some from transferring at all.

HOW CAN WE DO BETTER?

These issues have not gone unnoticed, and a budding "completion agenda" has focused policymakers on finding ways to promote the success of low-income students. In the remainder of this chapter, I explore some of the emerging reform ideas and summarize the relevant research.

Innovations in Financial Aid

Low- and middle-income students may not enroll in or complete college because it is becoming prohibitively expensive. Quasiexperimental studies suggest that $1,000 in need-based aid boosts enrollment by about three to six percentage points. Estimates of aid's impact on completion are less conclusive, though a recent longitudinal study found that a Florida grant program increased persistence and degree completion.[62]

Additional grant money might help increase access, but there is also a sense among reformers that we must go beyond simply pouring more aid into the system. After all, the federal government has invested billions in grants and subsidized loans—including record amounts in recent years—yet income-attainment gaps have widened and college-completion rates remain flat. This discouraging track record has raised questions as to whether student aid programs as currently designed encourage students to graduate on time and what reforms might help better align those incentives.

In a recent review of the literature, Dynarski and Scott-Clayton highlight a series of lessons from existing literature, a few of which are worth highlighting here.[63] First, the complex and time-consuming application process for federal aid programs likely blunts their effects. Studies of programs with simple eligibility criteria (like state merit aid programs) and brief applications have found positive aid effects. Efforts to dramatically simplify the Free Application for Federal Student Aid and notify students earlier about their eligibility would help lower these transaction costs.

Second, aid programs that incentivize academic performance appear to have a positive effect. Currently, recipients of federal aid must make "satisfactory academic progress" each semester to remain eligible for aid, but the threshold varies by campus and it is not clear that students are aware of the incentive. MDRC has conducted a series of experiments using incentive-based grants, where additional grant money is conditional on meeting academic benchmarks. In general, they have found that the incentives had significant, positive effects on retention and credits earned.[64] A study of incentive-based grants combined with additional student services at a Canadian university also found positive effects on student success.[65]

Reformers have generally focused on public aid programs, but private financing can also play a fruitful role. In general, publicly funded grants and loans provide few signals to students about the value of the different programs they are considering. In contrast, private financing—like "Income-Share Agreements" (ISAs)—could help steer low-income students toward worthwhile programs.

Under an ISA, private investors provide the funding a student needs in return for a percentage of that student's future income over a fixed period of time. Because investors only reap a return if the student is successful, they have incentive to guide students toward quality programs (thus helping to solve information problems) and to support students while they are in school and searching for a job. This market is currently stunted by legal and regulatory uncertainty, though federal lawmakers have set out to remove these obstacles.[66]

Solving Information Problems

In response to the information problems described previously, policymakers have worked to improve the supply of information and researchers have tested new ways of providing information. The latest reauthorization of the Higher Education Act required that colleges create "net price calculators" to provide prospective students with a realistic estimate of out-of-pocket costs. The Obama administration has created a financial aid shopping sheet and a College Scorecard, and it recently pledged to develop a new set of federal college ratings. A handful of states—including Colorado, Tennessee, Florida, and others—have begun to publish data on earnings and employment outcomes linked to particular postsecondary programs.

Recent research suggests that providing information directly to students can have an affect on aspirations, application behavior, college choices, and enrollment. In a field experiment with Canadian high school students, Oreopolous and Dunn found that access to a multimedia website and video containing information on college-going led treated respondents to have higher aspirations and more awareness of financial aid and likely returns even three weeks later.[67] Castleman and Page found that sending personalized text-message reminders to college-bound students helped reduce summer melt by three to four percentage points.[68]

In the largest information experiment to date, Hoxby and Turner identified high-achieving low-income students and tested whether providing personalized information about college options could change behavior. The experiment sent randomly chosen strivers a guide with information on their college options, the application process, and financial aid, as well as application fee waivers. Hoxby and Turner found that for about six dollars per student, the intervention raised the probability of applying to a matched college by 56 percent and the probability of enrolling in one by 46 percent.[69]

These interventions are only as good as the data upon which they are based. Unfortunately, critical data on postgraduation earnings and grant recipients' graduation rates are still not systematically available. Better federal and state-level data collection and dissemination systems could provide the information on postprogram earnings and completion rates that consumers need.[70]

Reforms to Increase the Supply of Quality Seats

Helping low-income students navigate to programs where they are likely to be successful is a worthwhile enterprise, but the impact of demand-side reforms will depend on the supply of quality seats. If the capacity of good programs is more or less fixed, then helping students make better choices will be a zero-sum game: every low-income student who gets a seat will displace one who also would have benefited from it. That means we have to tackle the supply side of reform, as well.

We are starting to learn what it takes to design postsecondary programs that set low-income students up for success, and it often requires significant organizational change. New research suggests that immersive, structured programs—with clear expectations for student performance and behavior—can promote student success.

For instance, the Accelerated Study in Associates Programs (ASAP), a comprehensive effort to improve persistence and completion for developmental education students at the City University of New York, has substantially improved student success. ASAP requires that students enroll full time; in return, they receive a tuition waiver, enhanced advising, tutoring, free Metro Cards, and money for textbooks for three years. Students are also grouped into cohorts and take block-scheduled courses. A randomized study found that ASAP students earned almost eight more credits than a control group and that graduation rates were six percentage points higher three years after implementation.[71]

Beyond ASAP, reformers have begun to implement "structured pathways" to a credential—programs where students are guided into a field of study quickly, are provided with a clear map of the courses they need to finish, and are given less discretion in choosing courses. In addition, structured pathways transform services that are traditionally passive and "opt in," such as orientation, academic advising, and student success courses, to services that are mandatory and proactive.[72] Similarly, a randomized study found that student success coaching—where a mentor calls students directly every week or so to help them set goals, build study skills, and manage their time—boosts persistence in a cost-effective way.[73]

At the system level, states have taken pains to facilitate credit transfer, with some going so far as to create fully "stackable" credentials that allow students to accumulate stand-alone certificates that count toward a larger degree. In Texas, for instance, community colleges have partnered with energy companies to create a set of core courses for energy workers that will transfer to institutions across the state and count toward an associate's degree (and potentially a bachelor's) later on.[74] Stackable credentials lower the stakes of schooling decisions made at age eighteen or nineteen and can assuage fears of "tracking" low-income students into vocational programs that may have a low ceiling.

Note that these reforms are not simply tweaks to the existing model but are fundamental changes to the way a college education is delivered, how colleges interface with students, and how institutions work with one another. In ASAP's case, it is not just "free college" but a structured program that demands a full-time enrollment. Creating stackable credentials requires changes to longstanding credit-transfer policies and traditions of academic autonomy.

The effort to figure out "what works" is just beginning, but providing colleges and systems with incentives to adopt promising strategies is another question entirely. As a start, the federal government could put colleges on the hook for a portion of any loans on which their students default. Giving colleges "skin in the game" would do two things. First, it would dissuade colleges from enrolling students who are not college-ready and are unlikely to be successful. Second, it would encourage colleges to do their best to ensure that those students they do enroll are successful.

States, meanwhile, continue to experiment with outcomes-based funding policies, where public institutions are subsidized according to how well they perform. The research on these systems is decidedly mixed, with the latest analysis showing that they had little or no effect on productivity.[75] Going forward, policymakers should consider rewarding institutions on the basis of student learning or the labor-market success of graduates in addition to (or instead of) graduation rates.

THE FUTURE: NEW OPTIONS AND MULTIPLE PATHWAYS

Up to now, I've focused on changes to the existing postsecondary system that could promote low-income student success. These are worthwhile steps, but many of them amount to "retrofitting" institutions and policies that were designed in a different era to accomplish new goals.[76] As such, policymakers must also look beyond higher education as traditionally conceived—the two- or four-year degree-granting college—and create space for new options that can provide additional pathways to the middle class. In particular, mobility-seeking students would benefit from a more flexible system that allows them to jump in when they need to learn new things and jump out when they are ready to rejoin the workforce.

For instance, helping people learn the skills they need for a particular job may not require multiple semesters of fifteen-week courses, general education requirements, and the like but short bursts of intensive, targeted instruction followed by a chance to apply what they've learned. Learners could repeat this sequence a few times over a decade to keep up with industry demands, all while earning credentials that add up to a larger whole.

Career "bootcamps" like General Assembly and Dev Bootcamp provide one possible model; these private firms teach short, immersive courses that are linked directly to high-demand tech jobs. Udacity's "Nanodegrees"—sequences of five online courses designed in concert with employers to prepare students for particular roles—are another. Students pay $200 a month and can move through the coursework and assignments at their own pace. These models are new and unproven, but they illustrate what's possible when we think outside of the two- and four-year degree box.

Low-income students looking to climb the economic ladder may well want to pursue such alternate routes to productive careers (in addition to routes that Tamar Jacoby describes in her chapter), especially as the cost of college grows. But they will often need financial aid to do so, aid that is currently limited to accredited degree- or certificate-granting institutions. Without access to aid, less-traditional offerings—even those that are exceptionally inexpensive—cannot hope to compete with publicly funded options that are essentially free to low-income students who qualify for grants.

Policymakers who want to foster new, more affordable pathways to the middle class should work to lower barriers to entry like accreditation and allow new competitors to prove their mettle. Existing colleges and universities can promote upward mobility, but they are not miracle workers. They will be hard-pressed to overcome twelve years of slipshod instruction. Reformers must therefore not lose sight of the need for both reform of the pre-K–12 system and the development of worthwhile alternatives to the traditional college degree. It is time for America to once again redefine what postsecondary education can look like and whom it should serve.

NOTES

1. "John Adams to Matthew Robinson, Jr.," March 23, 1786, Founders Early Access, http://rotunda.upress.virginia.edu/founders/FOEA-03-01-02-0563.
2. "Extract from Thomas Jefferson to James Breckenridge," February 15, 1821, The Jefferson Monticello, accessed at: http://tjrs.monticello.org/letter/1611.
3. Lyndon Johnson, "Remarks at Southwest Texas State College," November 8, 1965, LBJ for Kids! http://www.lbjlib.utexas.edu/johnson/lbjforkids/edu_whca370-text.shtm.
4. Richard J. Murnane and Stephen Hoffman, "Graduations on the Rise," *Education Next* 13, no. 4 (2013), http://educationnext.org/graduations-on-the-rise/.
5. *Recent high school completers and their enrollment in 2-year and 4-year colleges, by sex: 1960 through 2010* (Washington, DC: National Center for Education Statistics, 2011), https://nces.ed.gov/programs/digest/d13/tables/dt13_302.10.asp.
6. Martha Bailey and Susan Dynarski, "Inequality in Postsecondary Education," in *Whither Opportunity? Rising Inequality, Schools, and Children's Life Chances*, ed. Greg Duncan and Richard Murnane (New York: Russell Sage, 2011): 117–31.
7. Jennie Brand and Yu Xie, "Who Benefits Most from College? Evidence for Negative Selection and in Heterogeneous Economic Returns to Higher Education," *American Sociological Review* 75, no. 2 (2010): 273–302.

8. *Pursuing the American Dream: Economic Mobility Across Generations* (Washington, DC: The Pew Charitable Trusts, July 2012), http://www.pewtrusts. org/~/media/legacy/uploadedfiles/wwwpewtrustsorg/reports/economic_mobility/ PursuingAmericanDreampdf.pdf.

9. Raj Chetty et al., "Is the United States Still a Land of Opportunity? Recent Trends in Intergenerational Mobility," NBER Working Paper (Cambridge, MA: National Bureau of Economic Research, 2014), http://obs.rc.fas.harvard.edu/chetty/ mobility_trends.pdf.

10. Daniel Carroll and Amy Higgins, *A College Education Saddles Young Households with Debt, but Still Pays Off* (Cleveland, OH: Federal Reserve Bank of Cleveland, 2014) http://www.clevelandfed.org/research/trends/2014/0714/01labmar.cfm.

11. Mary Ann Fox, Brooke A. Connolly, and Thomas D. Snyder, *Youth Indicators 2005: Trends in the Well-Being of American Youth* (Washington, DC: US Department of Education, National Center for Education Statistics, 2005), http://files.eric.ed.gov/ fulltext/ED485721.pdf.

12. For the purposes of this discussion, I focus on relative mobility, or the probability that a child born into a particular income group moves up and out of that group by the time he or she reaches adulthood.

13. Ron Haskins, Harry Holzer, and Robert Lerman, "Promoting Economic Mobility by Increasing Postsecondary Education," (Washington, DC: The Pew Charitable Trusts, May 2009).

14. Jaison Abel, Richard Deitz, and Yaqin Su, "Are Recent College Graduates Finding Good Jobs?" *Current Issues in Economics and Finance* 20, no. 1: 1–8, http:// www.newyorkfed.org/research/current_issues/ci20-1.pdf.

15. Ibid., 2014; Anthony P. Carnevale, Stephen J. Rose, and Ban Cheah, *The College Payoff: Education, Occupations, Lifetime Earnings* (Washington, DC: Georgetown University Center on Education and the Workforce, 2011); Claudia Goldin and Lawrence F. Katz, *The Race Between Education and Technology,* (Cambridge, MA: Harvard University Press, 2008).

16. For analysis of the Economic Policy Institute's data, see David Leonhardt, "Is College Worth It? Clearly, New Data Say," *New York Times,* http://www.nytimes. com/2014/05/27/upshot/is-college-worth-it-clearly-new-data-say.html.

17. See David Card, "Estimating the Return to Schooling: Progress on Some Persistent Econometric Problems," *Econometrica* 69, no. 5 (2001): 1127–60.

18. Thomas J. Kane and Cecilia Elena Rouse, "Labor-Market Returns to Two- and Four-Year College," *The American Economic Review* 85, no. 3 (1995): 600–614; Louis S. Jacobson and Christine Mokher, *Pathways to Boosting the Earnings of Low-Income Students by Increasing Their Educational Attainment* (Washington, DC: The Hudson Institute, 2009).

19. David A. Jaeger and Marianne E. Page, "Degrees Matter: New Evidence on Sheepskin Effects in the Returns to Education," *Review of Economics and Statistics* 78, no. 4 (1996): 733–40.

20. Brand and Xie, "Who Benefits Most from College?"

21. Stacy Dale and Alan B. Krueger, "Estimating the Return to College Selectivity Over the Career Using Administrative Earnings Data," NBER Working Paper No. 17159 (Cambridge, MA: National Bureau of Economic Research, 2011).

22. Louis S. Jacobson, Robert J. LaLonde, and Daniel G. Sullivan, "Estimating the Returns to Community College Schooling for Displaced Workers," Discussion Paper No. 1017 (Bonn, Germany: Institute for the Study of Labor, 2004).

23. Jason R. Abel and Richard Deitz, "College May Not Pay Off for Everyone," September 4, 2014, Liberty Street Economics, http://libertystreeteconomics.newyork-fed.org/2014/09/college-may-not-pay-off-for-everyone.html#.VBYS7mSwLtV.

24. Richard Arum and Josipa Roksa, *Aspiring Adults Adrift: Tentative Transitions of College Graduates* (Chicago: University of Chicago Press, 2014).

25. Anthony P. Carnevale, Jeff Strohl, and Michelle Melton, *What's It Worth? The Economic Value of College Majors* (Washington, DC: Georgetown University Center on Education and the Workforce, 2011), https://georgetown.box.com/s/5bgczqc0nefsx68bj4u4.

26. Mina Dadgar and Madeline Joy Trimble, "Labor Market Returns to Sub-Baccalaureate Credentials: How Much Does a Community College Degree or Certificate Pay?" *Educational Evaluation and Policy Analysis* (November 2014).

27. This may help explain why the Pew study of mobility—using more recent data than Haskins—found that 37 percent of degree holders born in the bottom only rose as high as the second quintile as adults. See *Pursuing the American Dream: Economic Mobility Across Generations.*

28. *Completing College: A National View of Student Attainment Rates—Fall 2007 Cohort* (Herndon, VA: National Student Clearinghouse, 2013), http://nscresearchcenter.org/wp-content/uploads/NSC_Signature_Report_6.pdf.

29. Kane and Rouse, "Labor-Market Returns to Two- and Four-Year College"; Jacobson, LaLonde, and Sullivan, "Estimating the Returns to Community College Schooling for Displaced Workers."

30. Carroll and Higgins, *A College Education Saddles Young Households with Debt, but Still Pays Off,* July 16, 2014.

31. See figure 18 of *Pursuing the American Dream: Economic Mobility Across Generations.*

32. Bailey and Dynarski, "Inequality in Postsecondary Education."

33. Strong American Schools, *"Diploma to Nowhere"* (Los Angeles: The Broad Foundation, 2008) http://www.broadeducation.org/asset/1128-diploma%20to%20nowhere.pdf.

34. ACT, *"The Condition of College and Career Readiness 2014: National"* (Iowa City, IA, 2014), www.act.org/research/policymakers/cccr14/pdf/CCCR14-NationalReadinessRpt.pdf.

35. *Higher Education's Bridge to Nowhere* (Washington, DC: Complete College America, 2011), www.insidehighered.com/sites/default/server_files/files/CCA%20Remediation%20ES%20FINAL.pdf.

36. See College and Career Tables Library Table 2-A "Remedial Courses" here: "College & Career Tables Library," 2009, National Center for Higher Education Statistics, http://nces.ed.gov/datalab/tableslibrary/viewtable.aspx?tableid=8888.

37. For a summary of this literature, see Eric Bettinger, Angela Boatman, and Bridget Terry Long, "Student Supports: Developmental Education and Other Academic Programs," *Future of Children* 23, no. 1 (2013): 93–115.

38. *Higher Education's Bridge to Nowhere.*

39. Jessica S. Howell, Michal Kurlaender, and Eric Grodsky, "Postsecondary Preparation and Remediation: Examining the Effect of the Early Assessment Program at California State University," *Journal of Policy Analysis and Management* 29, no. 4 (2010): 726–48.

40. Nikki Edgecombe, *Accelerating the Academic Achievement of Students Referred to Developmental Education*, Working Paper No. 30 (New York: Community College Research Center, Columbia University, 2011).

41. Louis S. Jacobson and Robert J. LaLonde, *Using Data to Improve the Performance of Workforce Training* (Washington, DC: The Hamilton Project, The Brookings Institution, 2013), www.hamiltonproject.org/files/downloads_and_links/ THP_JacobsonLaLondePaperF2_4-13.pdf.

42. Anthony P. Carnevale, Stephen J. Rose, and Andrew R. Hanson, *Certificates: Gateway to Gainful Employment and College Degrees* (Washington, DC: Georgetown University Center on Education and the Workforce, 2012), https://georgetown. app.box.com/s/w6bzsdoxvqcywwoog6yl.

43. Brian Bosworth, *Certificates Count: An Analysis of Sub-Baccalaureate Certificates* (Washington, DC: Complete College America, 2010).

44. Fox, Connolly, and Snyder, *Youth Indicators 2005: Trends in the Well-Being of American Youth.*

45. The College Board, "Trends in College Pricing, 2013" (Washington, DC: The College Board, 2013).

46. Rajashri Chakrabarti, Maricar Mabutas, and Basit Zafar, "Soaring Tuitions: Are Public Funding Cuts to Blame?," Liberty Street Economics, September 19, 2012, http://libertystreeteconomics.newyorkfed.org/2012/09/soaring-tuitions-are-public-funding-cuts-to-blame.html#.VG46jPnF98E.

47. Congressional Budget Office, *The Federal Pell Grant Program: Recent Growth and Policy Options* (Washington, DC: Congressional Budget Office, September 2013).

48. Andrew P. Kelly, "New Data on Tuition Prices: Is It Possible It's Even Worse Than We Thought?" AEIdeas, October 24, 2013, www.aei.org/publication/new-data-on-tuition-prices-is-it-possible-its-even-worse-than-we-thought/.

49. Xianglei Chen, *Part-Time Undergraduates in Postsecondary Education: 2003–04* (Washington, DC: US Department of Education, National Center for Education Statistics, 2007).

50. Laura Horn, Xianglei Chen, and Chris Chapman, *Getting Ready to Pay for College: What Students and Their Parents Know About the Cost of College Tuition and What They Are Doing to Find Out* (Washington, DC: US Department of Education, National Center for Education Statistics, 2003).

51. Eric Grodsky and Melanie T. Jones, "The Real and Imagined Barriers to College Entry: Perceptions of College Costs," *Social Science Research* 36, no. 2 (June

2007): 745–66; *Financial Aid: The Information Divide* (Newark, DE: Sallie Mae Fund and Harris Interactive, 2003).

52. Caroline M. Hoxby and Christopher Avery, *The Missing "One-offs": The Hidden Supply of High-Achieving, Low Income Students,* Working Paper No. 18586 (Cambridge, MA: National Bureau of Economic Research, 2012); Melissa Roderick, et al., *From High School to the Future: Potholes on the Road to College* (Chicago: University of Chicago, Consortium on Chicago School Research, 2008), http://ccsr. uchicago.edu/sites/default/files/publications/CCSR_Potholes_Report.pdf.

53. William G. Bowen, Matthew M. Chingos, and Michael S. McPherson, *Crossing the Finish Line: Completing College at America's Public Universities* (Princeton, NJ: Princeton University Press, 2009).

54. Jacobson and LaLonde, *Using Data to Improve the Performance of Workforce Training.*

55. Eleanor Wiske Dillon and Jeffrey Andrew Smith, *The Determinants of Mismatch Between Students and Colleges,* Working Paper No. 19286 (Cambridge, MA: National Bureau of Economic Research, 2013).

56. Benjamin L. Castleman and Lindsay C. Page, *Summer Melt: Supporting Low-Income Students through the Transition to College* (Cambridge, MA: Harvard Education Press, 2011).

57. "Institutional Retention and Graduation Rates for Undergraduate Students," The Condition of Education 2014, National Center for Education Statistics, http:// nces.ed.gov/programs/coe/indicator_cva.asp.

58. See Josipa Roksa, "Equalizing Credits and Rewarding Skills: Credit Portability and Bachelor's Degree Attainment," in *Getting to Graduation: The Completion Agenda in Higher Education,* ed. Andrew P. Kelly and Mark Schneider (Baltimore, MD: Johns Hopkins University Press, 2012): 201–22.

59. In California, for instance, community colleges reduced course sections 21 percent between 2007–2008 and 2011–2012. See Sarah Bohn, Belinda Reyes, and Hans Johnson, *The Impact of Budget Cuts on California's Community Colleges* (San Francisco: Public Policy Institute of California, 2013).

60. See Barbara Means et al., *Evaluation of Evidence-Based Practices in Online Learning: A Meta-Analysis and Review of Online Learning Studies* (Washington, DC: Department of Education, Office of Planning, Evaluation, and Policy Development, 2010).

61. Don Hossler et al., *Transfer and Mobility: A National View of Pre-Degree Student Movement in Postsecondary Institutions* (Washington, DC: National Student Clearinghouse Research Center, 2012).

62. For a recent review of literature, see David Deming and Susan Dynarski, *Into College, Out of Poverty? Policies to Increase the Postsecondary Attainment of the Poor,* Working Paper No. 15387 (Cambridge, MA: National Bureau of Economic Research, 2009); Benjamin L. Castleman and Bridget Terry Long, *Looking Beyond Enrollment: The Causal Effect of Need-Based Grants on College Access, Persistence, and Graduation,* Working Paper No. 19306 (Cambridge, MA: National Bureau of Economic Research Working Paper, 2013).

63. Susan Dynarski and Judith Scott-Clayton, "Financial Aid Policy: Lessons from Research," *The Future of Children* 23, no. 1 (2013): 67–91.

64. LaShawn Richburg-Hayes, "Incentivizing Success: Lessons From Experimenting With Incentive-Based Grants," in *Reinventing Financial Aid: Charting a New Course to College Affordability*, ed. Andrew P. Kelly and Sara Goldrick-Rab (Cambridge, MA: Harvard Education Press, 2014).

65. Joshua Angrist, Daniel Lang, and Philip Oreopoulos, "Incentives and Services for College Achievement: Evidence From a Randomized Trial," *American Economic Journal: Applied Economics* 1, no. 1 (2009): 136–63.

66. For more on income-share agreements, see Miguel Palacios, Tonio DeSorrento, and Andrew P. Kelly, "Investing in Value, Sharing Risk: Financing Higher Education Through Income Share Agreements," (Washington, DC: AEI, February 2014), www.aei.org/wp-content/uploads/2014/02/-investing-in-value-sharing-in-risk-financing-higher-education-through-inome-share-agreements_083548906610.pdf.

67. Philip Oreopoulos and Ryan Dunn, *Information and College Access: Evidence from a Randomized Field Experiment*. Working Paper No. 18551 (Cambridge, MA: National Bureau of Economic Research, 2012).

68. Benjamin L. Castleman and Lindsay C. Page, *Summer Nudging: Can Personalized Text Messages and Peer Mentor Outreach Increase College-Going among Low-Income High School Graduates?* Working Paper (Charlottesville: University of Virginia, Curry School of Education, 2014).

69. Caroline Hoxby and Sarah Turner, *Expanding College Opportunities for High-Achieving, Low Income Students,* Working Paper No. 12-014 (Stanford, CA: Stanford Institute for Economic Policy Research, 2013).

70. Jacobson and LaLonde, *Using Data to Improve the Performance of Workforce Training*.

71. Susan Scrivener and Michael J. Weiss, *More Graduates: Two-Year Results from an Evaluation of Accelerated Study in Associate Programs (ASAP) for Developmental Education Students* (New York: MDRC, 2014), www.wsac.wa.gov/sites/default/files/2014.ptw.%2823%29.pdf.

72. Lara K. Couturier, *Cornerstones of Completion: State Policy Support for Accelerated, Structured Pathways to College Credentials and Transfer* (Washington, DC: Jobs for the Future, 2012), http://www.jff.org/sites/default/files/publications/CBD_CornerstonesOfCompletion_111612.pdf.

73. Eric Bettinger and Rachel Baker, *The Effects of Student Coaching in College: The Evaluation of a Randomized Experiment in Student Mentoring*, Working Paper No. 16881 (Cambridge, MA: National Bureau of Economic Research, 2011).

74. Paul Fain, "Have Credential, Will Travel," *InsideHigherEd* (blog), September 25, 2013, www.insidehighered.com/news/2013/09/25/stackable-credentials-energy-industry-take-texas.

75. David A. Tandberg and Nicholas W. Hillman, *State Performance Funding for Higher Education: Silver Bullet or Red Herring* (Madison: University of Wisconsin-Madison, Wisconsin Center for the Advancement of Postsecondary Education [WISCAPE], 2013).

76. See Andrew P. Kelly and Frederick M. Hess, *Beyond Retrofitting: Innovation in Higher Education* (Washington, DC: The Hudson Institute, 2013).

Chapter Three

The Certification Revolution

Tamar Jacoby

Daniel Gamez is no one's idea of a traditional postsecondary student. He finished high school decades ago and at the time had no interest in college. The San Antonio economy was booming, and he was in a hurry to get to work. He started as a construction laborer, then headed off to the military, where he got some exposure to computers. When he got home to Texas, he went back into construction in a well-paying technical job—designing and assembling roof trusses.

Then, during the downturn, technology caught up with him. Automated roof truss assembly replaced manmade design, and Daniel found himself once again wondering how to make a living. He fell on hard times, moved back in with his parents, and ended up in an accident that ruled out any job requiring physical labor. By 2014, he was at a loss, uncertain where the next paycheck would come from.[1]

That's when he heard about the course in information technology (IT) networking being offered at a local vocational training center, the Goodwill Good Careers Academy. No one would mistake the academy for a college. It's a small storefront building in a neglected neighborhood near downtown. Many of the other students, struggling to get off public assistance, would be intimidated even at community college. But for Daniel, it was a lifeline—and unlike college, within his reach. The course he signed up for required three hundred hours over six months, half in a classroom and half in a computer lab. Daniel could live at home and work almost full-time while he was studying. Goodwill staff had to be attentive and encouraging, and tuition was a fraction of what he'd have had to pay at college—just $3,200.

But the prize Daniel was aiming for was as valuable as many college degrees: A+ and Network+ certifications from the computer-industry trade association CompTIA. Recognized around the world in the IT business and beyond, CompTIA certifications are widely seen as the entry-level qualifications for computer technicians.[2]

Unlike a degree, certification says nothing about how or where you studied, simply that you passed a performance-based test demonstrating required knowledge and abilities. Test-takers prepare in a broad array of venues: high schools, community colleges, franchised for-profit learning centers, vo-tech academies like Goodwill, or, very often, self-study on the Internet. A basic certification can get you a first job. Many technicians then continue studying while they work, adding test-based credential on top of test-based credential over the course of a lifetime. The average salary for technicians with Network+ is $71,000.[3]

Daniel's story isn't unusual. On the contrary, he's on the cutting edge of a burgeoning trend: alternative, competency-based credentials. It's the hottest new idea you've never heard of, and it's coming soon to a theater near you—if it isn't showing already.

CompTIA credentials capture the essence of the idea, which can be broken down into two components: learning targeted at a specific job and learning certified by a test that can be prepared for in many ways, in school and out. But this isn't just about IT; it's an approach transforming training in diverse technical fields ranging from advanced manufacturing and health care to construction, energy, and logistics, among others. It isn't just for at-risk kids or people like Daniel, down on their luck—although for many, including disadvantaged youth, it can be a fast track to middle-class earnings. And in truth it isn't just about vocational training. Job-focused, competency-based learning is poised to transform academic and vocational education as we know them.

According to the Census Bureau, 25 percent of US adults, or more than fifty million people, hold a nondegree credential such as a professional certification, license, or educational certificate.[4] Business owners are changing how they do business to accommodate the new approach. Ferment and enthusiasm stretch across the political spectrum, from big-government Democrats to free-market Republicans. And the nation's leading education foundations are pouring money into refining and advancing what they see as a transformative idea with ramifications for both secondary and postsecondary education.

AN IDEA WHOSE TIME HAS COME

Where did the idea come from, and why is it taking off now?

Both nondegree credentials and competency-based learning have been around a long time, albeit mostly below the radar and often looked down upon by the education establishment. Before there were industry-recognized credentials, there were licenses. Tests, usually administered by a state or municipality, assessed workers' knowledge of their trade and certified them to work as a nurse or plumber or commercial truck driver.

Community colleges worked in parallel to offer occupational training that culminated in a certificate: usually a year-long program of study, though often not for credit and not captured in national education statistics. And going back as far as World War II, it was possible for students who had learned a skill in the military or the corporate world to translate that knowledge into college credit. But few young people aspired to come up this way. It was a path of last resort.

What changed? Massive open online courses and other online learning are part of what's propelling the new approach. Millions of students taking courses online find it difficult to get credit for what they're learning; most colleges are still hesitant to acknowledge online courses they don't provide themselves. For many students and would-be students, this is just one more affront fueling a broader crisis of faith—the spreading wave of doubt about higher education being driven by rising debt and falling return on investment.

And it's not just students feeling the dissatisfaction. Public figures like Vice President Joe Biden and Florida senator Marco Rubio are already beginning to push back, demanding that colleges find a way to incorporate what students learn elsewhere into the mix of knowledge and skills they reward with credit.

A second important change is taking place out in the world of work: the skills gap. Information technology and globalization are transforming the American workplace, phasing out many low-end jobs and putting a premium on technical skills. Many more Americans go to college today than even a generation ago, but they often aren't learning the right skills. In 2014, even with 9 million Americans unemployed, businesses across the country were struggling to fill 4.7 million job openings.[5] Companies in a range of sectors—IT, finance, manufacturing, health care, construction, and still others—report worker shortages and often crippling skills mismatches. And those mismatches are likely to grow worse in years to come.

Labor economists predict that at least one third and perhaps half of all jobs coming online in the next five years will be "middle skill"—requiring less than a bachelor's degree but more than a high school diploma (in most cases some kind of technical training).[6] These aren't old-fashioned factory jobs. Today's technical workers are more likely to man computer controls than greasy machines, and they often take home a middle-class paycheck. Yet many Americans still look down on technical skill.

And few educators see it as their role to prepare students for the world of work. It's viewed as somehow dirty or ignoble, mere training instead of education. But increasingly strapped employers are clamoring for change—education geared more closely to skills needed on the job. And if they can't get what they need from the education system, many are determined to find another route, working around the system by developing their own credentials.

Finally, the more Americans cling to the dream of college for all, the clearer it becomes that it isn't always the best or only path into the middle class. Most students who begin college do not finish. Even graduates often end up saddled with debt and working at jobs that don't require a college degree. It's widely understood that high school is no longer enough. Most middle-class jobs call for some postsecondary preparation, and that percentage will only grow in decades to come. For those who can finish college, it still pays to do so—there's no disputing the lifelong earnings premium. But studies increasingly show that some students in some fields do better with an alternative credential.

Anthony Carnevale was the first to notice the trend in a 2009 study comparing the return to various kinds of postsecondary awards. His surprising findings: Not only do 43 percent of license and certificate holders earn more than peers with associate's degrees, but 27 percent earn more than the average bachelor's recipient. Gains are even sharper in a few specialized fields, including computer and information services, electronics, business, and office management.[7]

Five years later, another trio of scholars took this line of inquiry a step further, focusing in on disadvantaged and minority students. Benjamin Backes, Harry Holzer, and Erin Dunlop Velez compared postsecondary attainment and later earnings for a large cohort of Florida students. The study found that many disadvantaged young people who had a hard time in high school gravitated in college toward general humanities courses, but then often ran into difficulty and failed to finish. Those who graduated did relatively poorly in the labor market. Only a small percentage of their peers opted for a technical education—a certificate or an associate's degree in a practical field such as manufacturing, health care, or construction. But those who did were more likely to finish and earn better salaries, particularly if they combined the certificate with more than a year of work experience.[8]

For these and other students, an alternative credential is a key to economic mobility—a cheaper, quicker, streamlined postsecondary education, targeted and purpose-driven preparation for the world of work.

WHAT IS AN ALTERNATIVE CREDENTIAL?

Alternative credentials come in a variety of shapes and sizes, and the movement behind them is so new that many terms and definitions are still in flux. It doesn't help that the terminology itself is a little confusing: A certificate is not the same as a certification, and neither is the same as a license or digital badge or prior learning assessment. All are tools for translating competency into terms that mean something in the academy or the workplace.

The three biggest-ticket items are certificates, certifications, and licenses—and the terms cannot be used interchangeably.[9] A certificate is the closest to a degree—awarded by an educational institution on completion of a course of study. The subject is often more narrow and more occupationally focused than the subjects in which students get degrees, and the duration of study is generally shorter (most certificates require only a year or two).

But as with a degree, earning a certificate requires attendance at an educational institution and seat time in class. And once you've earned it, it lasts forever—there's no need to renew it with continuing training or periodic exams. Some of the most commonly awarded occupational certificates are geared toward electronics, auto mechanics, construction, health care, cosmetology, and basic office work. Over the past decade, the number of certificates awarded has skyrocketed from three hundred thousand in 1994 to roughly one million in 2012, a testament to students' interest in occupationally focused education and training.[10]

Certifications and licenses are altogether different. Unlike certificates, neither requires time in class. What they signal is not attendance, but mastery of a set of occupational skills, usually assessed by tests—often a conventional pen-and-paper test and a hands-on, performance-based assessment. As with CompTIA Network+, the skills certified by the credential can be learned either at a traditional educational institution or through some other means, including self-study. It's the essence of competency-based learning. What matters is knowledge and ability, not where or how it was learned.

The difference between licenses and certifications is that licenses are issued by government agencies, usually a state or municipality; they grant legal permission to perform an occupation in that jurisdiction. Occupations for which licenses are commonly required include electrician, cosmetologist, nurse, commercial driver, and real-estate broker.

Certifications are more likely to be awarded by an independent third party—a company like Microsoft, a trade association like CompTIA, a professional association like the Association of Clinical Research Professionals, a nonprofit like the Wildlife Society, or some other autonomous group with an interest in maintaining occupational skills standards. Health care, IT, advanced manufacturing, and the construction trades are some of the most fruitful occupations for certifications.

Unlike certificates or degrees, both licenses and certifications must be renewed. Their holders often have to take the test again three or five years later; in other cases, it's enough to provide evidence of ongoing learning.

A number of realities flow from this basic difference between licenses and certifications. After all, if what's being measured are your qualifications to work, it makes a big difference whether those qualifications are established by someone likely to employ you or by the government.

Employers are by definition more likely than state agencies to be concerned about ability. An employer-driven certification is more likely to be up to date. After all, employers need employees with state-of-the-art skills, whereas government agencies often lag behind the times. Licenses are mandatory in the jurisdictions where they apply. They determine who may and may not work. Certifications are generally voluntary, and most of the employer groups behind them hope to enlarge the pool of qualified employees, not restrict or bar workers.

In theory, government licensing agencies exist to protect public safety, but in practice, many licenses work to restrict competition among service providers—erecting barriers to entry, creating labor market shelters, and suppressing innovation. No one has yet leveled these charges against the new generation of employer-driven certifications.

The Census Bureau has only just begun to count the number of Americans who hold nondegree credentials. The first inquiry was in 2012, part of the Survey of Income and Program Participation (SIPP).[11] Licenses are the most common nondegree credential. Professional licensing has mushroomed since the 1950s, when only 5 percent of occupations required a license, compared to nearly one in three occupations today.[12] According to the SIPP survey, some 13 percent of Americans sixteen and older hold a license to work. Some are highly educated professionals, some lowly skilled-trade workers.

Certificates, though also growing fast, are by definition a narrower category: 10 percent of adults hold occupational certificates. And certification is rarer still, in part because it's newer. According to SIPP data, 5 percent of adults hold certifications issued by a company, a trade association, or a nonprofit organization. (By comparison, according to the same survey, 8 percent of Americans hold associate's degrees and 17 percent have bachelor's degrees.)[13]

Certifications are the smallest slice of the pie, but they are the credential generating the most excitement in reform circles. The rapid growth of both certificates and certifications attests to growing interest in occupational training—instruction designed expressly to prepare students for the world of work.

The problem with some certificates is that without input from employers, many community college courses teach outmoded computer code or old-fashioned welding techniques no longer in use in the workplace. Additionally, college courses don't always include hands-on training. Certifications, usually developed by employers, are far more likely to produce workers with skills needed in the marketplace. Their promise to students: This is the content you need to know to get a job. Their promise to employers and potential employees alike: These are workers equipped with the skills to succeed in today's economy.

Chapter Three

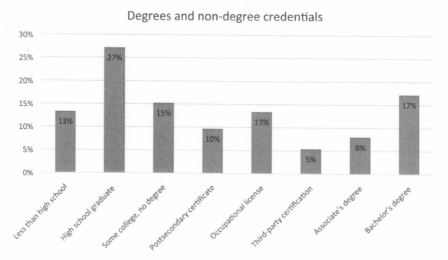

Figure 3.1. **Degrees and nondegree credentials.**

THE BRAVE NEW WORLD OF INDUSTRY CERTIFICATIONS

The certifications issued by the National Institute for Metalworking Skills (NIMS) aren't new. They were launched around 1995. But they are among the most successful industry credentials to take off in recent years—and a telling example of how third-party certification works. How does an industry develop a credential that truly reflects the skills needed in a changing technical workplace? And how is it used on the ground by employers, educators, and trainees?[14]

Precision machining is the high end of the manufacturing business. These are the firms that make the machines that make the things consumers use. Products are metal parts, instruments, and tools, and in the age of robotics, they have reached a level of complexity and accuracy almost beyond imagining.

Machinists used to wear goggles and overalls and get grease on their hands from dirty lathes. Today, many machinists work computer controls, standing outside booths that look something like magnetic resonance imaging machines. The grinding, stamping, tooling, and lapping happen inside the immaculate box. There's little dust or grease in the laboratory-like room. Parts are measured to 0.0005 or 0.0001 of an inch.

A precision machining firm's customers are mostly companies in the medical, automotive, and aerospace sectors, as well as construction and oil and gas exploration. And many downstream manufacturing firms also need machinists: people to operate the robots doing the machining on their production lines, for example. According to the Manufacturing Institute, the research arm of the National Association of Manufacturers, there's virtually no limit to the demand for machinists today, and a skilled technician can make $70,000 a year.[15]

The NIMS credentialing system operates on the same basic principles as CompTIA's. The institute doesn't write curriculum or offer courses. What it produces are tests that measure trainees' skills. But by designing tests and setting standards, it drives curricula and training nationwide. Training providers—high schools, community colleges, and vocational training centers—teach to the test. Trainees aspire to its standards and, when they pass an exam, get a nationally recognized credential.

Employers who hire credentialed workers know what they're getting. That's more than most can say now, because training quality varies from school to school and grade inflation often obscures whether trainees have the necessary skills. The credentialing system aims to standardize and upgrade the machining workforce so that everyone benefits—employers, employees, and educators, who can now be sure their courses are preparing students for the world of work.

A student who wants to become a NIMS-certified machinist starts by looking for a school that teaches to the exam. Venues, curricula, and teaching methods vary, and NIMS expects that. Some schools offer credit for their machining courses. Some don't. Some award certificates or degrees. It's all irrelevant to NIMS and to most employers who look to NIMS credentialing.

The assessment that matters to them is a NIMS test. Each test is made up of one written component, taken and graded on a computer, and one performance-based piece. Students get specifications for a series of machine parts that they produce on their own time, on whatever equipment they have access to. The one thing NIMS insists on is that the school, vo-tech center, or industry association that provides the training cannot administer or judge the test. The separation of instruction and assessment is an all-but-universal requirement of the new generation of industry certifications. After all, most teachers feel some stake in their students' success.

The parts submitted for the performance-based portion of the exam must be exactly as specified in order to pass—100 percent correct within the tolerance specified on the plan. "That's the standard that counts on the job," says NIMS executive director, James Wall. "One dimension off, and it's a scrap part."[16]

The NIMS system offers fifty-two different tests of varying rigor in two dozen different machining specialties, including machining, metal forming, stamping, machine maintenance and repair, and others. The goal is to create a clear, streamlined path from school to work and then from entry-level job up a ladder of machining skills—what educators call a "career pathway." Even the entry-level test can help you land a job. But one course leads to another, and each test builds on the one that came before. The term for this is "stackable," and it's another core requirement for nationally recognized industry credentials.

It's an ideal answer for struggling students and others who often can't commit at first to a very long or deep course of study. But once they get started on a job, many want to move up and will pursue training if it's available—especially short, bite-sized modules and a graduated sequence of credentials that allows them to progress at their own pace over a lifetime of learning. Some students start as early as high school, then attend a community college that recognizes their NIMS credential. Other machinists are still taking NIMS's most advanced exams well into their professional careers.

The cost of training for a NIMS test is considerably less than the cost of most academic programs, but sometimes harder to cover, thanks to federal government regulations. It takes far less time to get the first credential. Students can often complete several modules and take several tests in a single semester. Training is free at a public high school or public vo-tech center. Even at community college, a semester or two rarely costs more than $5,000 for in-state students, and many get federal help in the form of a grant or other Title IV funding.

The problem is that this assistance is not generally available to students who train outside an academic setting. Many companies that teach to a NIMS test cover the cost, some of them reimbursed through the federal workforce system. Still, some trainees fall through the cracks, unlike college students on an academic track, without access to financial aid, public or private.

The challenge for NIMS is to make sure the tests reflect the things employers want and need. That means the right skills and the right level of skill, changing with a cutting-edge industry buffeted by globalization and evolving technology. If the institute's tests don't meet this standard, they're just one more guild-driven barrier to entry, not likely to appeal to employers or educators and useless to students. So NIMS spends an extraordinary amount of time and money developing, refining, and revising its standards.

The tests are just the tip of the iceberg. What's difficult is deciding what should be measured. The institute manages an elaborate consultative process that draws on some six thousand employers nationwide to decide which skills matter and what level of performance is needed on the job. The process starts with subject-matter experts—practitioners from the field who analyze the skills and "competencies" that go into every machinist's task. Next comes regional validation by hundreds of employers in the NIMS network, then more deliberations by the original technical working group, then more national validation.

And this is all before there's even a test. That, too, is a consensus product, designed by a first group of experts, adjusted by others, beta-tested in the field on hundreds of trainees, and then revised again. Altogether, the process takes more than a year and costs $350,000. And every test is revisited on a regular basis, every five years.

NIMS works hard to create a market for certification in a field that had no industry standards in the past. It's a three-part effort: convincing community colleges and other schools to upgrade their training programs, convincing employers to adopt NIMS standards, and convincing students that it's worth their while to bother with the tests. Among these three potential consumer groups, community colleges are the most enthusiastic, followed by state high school authorities.

Hundreds of schools across the country are now teaching to NIMS tests, and many are also applying to be accredited by the institute. Student demand is mushrooming, and the number of credentials awarded annually increased by 60 percent in 2013, although the absolute number of trainees taking the tests is still relatively small (some fourteen thousand last year).

Ironically, the small- and medium-sized employers who make up most of the metalworking industry have been the slowest to adopt the system. So far, only about 10 percent are requiring that job applicants have NIMS credentials. But institute staff are both undeterred and optimistic about the future. "It's chicken and egg," says Executive Director James Wall. "You can't expect a critical mass of companies to sign on until there's a critical mass of trainees with credentials. Once it gets going, it snowballs."

IT educators and employers know all about this kind of snowballing. The world of IT credentialing has been growing exponentially for two decades. There is no official reporting system and little good data, but according to informal estimates, tens of millions of IT technicians around the world have been awarded certifications. The fastest growth is now in emerging countries. The hottest new technical area—as certifying bodies scramble to keep up with changes in the industry—is cloud computing.

QUALITY CONTROL?

As nondegree credentials take off, one of the biggest challenges ahead is quality control. The new experimentation layered on top of old programs has produced a baffling array of paper attesting to the qualifications of students and trainees. Many different types of institutions and programs are issuing paper: community colleges, for-profit colleges, high schools, apprentice-ship programs, franchised training centers, company-run training initiatives, union-run training initiatives, and ad hoc online courses.

Some credentials mean little or nothing. Students are paying for classes and taking on debt, but often can't be sure the training will lead anywhere. The difficult question is what to do about this rich but sometimes dysfunctional ferment—what one researcher has called a "Wild West of programs"—particularly in an American culture suspicious of regulation.[17]

The problem is most acute for industry credentials, growing fast and among the least tethered to conventional institutions of higher learning. Credentialing organizations like NIMS and CompTIA take great pains to ensure the quality of their certifications. That's the reason for the subject matter experts, the nationwide employer feedback, the beta testing, and the rest. They and organizations like them count on this bottom-up consensual process as a guarantor of quality and of their relevance in the marketplace.

NIMS and many other bodies like it also act as accreditors, evaluating and endorsing training programs at schools and companies. But not every industry group issuing credentials is as rigorous. And it's easy to imagine the system spinning out of control, with a welter of inferior credentials swamping the good ones and eventually undermining the currency.

This urgent need for quality control is Topic A among employers, educators, and policymakers working to promote industry credentials, which includes everyone from the Organisation for Economic Co-operation and Development to the Business Roundtable.[18] One response is to create a system for accrediting the accreditors—an oversight body that promulgates and enforces standards. And leading education foundations like Gates, Lumina, Joyce, and the ACT testing service have funded several initiatives to explore the options.

One group of large national trade associations in sectors projected to generate 75 percent of US job growth in the next five years recommends a consensual process much like the one in use at NIMS and CompTIA.[19] Still another group, based at George Washington University and involving many of the same experts, is working on a different project that one scholar compares to a twenty-first century e-version of *Consumer Reports*.[20] An alternative approach, distinct from these efforts to oversee process and evaluate quality, would rely on data about credential holders' success in the labor market.

Are trainees with industry certifications more likely to get jobs than workers without credentials? Do they get jobs in the fields in which they're certified? Do they earn more? Surprisingly, even after twenty years of competency-based credentialing, little is known about labor market outcomes. What accounting there is draws largely on circumstantial evidence: anecdotes, surveys, mentions in want ads.

A more reliable method would match information about who earns what credentials with government data about employment and earnings. One option is state wage records: information about wages reported by employers to the state agencies that manage unemployment insurance. Even better would be federal data collected by the Social Security Administration. Both sources have been largely off limits until recently, thanks largely to privacy and liability concerns. But researchers are breaking through.

In one promising pilot project in Illinois, CompTIA, the Illinois community college system, and the state agency responsible for unemployment insurance shared information about students who took CompTIA tests. The study found that those who passed the test were more likely to have a job and their median quarterly earnings were up to 150 percent higher. Still another interesting project, this one spearheaded by officials from California and North Carolina, involves government agencies and community college administrators from twenty-one states.[21] Their pilot will match test results from NIMS and other credentialing bodies with community college transcripts and wage record data. The goal is to assemble a national repository of data about labor market returns to industry credentials and the courses that prepare students for them.

One of the most promising initiatives at the federal level may be legislation introduced in 2013 by an incongruous pair of liberal and conservative senators, Democrat Ron Wyden of Oregon and Republican Marco Rubio of Florida.[22] Like the California and North Carolina project, the "Student Right to Know Before You Go Act" would create a single national reporting site that collects data on the return to all postsecondary programs, degree and nondegree. But rather than rely on spotty state wage records, it would use earnings data from the Social Security Administration.

Which one of these projects is most likely to succeed in taming the Wild West of alternative credentialing? The answer will surely be some combination, and perhaps all of the above. There's no substitute for bottom-up, employer-driven confirmation that credentials certify skills actually needed in the workplace. But there's also no gainsaying data about labor market outcomes.

The one thing most reformers hopeful about certification seem to agree on is that the system shouldn't be run or regulated by the federal government. Standards are essential, and so is transparency. But the measure that counts is the skills employers need and want in employees—and the government can't assess that. Only an employer-driven process can.

WHAT ALTERNATIVE
CREDENTIALS MEAN FOR EDUCATORS

What does this new vogue mean for traditional K–12 and college educators? At first blush, the new credentials may seem irrelevant to most teachers—an alternative path, helpful perhaps for some struggling students but with little bearing for the vast majority of young people going to class and concentrating on academics. These skeptics couldn't be more wrong.

Many more students than most teachers imagine are drawn to the prospect of job-oriented education and training where they learn skills on demand in the workplace. Schools should be helping them find career paths that suit them. Besides, the big new ideas behind alternative credentialing are already driving change at many traditional schools. Just look around; the revolution has already begun.

Industry-driven credentialing bodies like NIMS and CompTIA don't care where students prepare for their tests, and both have relationships with scores of high schools as well as community colleges and vo-tech centers. High school courses teaching to technical certification tests are usually electives. The teachers generally come up out of the school system, but often get training and certification from a national credentialing body. Students earn credit toward their high school diplomas and can also earn an industry credential that may open a door to a job. And in many schools, the industry award is worth credit at a local community college, the technical equivalent of Advanced Placement.

The big advantage for students is to get an early start on a career path that can carry them through the transition from school to work—a perilous passage for many teenagers. A kid who gets excited about metalworking isn't just less likely to drop out of high school. He now has a reason to go on for more schooling and a clear path to follow to the next level and beyond.

Lake Brantley High School in Altamonte Springs, Florida, has a fairly typical program that demonstrates how credentialing can work in high school. Altamonte Springs is a suburban enclave just north of Orlando, and Lake Brantley is a nationally recognized, award-winning school. It complements its rich academic offerings with a career and technical education (CTE) division that prepares students for sixteen industry certifications: CompTIA, Microsoft, Cisco, Apple, and nationally recognized first-rung tests in nursing, accounting, architecture, engineering, and basic construction skills.

Students who complete Lake Brantley CTE courses are eligible to take college-level assessment tests. If they pass and then enroll in nearby Seminole State College, they receive credit toward a technical certificate or an associate of science degree.[23] This overlap, called *dual enrollment,* saves students both time and money. Students who study computer programing at Lake Brantley can earn up to nine credits worth $939, and those who take allied health courses can earn twelve credits worth $1252.

A student who then pursues, say, nursing at Seminole State can earn not just an associate's degree, but also concurrent credit toward a bachelor's degree at the University of Central Florida. This too saves time and money and puts the student on a guided path that can make it much easier to keep going. Other certifications available at Lake Brantley open the door to internships, apprenticeships, and industry-sponsored craft training. Still other students may use their industry credentials to head straight for the job market, but then after a few years come back for more schooling, whether at a community college or other training center that recognizes their certification.

What makes this work are the stackable, bite-sized pieces. These are relatively short learning modules validated by nondegree credentials. And the best time to start on a path is often in high school. For kids who know where they're going, it's a head start. For those who have reached high school without a clue, it can be a new lease on life.

Employers and educators from the world of alternative credentialing are adamant: A technical career is not an inferior track. "We don't want the C and D students," says Neil Ashbaugh, training and development specialist at the precision machining firm Oberg Industries, an early adopter of NIMS credentialing. "We want the As and Bs."[24] NIMS and CompTIA executives agree that students need good writing and math skills, especially for higher-level credentials. Technical training is not a last resort for young people who aren't "college and career ready."

It's also not an alternative to community college remedial courses. "Remedial students often have trouble in our programs," says Ashbaugh. "It's hard for them to keep up with the math." Students who end up in technical training may have a different kind of mind than those who do well in academic courses. They're generally more practical and hands-on. But that doesn't let K–12 teachers off the hook. On the contrary, says Asbaugh, who feels that many schools are failing the kind of young people he hires. "We need more schools that teach math more practically, that show kids the applications of the math they're learning. 'Why do I need to learn that? Where will I use sines and cosines—and how, exactly?'"

This needn't involve tracking. On the contrary, it's about choices—and the challenge for K–12 educators is to keep choices open, all the way from kindergarten through graduation. As it is, most students have few if any choices. Most schools are single-mindedly focused on academic achievement. Most counselors neglect or actively denigrate potential alternatives to college. Students get little exposure to the world of work, and the only second track open to many—other than academics—is failure.

This failure shows up first in high school dropout rates and then again later in life. According to a recent ACT survey, 80 percent of students who sit for the organization's standardized readiness test aspire to earn a bachelor's degree or higher, while only 6 percent are aiming for an associate's degree or technical certificate.[25] According to another study, even among high school seniors in the bottom quarter of their class, more than 90 percent expect to go to college.[26] But the fact is that only four in ten Americans graduate from college, so the system is failing 60 percent of students.

Surely it makes sense to offer some other options. For K–12 students, this means mostly exposure. It can start as early as elementary school, with field trips to a broad range of workplaces. For middle school kids, there's job shadowing; for high school students, internships. Hundreds of trade associations and professional societies offer mentoring programs, summer camps, co-op jobs, practicums, and other introductory programs designed to expose students to a practical field and interest them in future careers.

Annual skills competitions in IT, construction, culinary arts, and a host of other trades whet students' appetites and give them a sense of accomplishment. Courses like "tape measure math"—students learn about fractions from a ruler or a measuring tape—can help technically minded young people excel and also discover what interests them.

Counseling is key. Perhaps the most important imperative in an elementary or high school setting is to do no harm, to avoid disparaging practical or technical work and stop sending the signal that the only success that counts is academic. What educators need to remember is that this isn't an either/or proposition. A student who does well in high school because a course in computer networking, nursing, or welding finally grabbed his interest may go on to college and eventually professional school.

TRANSFORMING COLLEGE AS WE KNOW IT

Industry-driven credentials are putting the dignity back in technical work, but that's not the only way they are changing American education. The principles behind nondegree credentialing are already catching on at an array of colleges. Small, stackable units, education to prepare students for jobs, credit given for demonstrated learning rather than time spent in class: this is the cutting edge of new thinking about postsecondary education.

The evidence is everywhere. Prior learning assessments allow veterans to earn college credit for what they did in the military; learning portfolios help mid-career professionals go back to school to get that degree they skipped; Mozilla Open Badges validate work experience and extracurricular skills; and the best for-profit colleges focus unabashedly on preparing students for the world of work. But perhaps the most exciting example is what's happening at Western Governors University (WGU), the only college in the country where the learning is entirely competency-based.

Established less than two decades ago by a group of governors concerned that American colleges weren't preparing the workforce of the future, WGU now serves some thirty-eight thousand students in fifty states.[27] All courses are online. Students work from wherever they live and do not meet a teacher or a counselor in person until graduation day. Degrees are concentrated in four disciplines that lead directly to jobs: business, IT, teaching, and the health professions. The average tuition is $15,000, about half the price of a typical public college. And the average student gets a bachelor's degree in just 2.5 years, about half what it takes most students at conventional four-year schools.

There is so much innovation at WGU that it can be hard to know where to start in explaining its success. But the core idea is the same core idea that drives nondegree industry credentials: identify the skills that students need on the job, then help them learn those skills the most efficient way, focusing on and measuring what they learn rather than who they learn it from or how long it takes them.

Student begin their careers at WGU with a high-stakes assessment test. The result determines where they start on a series of modules that lead to a degree. Some students begin at the beginning of the series. Others place out of much or most of it (industry credentials can help you skip ahead). Students proceed through online courses at their own pace—one may struggle to complete three credits in a semester while another aces ten or twenty courses.

Many WGU courses require a performance-based assessment as well as a written test. Often this assessment is the same test required for an industry credential, and many WGU students graduate with industry certifications alongside their degrees. Indeed, the methods pioneered by industry credentials are everywhere in evidence at WGU, from a strict separation of instruction and assessment to the design of the curriculum. Like industry certifications, WGU degree programs are built around competencies required on the job, and university administrators work with industry representatives to identify these competencies in a deliberative process much like the process behind NIMS and CompTIA credentials.

WGU president Robert Mendenhall makes an important distinction between industry certifications and the education offered at WGU. "We're not in the business of mini-credentialing," he explained to me. "We're a university, and our students come away with a full, well-rounded education—the skills they need for life." But this is not at odds with the principle of job-focused, competency-based education.

For Mendenhall and others at WGU, there's no tension between purpose-driven training and a foundational education that teaches students essential skills like critical thinking and problem solving. Western Governors University proves that there's no reason a well-designed practical course can't also teach broader skills.

TWO ROADS AHEAD

For every reformer excited about nondegree credentialing, there's a skeptic who looks down on it as narrow, unworthy, or anti-intellectual. Even many who champion job-driven technical training see it as a second, inferior track, of value for society perhaps, but not for *their* children. The new credentials are gathering momentum, but they collide at every turn with this disdain from parents, teachers, guidance counselors, government funders, and society at large.

Deep-seated cultural attitudes of this kind do not change easily. There's no magic bullet—information about the payoff to alternative credentials should eventually puncture old prejudices, but even that will take time. Still, there are many steps that can be taken in the meantime. Federal and state policymakers can create incentives for schools to teach to industry credentials. Title IV education funding should be reformed to put technical training that leads to an industry credential on a par with academic programs that culminate in degrees. Business and industry can put their own house in order, creating whatever frameworks or other processes are needed to distinguish meaningful credentials from those that lead nowhere. Educators and employers can learn to collaborate more effectively, reaching across the cultural gulf that divides them to provide education and training with clearer value in the workplace. And many other entities can help structure ways for these two critical sectors to come together.

Alternative credentials are themselves a powerful weapon in this battle. Today, the gold standard is a degree—every young person wants a college degree. But it's not hard to imagine a time when nondegree credentials enjoy a similar status and cachet, to the point that they eventually compete with degrees. For many young people, skills in welding, nursing, machining, or computer programing are already proving more navigable than college as a pathway to the middle class.

For these young people and others, including many who start with a degree, stackable nondegree awards open up otherwise unimaginable opportunities for lifelong learning and growth. In these and other ways, nondegree credentialing is already starting to take the stigma out of job-oriented training. What's wrong, after all, with learning a skill that gets you a job? Isn't that why most people go to college in the first place?

NOTES

1. Daniel Gamez, interview by author, San Antonio, TX, August 8, 2014.
2. Gretchen Koch, executive director of workforce development at CompTIA, and Steven Ostrowski, director of corporate communications at CompTIA, telephonic interview by author, August 13, 2014.

3. "Top IT Certifications for 2014," *The Night Owl Blog,* Western Governors University, March 7, 2014, http://www.wgu.edu/blogpost/top-it-certifications-2014 (accessed September 10, 2014).

4. US Department of Commerce, Census Bureau, *Measuring Alternative Educational Credentials: 2012,* by Stephanie Ewert and Robert Kominski (Washington, DC: US Census Bureau, January 2014), http://www.census.gov/prod/2014pubs/p70-138.pdf (accessed September 8, 2014).

5. US Department of Labor, Bureau of Labor Statistics, *The Employment Situation—October 2014,* USDL-14-2037 (n.p.: US Bureau of Labor Statistics, November 7, 2014), http://www.bls.gov/news.release/empsit.nr0.htm (accessed December 1, 2014); US Department of Labor, Bureau of Labor Statistics, *Job Openings and Labor Turnover—September 2014,* USDL-14-2064 (Washington, DC: US Bureau of Labor Statistics, November 13, 2014), http://www.bls.gov/news.release/pdf/jolts.pdf (accessed December 1, 2014).

6. Harry J. Holzer and Robert I. Lerman, *The Future of Middle-Skill Jobs* (Washington, DC: Brookings Institution, Center on Children and Families, February 2009), http://www.brookings.edu/~/media/research/files/papers/2009/2/middle%20 skill%20jobs%20holzer/02_middle_skill_jobs_holzer.pdf (accessed September 8, 2014); Anthony Carnevale, Nicole Smith, and Jeff Strohl, *Help Wanted: Projections of Jobs and Education Requirements through 2018* (Washington, DC: Georgetown University Center on Education and the Workforce, June 2010), https://georgetown. app.box.com/s/ursjbxaym2np1v8mgrv7 (accessed September 10, 2014).

7. Carnevale, Smith, and Strohl, *Help Wanted.*

8. Benjamin Backes, Harry J. Holzer, and Erin Dunlop Velez, "Is It Worth It? Postsecondary Education and Labor Market Outcomes for the Disadvantaged," *IZA Discussion Paper Series No. 8474* (September 2014): 1–36, http://edexcellence.net/ articles/is-it-worth-it-postsecondary-education-and-labor-market-outcomes-for-the-disadvantaged (accessed December 1, 2014).

9. US Department of Commerce, Census Bureau, *Measuring Alternative Educational Credentials: 2012*; "What is a Credential?" Association for Career and Technical Education, www.acteonline.org/WorkArea/DownloadAsset.aspx?id=1917 (accessed September 12, 2014).

10. Anthony Carnevale, Tamara Jayasundara, and Andrew Hanson, *Career and Technical Education: Five Ways That Pay Along the Way to the B.A.* (Washington, DC: Georgetown University Center on Education and the Workforce, September 2012), https://georgetown.app.box.com/s/jd4r0nwvjtq12g1olx8v (accessed September 11, 2014); US Department of Education, National Center for Education Statistics, *The Condition of Education 2014,* by Grace Kena et al., NCES 2014-083 (Washington, DC: National Center for Education Statistics, May 2014), http://nces.ed.gov/ pubs2014/2014083.pdf (accessed September 11, 2014).

11. US Department of Commerce, Census Bureau, *Survey of Income and Program Participation 2008,* Panel Wave 13 (Washington, DC: US Census Bureau, 2012), http://www.census.gov/programs-surveys/sipp/data/2008-panel/wave-13.html (accessed September 12, 2014); Census Bureau, *Measuring Alternative Educational Credentials: 2012.*

12. Morris M. Kleiner and Alan B. Krueger, "Analyzing the Extent and Influence of Occupational Licensing on the Labor Market," *Journal of Labor Economics*, 31, no. 2, pt. 2 (April 2013): S173–S202, http://www.hhh.umn.edu/people/mkleiner/pdf/Final.occ.licensing.JOLE.pdf (accessed September 11, 2014).

13. US Department of Commerce, Census Bureau, *Measuring Alternative Educational Credentials: 2012.*

14. James A. Wall, executive director at NIMS, Melanie Stover, director of strategic initiatives at NIMS, and Jacey Wilkins, communications consultant at NIMS, interview by author, Fairfax, VA, August 8, 2014.

15. Gardner Carrick, vice president of strategic initiatives at the Manufacturing Institute, interview by author, Washington, DC, July 21, 2014; US Department of Labor, Bureau of Labor Statistics, *Occupational Outlook Handbook 2014–2015 edition,* Machinists and Tool and Die Makers, (Washington, DC: Bureau of Labor Statistics, January 2014), http://www.bls.gov/ooh/production/machinists-and-tool-and-die-makers.htm#tab-5 (accessed September 15, 2014).

16. James A. Wall, executive director at NIMS, interview by author, Fairfax, VA, August 8, 2014.

17. Amy Laitinen, comments at "Skills Beyond School," (New America Foundation, Education Policy Program and OECD event, Washington, DC, July 10, 2013).

18. Malgorzata Kuczera and Simon Field, "A Skills Beyond School Review of the United States," *OECD Reviews of Vocational Education and Training,* OECD Publishing, 2013, http://www.oecd.org/edu/skills-beyond-school/ASkillsbeyondSchool-ReviewoftheUnitedStates.pdf (accessed December 1, 2014); "Connecting Business to Working Learners," ACT Foundation, accessed December 1, 2014, http://actfdn.org/what-we-do/optimize-solutions/national-network-business-industry-associations/.

19. "Connecting Business to Working Learners," ACT Foundation.

20. Stephen Crawford, research professor at the George Washington Institute of Public Policy at George Washington University, telephonic interview by author, August 19, 2014.

21. Matthew Meyer, associate vice president of STEM innovations at North Carolina Community College System, telephonic interview by author, August 20, 2014; Michelle Massie, *Credential Data Pioneers: Forging New Partnerships to Measure Certifications and Licenses* (Washington, D.C.: Workforce Data Quality Campaign, April 2014), http://www.workforcedqc.org/sites/default/files/images/WDQC%20Credentials%20Paper%20April%202014.pdf (accessed September 14, 2014).

22. *Student Right to Know Before You Go Act of 2013,* S. 915, 113th Cong., 1st sess., *Congressional Record* 159 (May 9, 2013): S 3326, http://www.gpo.gov/fdsys/pkg/BILLS-113s915is/pdf/BILLS-113s915is.pdf (accessed September 10, 2014).

23. Mike Gaudreau, *Curriculum Guide 2014–2015,* Lake Brantley High School (Altamonte Springs, FL: 2014), http://lakebrantley.com/Portals/105/assets/pdf/Guidance%20pdf/LBHS%20Curriculum%20Guide%202014-2015%20REVISED%202-21-14.pdf (accessed September 15, 2014); Cheryl Cicotti, associate dean of nursing at Seminole State College, interview by author, Sanford, FL, June 3, 2014.

24. Neil Ashbaugh, training and development specialist at Oberg Industries, interview by author, November 13, 2014.

25. Mark Schneider, "2014 ACT Reports: Mismatch between College Aspiration and Preparation," *The Quick & the Ed,* American Institutes for Research, August 21, 2014, http://www.quickanded.com/2014/08/2014-act-reports-mismatch-between-college-aspiration-and-preparation.html (accessed September 15, 2014).

26. James E. Rosenbaum, *Beyond College for All: Career Paths for the Forgotten Half* (New York: Russell Sage Foundation, 2001).

27. Robert Mendenhall, president of Western Governors University, telephonic interview by author, August 4, 2014; The White House, *Ready to Work: Job-Driven Training and American Opportunity*, https://www.whitehouse.gov/sites/default/files/docs/skills_report.pdf.

Chapter Four

How Apprenticeship Approaches Can Spur Upward Mobility in the United States

Robert I. Lerman

The United States faces a pressing economic challenge: the weakening of the middle class. Slow economic growth, the stagnancy of wages in middle-wage jobs, and the decline of the two-parent family have all contributed to the problem. Young people are facing high unemployment and underemployment that may limit their long-term success. Young men, particularly those from low- and even middle-income families, are falling behind in schools and experiencing large declines in job prospects. Their inability to earn a good salary and to find satisfying jobs with upward mobility likely contribute to the large increase in female-headed families and delays in starting viable, two-parent families. Meanwhile, many firms, especially in manufacturing, are experiencing difficulties when hiring workers with relevant occupation skills. Can any policies and public-private initiatives change these realities?

State and federal governments have attempted to increase skills, mobility, and earnings almost entirely through an "academic-only" strategy. Unfortunately, the results are uneven at best. Although the vast majority of high school graduates attend college, only about 40 percent of American workers ages twenty-five to thirty-four achieve an associate's or bachelor's degree. For each full-time-equivalent student at a two-year public college, federal, state, and local governments spend about $11,400 per year. Yet only about 20 percent graduate within 1.5 times the normal period; for African-American students, the graduation rate is only about 11 percent.

Expanding apprenticeship training can make a major difference in these outcomes. What is apprenticeship? Apprenticeship is an approach that combines classroom-based vocational education, structured work-based learning, and paid work and production aimed at helping workers to master an occupation.

Apprenticeships are subject to externally imposed training standards, particularly for their workplace component. They usually last between two and four years and lead to a recognized credential certifying the apprentice's capabilities to perform the required tasks of a fully qualified worker in the occupation. In the United States and many other countries, apprenticeship takes place after high school when the participant is twenty years old (or older).[1] Unlike internships, apprenticeships require far more in-depth training, involve paid work, and lead to a recognized occupational credential. Unlike paid work experience, apprentices learn skills in formal classes and absorb their learning at the workplace in a highly structured setting.

Overall, the evidence demonstrates that apprenticeships (1) increase earnings of participants; (2) increase productivity and yield positive returns to firms; (3) enhance the quality and pay in jobs not requiring a bachelor's degree; (4) can expand substantially with modest government funding; (5) yield long-run savings of public money by lessening the need for high-cost, postsecondary education; (6) rely on learning by engaging in real production and earning while learning; (7) offer routes to rewarding careers not tied to an academic-only approach; (8) avoid the pitfalls of other training programs that are a poor fit for employer needs; (9) improve the transition from school to careers; and (10) provide a sense of occupational pride and identity in apprentice graduates.

The next sections briefly explain how apprenticeship systems work and describe the benefits of apprenticeship to individuals and society. I then look at specific programs that show promise at the high school, postsecondary, and college levels. The chapter concludes with recommendations for policy changes that can help bring apprenticeship to scale—and make apprenticeship options as accessible as traditional higher education.

HOW DO APPRENTICESHIP SYSTEMS WORK, GLOBALLY AND IN THE UNITED STATES?

Apprenticeship is a mainstream method for preparing for careers in a number of countries.[2] In Austria, Germany, Switzerland, and Denmark, apprenticeships take place during upper-secondary education or early postsecondary education.[3] Students typically enter apprenticeships by age seventeen and combine paid work, a work-based learning component, and a classroom-based component to gain the skills required to earn a credential in a specific profession. In several countries, the majority of all students enter apprenticeships (70 percent in Switzerland).

To engage such high shares of youth, apprenticeship systems cover a wide range of occupations, well beyond the construction and manufacturing trades. Tax specialist, hotel manager, costume designer, police officer, marketing designer, dental technician, and air traffic controller are a few of the hundreds of occupations in which employers use apprenticeships as the primary approach to training and ensuring a qualified workforce.[4]

In all countries, employers provide the structured work-based learning based on skill standards for the relevant occupation, pay the wages of apprentices, and assign trainers and mentors to work with apprentices. The apprentices are employees who contribute to the production process and are simultaneously students taking one or more courses. Countries that primarily involve adults as apprentices, including Canada and the United States, generally cover smaller shares of the population and fewer occupations outside the traditional trades. Still other countries offer large numbers of apprenticeship opportunities to both youth and adults.

Generally, training can be undertaken at a public training provider funded by the government or at a range of other training providers. For example, in Canada the training might be at a public college, a private training provider, or a union training center; in France, the centers may be run by private organizations, companies, or chambers. Countries sometimes use higher education institutions as training providers, but companies sometimes build their own courses. In Australia, companies and other organizations can be registered as a training provider and provide the "off-the-job" training for their apprentices or trainees in-house.

Countries vary in their certification and credentialing processes. Germany is well known for developing standards through a tripartite system involving labor, businesses, and the government—and by using chambers of commerce to test apprentices and ensure quality. In the United States, the system is quite decentralized. While the Office of Apprenticeship (OA) sends certifications of completion to apprenticeship sponsors when their apprentices complete their programs, OA lacks the resources to monitor the effectiveness of the training. In joint union-management programs in the United States, unions play a central role in ensuring quality.

Another key function is marketing to employers. In mature systems, where apprenticeships are a well-known phenomenon, companies can simply increase or decrease apprentice offers as their skill needs change. Most will know how to engage academic partners and how to recruit apprentices. In other areas, direct marketing to employers is necessary, as is the provision of general information and even branding.

England's ability to scale its apprenticeship program from about 150,000 in 2006–2007 to over 800,000 today depended in part on the activities of private training providers and units in further education colleges to market apprenticeships to employers. Governments have provided incentives for these training institutions to sell these services to employers. Similarly, South Carolina's success at scaling its apprenticeship programs is in no small part due to the effectiveness of the staff of Apprenticeship Carolina.

Apprenticeships are sometimes perceived to be holdover institutions that work only in the context of highly regulated labor markets, such as those in many European countries. As an example, a common misperception is that apprenticeship is an example of German exceptionalism and Germany's cultural heritage. By implication, adopting a robust apprenticeship system is unrealistic in the United States because it lacks the appropriate culture and regulated labor market of Germany. In fact, it is the United States, not Germany, which is the outlier. Most industrial countries—even those with unrelated labor markets—have much larger apprenticeship programs than the United States. Apprentices make up 3.7 percent of Australia's workforce, 2.2 percent of Canada's, and 2.7 percent of Britain's. In stark contrast, apprentices make up only 0.2 percent of the American labor force.

THE EVIDENCE ON APPRENTICESHIPS

Robust apprenticeship systems fundamentally influence the transition to jobs and careers, employer recruitment and training policies, credentials recognizing skill attainment, and the relationships among schools and employers. Large-scale apprenticeship systems can create network effects. Having many employers offer apprenticeships makes it easy for new employers to do so; wide dissemination of information about apprenticeship improves the likelihood that workers and businesses will see the benefits of participating; an abundance of apprenticeship opportunities lowers the unit costs of providing related courses through education and training organizations. Most studies are unable to account for these network effects, but they do cover how individual programs affect skills, productivity, and the economic returns to firms. This section examines the evidence from these studies.

Apprenticeship and Economic Returns to Workers

What is the economic return to workers from investing in apprenticeship? Do the gains persist in the long run—or are short-term gains offset by long-term losses? In particular, in teaching mastery of an occupation, do apprenticeships weaken the mobility of workers to move to other, high-wage occupations?

The two most in-depth studies of the American experience find high economic returns to apprentices. One study examined individuals using employment offices in Washington State. The study matched individuals entering apprenticeships with other individuals with the same preprogram earnings and same age and sex. Within two and a half years of completing the program, apprentices accumulated $78,000 more in earnings and fringe benefits than a comparison group, and are projected to earn over $400,000 more through age sixty-five.[5]

The gains for graduates of community college vocational programs were far smaller—$17,000 in the short run and about $210,000 by age sixty-five. In the early post-training period, 84 percent of apprentice completers held jobs, compared with only 70 percent of community college professional/technical graduates. Of those employed, only 11 percent of apprentices reported that their program was not related to their jobs; for community college graduates, the figure jumped to 25 percent.

Another study of apprenticeship in ten states also documents large and statistically significant earnings gains from participating in apprenticeship.[6] It estimates how the length of participation in an apprenticeship affected earnings, holding constant for preenrollment earnings of apprenticeship participants. At six years after starting a program, earnings of the average apprenticeship participant (average duration in an apprenticeship) stood at 1.4 times the earnings of nonparticipants with the same preapprenticeship history.

The gains were highly consistent across states, although the earnings advantages narrowed between the sixth and ninth years after program entry. The study looks at government administrative and oversight costs as well as the costs of government-funded classroom instruction. Costs to employers and union-management sponsors of apprenticeship are not examined. Overall, the study finds that apprenticeship returns nearly twenty-eight dollars in benefits for every dollar of government and worker costs. The net dollar gains projected over a worker's career amounted to about $125,000.

Studies of apprenticeship training in European countries also generally find high rates of returns to the workers, often in the range of 15 percent.[7] Clark and Fahr estimate wage gains in this range (about 6 percent to 8 percent per apprenticeship year with duration of slightly less than three years), with gains only modestly lower by shifts from the training occupation to another occupation.[8] One quasiexperimental study of the returns to apprenticeship training in small Austrian firms examines the interaction between apprenticeship duration and failing firms.[9] A firm going out of business generally results in a sudden and exogenous end to the apprenticeship training in the firm. Thus, the timing of firm failure will affect the duration of apprenticeship training a particular worker experiences.

By looking at apprentices who obtained training in failed firms, one can examine a large number of trained workers with varying durations in their apprenticeships. The results show that apprenticeships raise wages by about 4 percent per year of training. For a three- to four-year apprenticeship, postapprenticeship wages end up 12 percent to 16 percent higher than they otherwise would be. Since the worker's costs of participating in an apprenticeship are often minimal, the Austrian study indicates high overall benefits relative to modest costs.

Two studies of apprenticeships in Canada reveal a high wage premium for apprenticeships for men but not for women.[10] Apprenticeship completion is the highest educational attainment for only about 7 percent of Canadian men. However, for this group, earnings are substantially higher than the earnings of those who have only completed secondary school and nearly as high as those who have completed college programs that are less than a bachelor's degree. Overall, the gains for men from apprenticeship training are in the range of 17 percent to 24 percent. Even evaluated after twenty years of experience, apprenticeship training in most occupations yields continuing returns of 12 percent to 14 percent.

Apprenticeship and Economic Mobility

The portability of the skills learned in occupation-specific programs is a common concern about apprenticeships or any occupation-specific training. How skill portability varies with the mode of learning and the curricula is unclear, *a priori*. As Geel and Gellner point out, learning even a highly specific skill can yield benefits outside the narrow occupation.[11]

All skills are general in some sense and occupation-specific skills are various mixes of skills.[12] After compiling the skills and their importance for nearly eighty occupations, Geel and Gellner estimate how skills are grouped within narrow occupations.[13] This approach recognizes that skills developed ostensibly for one occupation can be useful in other occupations. It identifies occupational clusters that possess similar skill combinations within a given cluster and different skill combinations between clusters.

The cluster approach captures the high degree of portability of German apprentices. While only 42 percent of apprentices stay in their initial occupation, nearly two-thirds remain with their apprentice occupation or another occupation in the same skill cluster. When they do move to another occupation in the same cluster, apprentices actually increase their wages. Further, those trained in occupations with more specific skill sets are more likely to remain in their initial occupation or move to occupations within the same cluster.

Another study indicates high returns and transferability of German apprenticeship.[14] The overall rates of return to each year of apprenticeship range from 8 percent to 12 percent for training in firms of fifty workers or more, and from about 5.5 percent to 6.5 percent for firms of two to forty-nine workers. As Geel and Gellner found, the wage penalty varies with the distance away from the original occupation.[15] There is no penalty at all from displacement into a somewhat related occupation. Finally, Clark and Fahr find only 18 percent of all former apprentices stated they used few or no skills learned in their apprenticeships.[16]

In the United States, when comparing how postsecondary alternatives relate to mobility, we should recognize that community college and private, for-profit college students often take highly specific occupational courses, while all apprentices take some general, classroom courses. Thus, apprentice electricians learn the principles of science—especially those related to electricity. In most countries, collaboration takes place between vocational schools and apprenticeship programs. From this perspective, apprenticeship programs can be viewed as "college plus" or "dual" programs that combine work-based and postsecondary courses, albeit with an emphasis on work-based learning.[18]

Apprenticeship and Social Development

Apprenticeship is one of the few approaches that incorporate both an economic and social dimension. From an economic standpoint, apprenticeships can help resolve a skills mismatch that seems to be emerging in the United States. A good indication of this mismatch is the complaints by foreign companies operating in the United States about the skill shortfalls in key jobs; these companies have no ideological stake in misstating the notion of worker shortages.

German companies operating in the United States are so concerned about finding workers with appropriate occupational skills that they have stirred the German embassy in Washington, DC, to launch its own skills initiative, bringing together German and American companies, local chambers of commerce, colleges, and other training providers. The goal of the initiative, the embassy says, is to "identify and spread best practices in sustainable workforce development," and "spread the message about the German apprenticeship system" and its potential benefits for the US economy.[17]

At the same time, apprenticeships can yield social benefits—first by upgrading jobs and the earnings of the middle class, and second by improving social outcomes. One analysis found that technical vocational education (including apprenticeship) is linked to higher confidence and self-esteem, improved health, higher citizen participation, and higher job satisfaction.[18] These relationships hold even after controlling for income. Other studies have indicated that apprenticeships improve vocational identity.[19]

Apprenticeship training limits the gaps between what is learned at school and how to apply these and other skills at the workplace. Transmitting skills to the workplace works well with supervisory support, interactive training, coaching, opportunities to perform what was learned in training, and keeping the training relevant to jobs.[20] The benefits extend to the developmental side of young people. Robert Halpern finds that youth apprenticeship helps young people develop independence and self-confidence through their ability to perform difficult tasks. He notes, "Apprentices learn through observation, imitation, trial and error, and reiteration; in other words through force of experience."[21]

While apprentices are expected to demonstrate professionalism and care, they are not expected opportunities to be perfect. From Halpern's perspective, apprenticeships offer youth opportunities to explore new areas in a structured environment. They can try out new identities in an occupational arena and experience learning in a context of production—of making things. By mastering tasks that other young people cannot, apprentices gain a strong sense of pride that a "B student" is unlikely to feel when passing a test or even completing a paper. Apprenticeships offer a way of evolving into constructive adults that makes sense to young people.

A robust apprenticeship system can narrow the gender gaps in postsecondary credentials. Young men, especially minority men, have fallen far behind young women in graduating college. As of March 2013, only 24 percent of African American men and 17 percent of Hispanic men ages twenty-five to thirty-four had attained an associate's or bachelor's degree. In contrast, associate's or bachelor's completion rates were 37 percent for African American women and 27 percent for Hispanic women. In Canada, young women also outpace young men in college completion. However, if one counts apprenticeship credentials as comparable to a postsecondary degree, the gender gap in postsecondary attainment narrows sharply.

Apprenticeships can accommodate differences in learning styles that may be relevant to gender gaps. Although learning-by-doing is appealing to most students, the difference between a model based solely on classroom learning and one taking place mostly on the job may be of special importance to men. Apprenticeships give workers who are bored in school, or who worry about the value of education, increased confidence that their personal efforts and investment in skill development will pay off. Minorities may find apprenticeships especially useful in enhancing their employability skills in such areas as communication, problem solving, and teaching others.

Benefits to Firms

It is common to ask the question: if apprenticeships are such good investments, why don't more employers offer them? The evidence from England and South Carolina demonstrates the importance of information and of making apprenticeships easy to implement. Both factors played a role in stimulating employers to adopt apprenticeships. Still, the long-term success of attracting employers to use apprenticeship requires knowledge of the costs and benefits to employers.

Employer net costs depend on the mix of classroom and work-based training, occupation, skill, and wage progression, and the productivity of the
apprentice while learning to master the required skill. Direct costs include
apprentice wages, the wages of trainer specialists for the time they oversee
apprentices, materials, and the costs of additional space required for apprenticeship.[22] The benefits depend on the extent to which apprenticeships save
on subsequent hiring and training costs, lower turnover costs, and enhance
productivity more than added wage costs.

Also valuable is the employer's increased certainty that apprentice graduates know all relevant occupational and firm-specific skills and can work
well alongside other skilled workers. In addition, having extra well-trained
workers, such as apprentice graduates, provides firms with a valuable option
of expanding production without reducing quality, in response to uncertain
demand shocks and covering for sudden absences of skilled workers. The
high level of occupational mastery achieved by apprentices may increase the
pace of innovation and the ease of implementing new technologies.

One analysis examined the costs and benefits to thousands of German and
Swiss firms while excluding the government-financed, school-based learning
linked to apprenticeships.[23] Looking only at the training period, the authors cal-
culate these gross costs—worker wages, trainer wages, and materials—and the
benefits to employers derived from the productive contributions of apprentices
during the training period. The study offers details on the wages of management and training personnel, wages of regular skilled and unskilled workers,
wage costs of apprentices, time at the workplace, share of apprentices' workplace time devoted to tasks normally undertaken by unskilled and skilled workers, and the relative productivity of apprentices compared to regular workers.

The results show firms recoup all or nearly all their investment in apprenticeships. The average gross costs per year, per apprentice amounted to
€15,500 for German firms and about €18,000 for Swiss firms. But the value
of production generated through apprentices amounted to over €19,000 per
year for Swiss firms and €8,000 per year for German firms. Most Swiss firms,
and about one-third of German firms, recouped their investment within the
training period.

The reason is that apprentices ascend quickly from taking on unskilled
to skilled tasks. In Switzerland, the productivity of apprentices rises from
37 percent of a skilled worker's level in year one to 75 percent in the final
year; the increase in Germany is just as rapid, increasing from 30 percent to
68 percent of a skilled worker's productivity over the apprenticeship period.

An extensive study of Canadian employers sponsored by the Canadian
Apprenticeship Forum estimated employer costs and benefits of four-year
apprenticeships in fifteen occupations.[24] For all fifteen occupations, employ-

ers earned a positive return on their apprenticeship investments during the apprenticeship period. The average benefit was 1.38 times the average cost. Any postprogram benefits would add to the economic returns.

A study of the United Kingdom program examined the returns to eight employers in each of four industries—engineering, construction, retail, and business administration, including foundation and advanced levels.[25] The authors estimate that employers recouped the costs during the apprenticeship period or by the early postapprenticeship period, when employers save on recruitment and training costs.

Savings in recruitment and training costs can be significant. One study found such savings average nearly €6,000 for each skilled worker trained in an apprenticeship and taken on permanently.[26] Other benefits accrue to employers, including reduced errors in placing employees, avoiding excessive costs when the demand for skilled workers cannot be quickly filled, and performance advantages favoring internally trained workers who understand company processes over skilled workers recruited from the job market.

One benefit to firms rarely captured in studies is apprenticeship's positive impact on innovation.[27] Another is the option value of having an abundance of well-trained workers. In a world of uncertainty about levels of production and irreversible investments in particular workers, firms investing in apprenticeship training create "real options." When workers complete their training, firms have the option—but not the obligation—to hire some or all of the trained workers. Having additional well-trained, apprenticed workers with a range of skills allows firms to deal with unexpected increases in demand or losses of other experienced workers. Though hard to quantify, the value of these real options raises the firm's returns on apprenticeship investments.

In the United States, reports by firms using apprenticeships are overwhelmingly positive. A majority of sponsors believe their programs are valuable and involve net gains.[28] Nearly all sponsors reported that the apprenticeship program helps them meet their skill demands. Other benefits of apprenticeship included reliably documenting appropriate skills, raising productivity and worker morale, and reducing safety problems.

One potential concern of employers is that the workers they train will move to other companies after completing their apprenticeship. Among US firms offering apprenticeships, the overwhelming majority did not view this problem as serious—and most of those that did still reported high levels of satisfaction with apprenticeship. The evidence from other countries suggests why "poaching" is not a deterrent to offering apprenticeship.

Overall, with sufficient information about setting up and maintaining an apprenticeship program and with an effective infrastructure for apprenticeship, firms are generally able to gain a high return by participating.

Promising Programs: Youth Apprenticeships

While most apprenticeship programs operate at the postsecondary level, Georgia and Wisconsin each have developed in-depth "youth apprenticeship" programs at the high school level. In both states, students fulfill all of the academic requirements for high school graduation while engaging in an apprenticeship, and use elective courses related to the apprenticeship. The occupations range widely—from agriculture and natural resources to finance, health, human services, logistics, printing, and security. In Wisconsin, students combine 450 to 900 hours of work-based learning with 180 to 360 hours of technical instruction. In Georgia, the work-based learning component—which includes working in the summer—is two thousand hours.

Sophomore students generally learn about the possibility of joining the apprenticeship program as juniors and seniors. Apprentices complete not only their high school diploma, but also a postsecondary certificate or degree, and certification of industry-recognized competencies applicable to employment in a high-skill occupation. Mentorship is a key part of the program, as are employer evaluations of the student's job performance and the building of professional portfolios. As of 2013, nearly seven thousand students in Georgia were participating in a youth apprenticeship. The program runs in all 165 school systems in the state. About two thousand Wisconsin students take up apprenticeships.

High schools recruit and counsel students, support career-focused learning, and assist in identifying industry partners. Businesses offer apprenticeship positions, provide each apprentice with a worksite supervisor, and ensure that apprentices gain experience and expertise in all the designated skill areas. The worksite supervisors must participate in mentor orientation and training so that they can guide students through all the skill areas and serve as coaches and role models. Parents must agree to and sign an educational training agreement and provide transportation to the student. Finally, apprentices must maintain high levels of attendance and satisfactory progress in classes (both academic and career-oriented) and in the development of occupational skills at the worksite.

Employers report high levels of satisfaction with the apprentices and the apprenticeship program. In Georgia, over 95 percent say the program has been highly beneficial to the company and that they would recommend the program to other companies. Participating companies also report good quality student performance in problem-solving and communication skills. Over three in four Georgia apprentices find jobs in their career of choice.

Promising Programs: Apprenticeships as a "College Plus" Initiative for the United States

Apprenticeship can be thought of as "college plus" in the sense that students take the equivalent of at least community college courses while pursuing a rigorous program of work-based learning and serving as a productive worker. Moreover, many programs at two-year public colleges involve courses and degrees with as much occupational specificity as apprenticeships.

The Obama administration is touting initiatives to count apprenticeships for community college credit, as part of the Registered Apprenticeship Community College Network (RACC). The RACC is a national network of postsecondary institutions, employers, unions, and associations. College members agree to provide credit for a Registered Apprenticeship completion certificate as recommended by a recognized third-party evaluator. The consortium will create a national network of colleges and Registered Apprenticeship sponsors allowing apprentice graduates to accelerate completion of their postsecondary degrees at member colleges.

BRINGING APPRENTICESHIPS TO SCALE IN THE UNITED STATES

Extend Use of Current Postsecondary and Training Subsidies to Apprenticeship

Several postsecondary programs could be set up to subsidize at least the classroom portion of apprenticeships. Already, localities can use training vouchers from the Workforce Investment Act for apprenticeship. To encourage the use of vouchers for apprenticeship, the federal government could provide one or two more vouchers to Workforce Investment Boards for one used in an apprenticeship program.

Another step is to encourage the use of Trade Adjustment Act (TAA) training subsidies to help companies sponsoring apprenticeships just as training providers receive subsidies for TAA-eligible workers enrolled in full-time training. In addition, policies could allow partial payment of TAA's extended unemployment insurance to continue for employed individuals in registered apprenticeship programs.

Allowing the use of publicly funded grants to pay at least for the classroom portion of a registered apprenticeship program makes perfect sense as well. As of 2015, a large chunk of Pell grants pays for occupationally oriented programs at community colleges and for-profit career colleges. The returns on such investments are far lower than the returns generated by apprenticeship.

The Department of Education can authorize experiments under the federal student aid programs; it has already allowed Pell grants for some students learning high-demand jobs as part of a certificate program.[29] Extending the initiative to support related instruction (normally formal courses) in an apprenticeship could increase apprenticeship slots and reduce the amount the federal government would have to spend to support these individuals in full-time schooling.

The GI Bill already provides housing benefits and subsidizes wages for veterans in apprenticeships. However, funding for colleges and university expenses is far higher than for apprenticeships. By amending the law, we could offer half the GI Bill college benefits to employers hiring veterans into an apprenticeship program. However, unless the liberalized uses of grants and GI Bill benefits are linked with an extensive marketing campaign, the take-up by employers is likely to be limited.

Expand Youth Apprenticeship

Although these programs reach only a very small share of young people, the United States could make a good start on building apprenticeship by replicating the numbers in Georgia throughout the country. To create about 250,000 quality jobs and learning opportunities, the gross costs of such an initiative would be only about $105 million—or about $450 per calendar year, or roughly 4 percent of current school outlays per student-year. Some of these costs would be offset by reductions in teaching expenses, as some students spend more time in work-based learning and less time in high school courses. The modest investment would pay off handsomely in the form of increased earnings and associated tax revenues, as well as reduced spending on educational and social expenditures.

Career academies are a good place to start. They are schools within high schools that have an industry or occupational focus. Over seven thousand operate in the United States, in fields ranging from health and finance to travel, construction, information technology (IT), hospitality and tourism, health, and arts and communication. Other sectors include agriculture, transportation, manufacturing, and public service.

These programs already include classroom-related instruction, and sometimes work with employers to develop internships in fields such as health, finance, travel, and construction. Compared with other high school students, Career academy students are exposed to a wider range of experiences linked to careers, including job shadowing, internships, and career fairs—plus guidance on how to look for a job, prepare a resume, and take an interview. Work-based learning varies, but the internships that many students experience are related to the academy's industry or occupation theme.

Evidence from an experimental study found that career academies induced striking gains in earnings, especially among minority young men.[30] In the period between four and eight years after applying for the academies, young men in the treatment group were earning 17 percent more than those in the control group. This represents an increase in earnings of about $3,700 per year. The percentage gains in earnings were highest for the students facing the highest risk of dropping out of school. Some observers believe that it was the work-based learning component that generated the most success in the program.

Since career academies already have an occupational and industry focus, adding a rigorous, structured apprenticeship could be attractive and feasible. A serious apprenticeship both adds skills and encourages the use of skills. Crediting these skills would reduce classroom time and the associated costs. If, for example, a student spent two days per week in a paid apprenticeship, the school should be able to save at least 15 percent of the costs. Applying these funds to marketing, counseling, and oversight for youth apprenticeship should allow the academy or other school to stimulate employers to provide apprenticeship slots. Success in reaching employers will require talented, business-friendly staff who are well-trained in business issues and apprenticeship.

To implement this component, state governments should fund marketing and technical support to career academies to set up cooperative apprenticeships with employers, either using money from state budgets or from federal dollars. The first step should be planning grants for interested and capable career academies to determine who can best market and provide technical assistance to the academies. Next, state governments should sponsor performance-based funding to units in academies so that they receive funds for each additional apprenticeship. Private foundations should offer resources for demonstration and experimentation in creating apprenticeships within high school programs, especially career academies.

Designate Best Practice Occupational Standards for Apprenticeships

To simplify the development of apprenticeships for potential employers, a joint team from the Labor Department's OA and the Department of Commerce should designate one or two examples of good practice with regard to specific areas of expertise learned at work sites and subjects learned through classroom components. The OA–Commerce team should select occupational standards in consultation with selected employers who hire workers in the occupation.

Once selected, the standards should be published and made readily accessible. Employers who comply with these established standards should have a quick and easy path to registration of the program. In addition, workforce professionals trying to market apprenticeships will have a model that they can sell, and that employers can adopt (and adjust as needed). Occupational standards used in other countries can serve as starting points to the OA–Commerce team and to industry groups involved in setting standards and in illustrating curricula.

The standards and certification development should link to an effort to reconcile apprenticeship standards with state licensing of occupations. Ideally, the initiative should modernize and limit licensing. But, to the extent licensing reform does not materialize, apprenticeship should become the prime route to licensure. Finally, the safe harbor or best practice standards should be available to all firms, independently of gaining approvals from other organizations, including state apprenticeship agencies.

Develop a Solid Infrastructure of Information, Peer Support, and Research

The federal government should sponsor the development of an information clearinghouse, a peer support network, and a research program on apprenticeship. The information clearinghouse should document the occupations that currently use apprenticeships—not only in the United States, but also in other countries—along with the list of occupation skills that the apprentices master. It should include the curricula for classroom instruction as well as the skills that apprentices should learn and master at the workplace. Included in the clearinghouse should be up-to-date information on available apprenticeships and on applicants looking for apprenticeships. The development of the information hub should involve agencies within the Department of Commerce as well as the OA.

The research program should cover topics especially relevant to employers, such as the return to apprenticeship from the employer perspective and the net cost of sponsoring an apprentice after taking account of the apprentice's contribution to production. Other research should examine best practices for marketing apprenticeship, for incorporating classroom and work-based learning by sector, and for counseling potential apprentices.

Widen the Occupational Scope and Expand the Marketing of Apprenticeship

Apprenticeships cover a wide range of occupations in several countries.[31] To reach 50 percent to 70 percent of young cohorts, as the Swiss and German systems do, apprenticeships have to include service and professional jobs as well as manufacturing and construction occupations. In mature systems, apprenticeships take place in banking, engineering, commercial sales, accounting, marketing, IT, security, natural and energy resources, and hotel management, just to name a few.

A broad-based apprenticeship system would mark a major change in the United States. Well over 50 percent of apprenticeships are in the construction trades; in many states, the figure is far higher. The building trade apprenticeships are generally high quality and yield high earnings upon completion. However, the very strength of apprenticeship in the building trades and in construction unions can cause government regulators to view apprenticeship in general from a construction perspective. The federal OA within the US Department of Labor has worked to attract employers to use apprenticeship for occupations outside of construction. However, OA's success has been limited, partly because of very small budgets and an inability to hire flexibly.

Few states have been dynamic in seeking out sponsors in new occupations or even in recruiting more employers in existing occupations. One reason is that their budgets for undertaking these efforts are minimal. In any event, the overall result is that the decline in the absolute number of apprenticeships associated with the drop in construction has not been offset by increases in apprenticeships in other fields.

Still, a few states have made headway in stimulating employers to start apprenticeship programs. South Carolina's successful example involved collaboration between the marketing unit (branded as *Apprenticeship Carolina*) in the technical college system and a federal representative from the OA. Apprenticeship Carolina uses talented, business-savvy salespeople to connect with businesses and encourage them to start apprenticeships, then handles all the paperwork and moves companies through the registration process.

With a state budget of $1 million per year—as well as tax credits to employers of $1,000 per year, per apprentice—the program managed to stimulate more than a sixfold increase in registered apprenticeship programs and a fivefold increase in apprentices. Nearly all of the increase in apprenticeships took place in nonconstruction fields. Especially striking is that these successes—including four thousand added apprenticeships—took place as the economy entered a deep recession and lost millions of jobs. The costs per apprentice totaled only about $1,250 per apprentice calendar year, including the costs of the tax credit.

Other approaches to marketing have worked to expand apprenticeship in England. In addition to a national branding effort by the National Apprenticeship Service, Apprenticeship Week activities, and speeches by government leaders on apprenticeship, England has devised a sales strategy for working directly with employers. The Skills Funding Agency funds Further Education colleges and private training providers (Association of Employment and Learning Providers) to recruit employers, manage the apprenticeship process and progress, and provide the related classroom training. The private training firms now account for about 70 percent of British apprenticeships.

For apprenticeship to achieve scale in the United States, policymakers will need to supply incentives to private and public organizations to reach individual employers and demonstrate to them why apprenticeships will have value. Additional options to promote apprenticeship training include the provision of tax credits to employers for adopting registered apprenticeship and technical assistance.

THE MODEST PROBLEM—PARENTAL AND SOCIAL INFLUENCES ON POTENTIAL APPRENTICES

One common concern about expanding apprenticeship in the United States is that parents will discourage their children from taking up an opportunity outside the traditional college framework. Fortunately, this is a far more hypothetical than real problem. Today, quality apprenticeship programs have little trouble attracting sufficient numbers of applicants to fill the apprenticeship slots available. Indeed, most have waiting lists filled with competent applicants. The central problem is insufficient apprenticeship offers.

In today's context, it would do no good—and in fact might harm the situation—if parents, schools, and workforce placement programs encouraged massive numbers of young people to seek apprenticeships. The constraint to expansion is on the employer demand side. As the number of positions expand, and as young people see others succeeding in apprenticeships, the stigma against apprenticeships as subpar options will erode further. At that point, the key government role is to improve job and career counseling, and to help young people think carefully about which occupation and pathway to pursue.

FUTURE VISION

Expanding apprenticeship training in the United States can make a major difference in the lives of young workers. Instead of performing at the mediocre level (or worse), more young people can gain mastery in an interesting profession. The learning-by-doing embedded in apprenticeship will give young people confidence in their ability to learn and sometimes encourage apprentice graduates to pursue and earn a bachelor's degree.

Apprenticeship is distinctive in affecting both the supply side (workers and their skills) and the demand side (employers and the jobs they create). As employers train and see the capabilities of the apprentices, they begin to raise expectations about the types of tasks that workers in a specific job category can undertake. This step encourages employers to require and use more skill on jobs, ultimately enhancing them.

The real question is not whether expanding apprenticeship is desirable, but rather whether it is feasible. The recent growth in England, from about 150,000 apprentices in 2007 to over 800,000 today, demonstrates the feasibility of expansion, even in countries with relatively free labor markets and similar scores on international literacy and numeracy scores as the United States.

Today, the United States is still absorbed in a "college for all" mentality, which has high returns for many young people. But for others, high costs, high failure rates, and weak links with the labor market dominate. One reason for the emphasis on "college," including occupational community college programs, is the limited number of alternative, well-structured learning opportunities. Building an extensive and high-quality apprenticeship system in the United States would diversify the routes to rewarding careers and potentially save government cost—as well as avoid the frustration of many young people who do not thrive in an "academic only" approach to learning.

If the United States apprenticeship system penetrated the same share of the workforce as in Australia, Canada, and England, there would be four million apprentices (about ten times the current number). Assuming apprenticeships last two to four years (an average of three), reaching this goal would provide nearly one-third of young people with the chance to master what is required to be well paid in a medium- or high-skill career. At this scale, and with bachelor's degrees at about 35 percent, over two out of three Americans would be attaining the skills and qualifications necessary for good jobs. The improvement in the middle class would be remarkable.

No single policy can deal with high youth unemployment, low youth skills, the rise in inequality, and the decline of middle-skill jobs. But expanding apprenticeship is one of the most productive and cost-effective ways of lessening these problems.

As these policy developments emerge, expanding the research base about apprenticeship will be important. We need a better understanding of the political, economic, business, and social attitude factors that constrain or help countries develop quality apprenticeship systems. What are the best systems for marketing apprenticeship to companies? What is the role of improved information for prospective apprentices and employers? What is the trade-off between national standards that ensure portability and company-based standards that might improve retention of workers after the apprenticeship? What is the tipping point at which there are sufficient apprenticeships—so that students see apprenticeships as viable paths to rewarding careers and employers become comfortable embracing apprenticeship in their recruitment, training, and upgrading policies? How best can apprentices smoothly transition to undergraduate and graduate university programs?

There is plenty of work to do at the policy, implementation, and research levels to use expanded apprenticeship as a way to make a better world for young people and the workforce. It is time to get started.

NOTES

1. See Robert Lerman, "Apprenticeship in the United States: Patterns of Governance and Recent Developments," in *Rediscovering Apprenticeship: Research Findings of the International Network on Innovative Apprenticeship (INAP)*, ed. Erica Smith and Felix Rauner (New York: Springer-Verlag, 2010). In Austria, Germany, and Switzerland, apprenticeship takes place in late school. Countries also vary in terms of occupational coverage, interactions with schools and training providers, and subsidies.

2. E. Smith and R. Brennan Kemmis, "Towards a model apprenticeship framework: a comparative analysis of national apprenticeship systems," International Labor Organization, World Bank, 2013.

3. Organisation for Economic Cooperation and Development (OECD), *Jobs for Youth: United States* (Paris: OECD, 2009).

4. For a list of apprenticeships in each of ten clusters of occupations in five countries, see the occupational standards section at www.innovativeapprenticeship.org.

5. Kevin Hollenbeck, "State Use of Workforce System Net Impact Estimates and Rates of Return," presented at the Association for Public Policy Analysis and Management (APPAM) Conference, Los Angeles, CA, 2008, http://research.upjohn.org/confpapers/1.

6. Debbie Reed et al., "An Effectiveness Assessment and Cost-Benefit Analysis of Registered Apprenticeship in 10 States" (Washington, DC: Mathematica Policy Research, 2012), http://wdr.doleta.gov/research/Full-Text_Documents/ETAOP_2012_10.pdf.

7. Damon Clark and René Fahr, "The Promise of Workplace Training for Non-College-Bound Youth: Theory and Evidence from German Apprenticeship," IZA Discussion Paper No. 378 (Bonn, Germany: IZA, 2001), http://www.iza.org/en/webcontent/publications/papers/viewAbstract?dp_id=378; Josef Fersterer et al., "Returns to Apprenticeship Training in Austria: Evidence from Failed Firms," *Scandinavian Journal of Economics* 110, no. 4

(2008): 733–53; Regula Geel and Uschi Backes-Gellner, "Occupational Mobility within and between Skill Clusters: An Empirical Analysis Based on the Skill-Weights Approach," Working Paper No. 47, Swiss Leading House on Economics of Education, Firm Behavior, and Training Policies (Zurich, Switzerland: Swiss Federal Office for Professional Education and Technology, 2009), http://ideas.repec.org/p/iso/educat/0047.html.

8. Clark and Fahr, "The Promise of Workplace Training"; Natalia Aivazova, "Role of Apprenticeships in Combating Youth Unemployment in Europe and the United States," Peterson Institute for International Economics, Policy Brief, no. PB 13-20, 2013, http://www.iie.com/publications/pb/pb13-20.pdf.

9. Fersterer et al., "Returns to Apprenticeship Trainings."

10. Daniel Boothby and Torben Drewes, "Returns to Apprenticeship in Canada," Canadian Labour Market and Skills Researcher Network, Working Paper no. 70, http://www.clsrn.econ.ubc.ca/workingpapers/CLSRN%20Working%20Paper%20no.%2070%20-%20Boothby%20and%20Drewes.pdf; Morley Gunderson and Harry Krashinsky, "Returns to Apprenticeship: Analysis Based on the 2006 Census." Canadian Labour Market and Skills Researcher Network, Working Paper no. 99, http://www.clsrn.econ.ubc.ca/workingpapers/CLSRN%20Working%20Paper%20no.%2099%20-%20Gunderson%20and%20Krashinsky.pdf.

11. Geel and Backes-Gellner, "Occupational Mobility within and between Skill Clusters."

12. Edward Lazear. "Firm-specific Human Capital: A Skill-weights Approach," *Journal of Political Economy* 117 (2009): 914–40.

13. Geel and Backes-Gellner, "Occupational Mobility within and between Skill Clusters."

14. Clark and Fahr, "The Promise of Workplace Training."

15. Geel and Backes-Gellner, "Occupational Mobility within and between Skill Clusters."

16. Clark and Fahr, "The Promise of Workplace Training."

17. German Skill Initiative, German Missions in the United States, 2015, http://www.germany.info/skillsinitiative.com.

18. European Centre for the Development of Vocational Training (CEDEFOP), *Vocational Education and Training is Good for You: The Social Benefit of VET for Individuals* (Luxembourg: Publications Office of the European Union, 2011).

19. Alan Brown et al., *Identities at Work* (Dordrecht, Netherlands: Springer, 2007).

20. James Pellegrino and Margaret Hilton, eds., *Education for Life and Work: Developing Transferable Knowledge and Skills in the 21st Century* (Washington, DC: National Research Council, 2012).

21. Robert Halpern, *The Means to Grow Up. Reinventing Apprenticeship as a Developmental Support in Adolescence* (New York: Routledge, 2009), 6.

22. S. Muehlemann, P. Ryan, and S. Wolter, "Monopsony Power, Pay Structure, and Training," *Industrial and Labor Relations Review 66*, no. 5 (2013): 1097–1114.

23. S. Muehlemann, H. Pfeifer, and S. Wolter, "Cost and Benefit of Apprenticeship Training: A Comparison of Germany and Switzerland," *Applied Economics Quarterly* 55, no. 1 (2009): 7–36.

24. Canadian Apprencticeship Forum, "Apprenticeship—Building a skilled workforce for a strong bottom line: Return on apprenticeship training investment for employers—a study of 15 trades," 2006.

25. C. Hasluck and T. Hogarth, "The Net Benefits to Employers' Investments in Apprenticeships: Case Study Evidence from the UK," *Canadian Apprenticeship Journal* 2 (Summer 2010).

26. U. Beicht and J. Ulrich, "Costs and benefits of in-company vocational training," BWP Special Edition (2005): 38–40, http://www.bibb.de/dokumente/pdf/a1_bwp_special-edition_ beicht.pdf.

27. Stefan Bauernschuster et al., "Training and Innovation," *Journal of Human Capital* 3, no. 4 (2009): 323–53.

28. Robert Lerman et al., "The Benefits and Challenges of Registered Apprenticeship: The Sponsors' Perspective," Urban Institute Research Report, June 12, 2009, http://www.urban.org/UploadedPDF/411907_registered_apprenticeship.pdf.

29. Ben Olinsky and Sarah Ayres, "Training for Success: A Policy to Expand Apprenticeships in the United States," Center for American Progress, December 2013, http://www.americanprogress.org/wp-content/uploads/2013/11/apprenticeship_report.pdf.

30. J. Kemple (with C. Willner), "Career Academies: Long-Term Impacts on Work, Education, and Transitions to Adulthood," *MDRC Report,* June 2008, http://www.mdrc.org/publication/career-academies-long-term-impacts-work-education-and-transitions-adulthood.

31. For a detailed listing of apprenticeships by occupational cluster for five countries, go to the occupational standards page of the American Institute for Innovative Apprenticeship, www.innovativeapprenticeship.org.

Part II

MULTIPLE PATHWAYS IN HIGH SCHOOL: TRACKING REVISITED?

Chapter Five

Small High Schools of Choice

Peter Meyer

Safety-net and support programs can never do what a good education can.

—Joel Klein, former Chancellor,
New York City Department of Education[1]

If one is looking for a symbol of the rise and fall—and resurrection—of the American high school, one need but take the #1 IRT subway train to 225th Street in the Bronx, then walk a few blocks up Marble Hill, along the north shore of the Harlem River separating Manhattan from its poorest borough, finally arriving at an eight-story building covering some four city blocks and looking very much like it was lifted from the drafting table of a Soviet bloc architect.

Opened in 1972, John F. Kennedy High School housed, in its heyday, somewhere between 3,000 and 6,000 students—4,500 started that first September. According to Iris Zucker, who taught there in the 1990s, "It was as big as some towns. We had 350 teachers."[2] It had everything for everyone— except an education. By the end of the century, only one-third of its students graduated. Furthermore, it was dangerous, described in a 2004 *New York Times* story as a school that:

> has turned out more horrifying tales than success stories. There was the substi-
> tute teacher whose hair was set on fire, the assistant principal hospitalized after
> being knocked down by students, the assorted objects—trash cans, ceramics
> projects—hurled from windows, sometimes into teachers' parked cars. In 2002,
> one summer school student fatally stabbed another outside the school. A few
> months later, things became so rowdy after a fire drill that the police officers
> on duty used Mace.[3]

Today, the building still holds some three thousand students and three hundred teachers, but a huge banner hanging from its towering façade announces a makeover: It lists five high schools. And even that is behind the times, since there are now seven: Marble Hill High School for International Studies (MHHS), the Bronx Engineering and Technology Academy (BETA), the Bronx School of Law and Finance (BSLF), the English Language Learners and International Support Preparatory Academy (ELLIS), New Visions Charter High School for Advanced Math and Science (NVAMS), the Bronx Theatre High School (BTHS), and New Visions Charter High School for the Humanities (NVH).

Each of them educates the same, mostly poor, mostly African American and Hispanic students as entered the building in 1972. Most of them now graduate between 66 and 90 percent of their students[4] and boast more "success stories" than "horrifying tales." What happened to Kennedy happened all over New York City, in what could be considered one of the most radical education system turnarounds in American history.

Between 2002 and 2008, the number of high schools in New York increased from just over 250 to nearly 450, even as the number of high school students in the system remained the same. This resulted from closing thirty large schools, shrinking others (such as Kennedy), and creating dozens of small, themed high schools, with one hundred students per grade instead of one thousand. At the same time, discovering tens of thousands of high school students who were hopelessly behind and on the fast track to dropping out, the district created a system of even smaller transfer schools.

Not only did New York City, the largest school district in the country, take on a student population that had come to symbolize the impossibility of educating certain kinds of children—the urban poor who entered high school two and three grades behind; it actually succeeded in getting them to graduation. As a series of studies began to emerge in 2012,[5] it became clear that what Michael Bloomberg and Joel Klein had done in New York City was real.

Graduation rates in these new schools soared by nearly ten points—from 60 percent to 70 percent—and it was often even more dramatic, considering that many of the high schools that were closed had had graduation rates around 20 percent. In an era when a high school diploma is the difference between a career and a lifetime on the dole, New York's high school reform has increased the economic mobility of tens of thousands of students.

As the *New York Times* editorial board headline put it in October 2014, "Small Schools Work in NYC":

[T]he Bloomberg approach has been vindicated by an innovative, multiyear study[6] showing that the poor, minority students who attend small specialized schools do better academically than students in a control group who attend traditional high schools. . . . Among the startling results are these: Students at small high schools have a graduation rate of 71.6 percent, compared with 62.2 percent for their peers in larger schools. The small-school students are also more likely to graduate in four years and go straight to college. The gains are especially impressive among young black men, 42.3 percent of whom enroll in college as opposed to 31 percent of their peers in the control group.[7]

"So we can fix these kids," I suggested to Michele Cahill, a senior program officer at the Carnegie Corporation when Klein tapped her to lead the high school reform efforts in 2002.
"We don't fix kids," she replied. "We fix schools."[8]

THE (SLOW) SMALL SCHOOLS REVOLUTION

What worked in New York was a multifaceted, multibillion-dollar, multiyear overhaul of New York City's high schools. It wasn't easy, and it didn't happen by itself. In fact, before billionaire Bloomberg became America's education mayor, West Coast billionaire Bill Gates was already steering his Bill and Melinda Gates Foundation to education; it would eventually devote a billion dollars to the small high schools effort, spreading its largesse to some three hundred school districts across the United States, including New York City.

While the nation seemed transfixed by No Child Left Behind, Race to the Top, and Common Core State Standards, "one of the most wide-ranging reforms in public education" during that time, according to a group of researchers from Duke and Massachusetts Institute of Technology (MIT), was New York City's "reorganization of large comprehensive high schools into small schools with roughly 100 students per grade."[9]

Part of the reason that the small schools effort was so remarkable is that it bucked the reform instinct to start when kids are young; it was also notable because it was so long in coming. The failing American high school had become such a familiar trope that the common wisdom was that *some kids were not meant for high school graduation.*

The infamous 1983 blue ribbon presidential panel that produced *A Nation at Risk,* for instance, took aim at high schools and their "smorgasbord" curricula that were "homogenized, diluted, and diffused to the point that they no longer have a central purpose."[10] Other educators were taking aim at the structure of the comprehensive high school, complaining that it was simply too big to work and too impersonal to reach every child, much less hundreds of children who entered high school two and three grade levels behind.

Such large high schools emerged in the 1920s as the United States expanded its already ambitious public education effort to secondary school and began, for efficiency's sake, building bigger ones. Only 6.7 percent of 14- to 17-year-olds attended high school in 1890; by 1950, 76.5 percent did.[11] In 1950, there were about 24,500 high schools educating 5.7 million students; by the end of the century there were twice as many high school students, but only 1,900 more high schools. The segment of American high schools enrolling more than one thousand students grew from 7 percent to 25 percent.[12] What had been conceived as an educational melting pot had for many become a cauldron of educational failure.

Even James Bryant Conant, the former Harvard president whose 1959 book *The American High School Today* advocated the elimination of small high schools, admitted, fewer than ten years later, "I said not a word [in *The American High School Today*] to indicate that certain schools I visited were comprehensive only insofar as white youth were concerned."[13] A chastened Conant suspected that large comprehensive schools didn't work in the modern American city.

And the solutions—at least, the alternatives—were already in the works.

Deborah Meier, the modern godmother of personalized education, opened her small Central Park East Secondary School in 1985, to complement the elementary school she had opened ten years earlier. The year before, Ted Sizer had written the now-classic *Horace's Compromise: The Dilemma of the American High School*[14] and had launched his Coalition of Essential Schools (with twelve member schools).[15] Sizer proposed nine principles for his schools, setting an agenda for school organization that has guided reformers to this day:

- Learning to use one's mind well
- Less is more; depth over coverage
- High standards for all students
- Personalization of teaching and learning
- Student-as-worker, teacher-as-coach
- Demonstration of mastery of subjects
- Maintain a tone of decency and trust
- Commitment to the entire school
- School resources are dedicated to teaching and learning[16]

Though Sizer and Meier did not make school size a major focus of their education philosophies and practices, the assumption was that their principles of teaching and learning would be much harder in a large school. "Given its 'radical' nature," Deborah Meier says today, "why not improve the odds by going small? There are enough obstacles without size standing in the way."[17]

By the end of the 1980s, the Carnegie Corporation—which had supported James Conant's early comprehensive high school work—weighed in on size, recommending in its influential *Adolescent Development* report the creation of "small communities for learning."[18]

The most audacious reform effort during this period was the Annenberg Challenge, a $500 million initiative announced by media mogul and philanthropist Walter Annenberg at the White House in December 1993. Up to that point, it was the largest private gift to public education; Annenberg would eventually provide matching grants ranging from $1 million to $53 million to 2,400 schools in thirty-five states, much of it to create small high schools.[19]

Meanwhile, in New York City, which received Annenberg funds, the small school experiments continued. They got a sizable bump when New Visions for Public Schools, a nonprofit established in 1989, launched a small high schools effort in 1993 with Annenberg's help. Predating New York State's charter school law by seven years, the initiative, created by Beth Lief, founding president of New Visions, included close collaboration with the city's Department of Education (DOE); the United Federation of Teachers (UFT); and the administrators' union, the Council of Supervisors and Administrators (CSA).[20]

By 2000, when New Visions created a separate organization, New Century High Schools, to run and expand its small high schools effort, the collaboration had created forty such schools.[21] Though research would trickle in showing the effectiveness of education principles like those proposed and used by Sizer, Meier, and New Visions, and despite the Annenberg philanthropy devoted to the effort, the academic performance needle for most urban students barely moved.

THE BILLIONAIRES' CLUB

Whether by coincidence or conspiracy, the confluence of two billionaire education reform crusaders turning to the cause of high school reform cannot be underestimated. And coming after nearly two decades of work by other reformers, the timing was right.

According to Becky Smerdon and Kathryn Borman, who led the Gates-sponsored research team that evaluated the initiative, there was some consensus among reformers about what made schools successful: "a shared vision focused on student learning, common strategies for engendering that learning, a culture of professional collaboration and collective responsibility, high-quality curriculum, systematic monitoring of student learning, strong instructional leadership (usually from the principal), and adequate resources."[22]

Based on the assumption that these characteristics of success were more easily achieved in smaller schools than larger ones—an assumption then supported by a growing body of research—the Gates grant-makers created seven

"attributes of high-performing schools" that would guide its giving to those
who wanted to create small high schools:

* A common focus
* High expectations
* Personalization
* Respect and responsibility
* Time to collaborate
* Performance-based instruction
* Use of technology as a tool[23]

Properly implemented, the foundation believed, these attributes would
"lead not only to better outcomes for students attending the schools, but to
increased demand for such schools."[24]

Unfortunately, in the first five years of the initiative, according to the
*Evaluation of the Bill and Melinda Gates Foundation's High School Grants
Initiative: 2001–2005 Final Report,* released in August 2006, the results were
mixed at best. The researchers who studied the project, from the American
Institutes for Research and SRI International, analyzed the grants to a sample
of seventeen school districts in eleven states—from Anderson Union, Cali-
fornia, to Providence, Rhode Island; from Baltimore to Chicago; and from
Denver to New York.

Their report found that most districts in its sample registered positive
results with personalization and collaboration, but struggled with efforts to
raise the expectations bar and implement performance-based instruction. For
a program that was supposed to improve the educational outcomes of low-
income high school students, this was not good news.

In a book that Smerdon and Borman would curate for the Urban Institute in
2009, *Saving America's High Schools,* many of the members of the research
team expanded on the findings from the *Evaluation* report, offering a wealth
of specific findings for many of the larger districts receiving Gates funds. The
conclusions were the same: The major problem was implementation, specifically of the instructional programs.

The Chicago researchers, for example, "failed to find evidence that attending a small school promoted higher test scores," but they pointed out that this
was not surprising since they "did not see a CHSRI [Chicago High School
Reform Initiative] effect on instruction."[25] Many of the schools simply never
went beyond "abstract goals for teaching and learning," according to Gates
researchers, and "did not have particular curricular or pedagogical designs."
And, in a sad irony for those promoting personalization, in many of the new
schools, "as teachers learned that students were not prepared for the type of

instruction the school wanted to offer," they were unprepared to help. Other teachers "were surprised to find that students didn't have the work habits, basic skills, conceptual knowledge, self-motivation, and/or learning strategies required by the instructional approaches they intended to use."[26]

In the end, according to the final report, "both new and redesigned schools needed more help with issues of curriculum and instruction."[27] As Smerdon and Borman would conclude in their subsequent book, "there is good reason to expect that the success of this 'raise-the-bar' approach to school improvement will depend on stakeholders' abilities to provide the academic supports that students, particularly struggling students, need to be effective learners. Without these supports, the benefits of entering a 'rigorous' high school with more course requirements or a college-preparatory mandate may not be realized."[28]

Indeed, though the Gates foundation would move on to other things (prematurely, according to some[29]), Smerdon and Borman had, in effect, suggested why New York City's small schools program worked: academic instruction.

LESSONS FROM ANNENBERG: SOVEREIGNTY, NOT JOHNNY APPLESEED

Robert Hughes recalls his first meeting with Joel Klein, at an opening day ceremony at South Bronx High School in September of 2002, just two months after Klein assumed the chancellorship reins. South Bronx High was the newest of New Century's small high schools. "And it's a beautiful day and he sees what we're doing," recalls Hughes, who had taken the top job at New Visions in 2000, "and he turns to me and he says, 'Can you create two hundred more of these?' I said, 'Sure,' because you always say 'Yes' to the new chancellor."

But Hughes recognized immediately what that question meant. As he would later explain, one of the lessons from the Annenberg initiative was that, "You have to have superintendency"—by which he means authority—"so you start to change the system itself. . . . You want to find new ways of supporting education improvement as a matter of routine."

To make improvement a matter of routine may have been Bloomberg's and Klein's greatest contribution to New York's public school ethos. Most of those involved with creating the small school revolution agree that having the support of a mayor and a chancellor was important, even essential. "Another critique of Annenberg that we were really very aware of," says Hughes, "was that its theory of change was a little bit like Johnny Appleseed. You sprinkle good schools throughout a system and they'll start to grow and sprout and other people will replicate them."[30]

Greg Duncan and Richard Murnane echoed Hughes's Johnny Appleseed observation in their book *Restoring Opportunity: The Crisis of Inequality and the Challenge for American Education.* The Annenberg Challenge, which was largely considered a failure, was characterized by "a lack of a cogent framework for structuring these schools," the authors note. The central school administration "viewed [such schools] as exceptions in a system of central-ized control, tolerating them only because they pacified innovative educators who would otherwise have been more vocal critics of the system."[31]

Until Bloomberg and Klein, the system tolerated the new small school "seeds," but didn't fertilize them. By backing the reform efforts, Bloomberg and Klein provided the "cogent framework"—the fertilizer, the water, the sun—to the small high schools effort. And that was just the beginning.

Not only had Bloomberg assumed the mayoralty with an education reform agenda in hand, but his break-the-mold chancellor also hit the ground run-ning, talking to Cahill the day after his appointment to head the schools in July of 2002—and asking her to join his team the following month.[32] This sent a signal to the bureaucracy that change was coming. Cahill had been at the Carnegie Corporation for only three years, but she had gone there with vast experience.

She had served as vice president of the Fund for the City of New York, where she developed the Beacon Schools initiative with New York City. She also had served as vice president for Schools and Community Services at the Academy for Educational Development, leading several national demonstra-tion projects with more than twenty urban districts. While at Carnegie, she was working closely with New Visions and helped, in the spring of 2001, secure an additional $30 million for New Century High Schools from the Gates foundation, the Open Society Institute, and Carnegie.

That October—his first as chancellor—Klein announced, as he had sig-naled to Hughes at the school opening ceremony, the district's intent to open two hundred new small high schools.

A CLEAR DEFINITION OF ACADEMIC RIGOR
AND A CITYWIDE REQUEST FOR PROPOSALS

A full-throated comparison of what worked in New York and didn't work in other parts of the country would be a welcome addition to this subject's research library, but after reviewing the literature and interviewing many of those who led the effort in New York, I suggest that we can glean lessons of strategy and implementation that might help show other school districts how to proceed.

For starters, as suggested previously, one of the remarkable things to note about New York's success was that it came honestly and clearly: academic rigor meant Regents diplomas. And Regents diplomas meant earning twenty-two credits of core subject courses and passing five different (and rigorous) domain-specific tests (in English, math, science, US history, and global history).[33] And this was with students once considered uneducable.[34]

"All the programs had the same academic goal," recalls Michele Cahill, "getting a Regents diploma."[35]

Unlike many of the districts receiving Gates funds, the emphasis on academic rigor in New York City was clear and unwavering, as was the firm belief in the need for systemwide, capacity-building efforts to ensure implementation success. As Leah Hamilton, who joined the effort after earning master's degrees in social work and business administration, would note, "The design of the program is important, high standards for everyone are important, an investment from the system to make this kind of work a priority is important, and leadership at a high level is important."[36]

Many of these priorities were on the table when Bloomberg and Klein arrived. "Carnegie was interested in systems, how do we systematically think about reform, and wanted us to look at both small schools and large school transformations," recalls Hughes about the $30 million small schools grant he received in 2000. "Gates was about small, so small was an option that we put on the table. And Open Society was about highest need."[37]

Balancing those funder desires, New Visions talked to its other partners (the UFT, the CSA, and the DOE), and created a Request for Proposals to all community school districts and high school superintendents in the city, inviting any group of educators to propose a small high school—limited to some one hundred students per grade—with a focus on the Bronx, which had the highest concentration of low-performing schools.

Another lesson learned from Annenberg, says Hughes, was working with community-based organizations. "Annenberg was all about outside groups coming in—so we wanted to use community-based organizations to drive change and ensure that there was a sense of urgency from the community, a kind of youth development perspective or civic perspective, that could be incorporated in what was going on in education."[38]

The Requests for Proposals that had gone out had already created a stir in the bureaucracy that was still reverberating when Bloomberg became mayor on January 1, 2002. Veteran teachers and administrators were excited again about school. And dozens of new school team hopefuls had responded. "We all had a passion for this," recalls Kirsten Larson, an English as Second

Language teacher at Morris High School in the Bronx. Larson was one of four teachers, an assistant principal, and guidance counselor from Morris determined to take the plunge. "But the writing was also on the wall," she recalls. "They were going to close Morris."[39] Morris, like Kennedy, had become a dropout factory. Its last principal had described it, in 2001, as "a place out of control."[40]

New Visions and the DOE provided technical assistance to the seventy-five applicants, convening workshops and advising the teams about curriculum, parent engagement, student engagement, teacher recruitment, the grading system, the floor plan, administrative priorities, and New Century's ten principles. As with Sizer's characteristics of effective schools and Gates's seven attributes, New Century had a list of priorities.

Number one, setting it apart from the others, was "a rigorous instructional program." That meant a Regents diploma curriculum. In the end, Larson and her colleagues were among only fifteen of the seventy-five applicants that made that first cut.[41] They moved to the eighth floor of Kennedy High School, then in the process of being remade, and opened Marble Hill High School for International Studies in September 2002. Today, with 440 students, Marble Hill High has a four-year graduation rate of 89.7 percent.

Over the next six years, the small high schools team succeeded in creating the two hundred schools that Klein had imagined. All were mission-driven, most with a specific theme or subject, including college prep and career and technical specialties. And these were the schools that would prove so successful: raising graduation rates of previously underperforming students by ten percentage points.

"We never lost track of the fact that it was about graduating more kids career- and college-ready," says Hughes. "But I think equally important was the fact that you had everybody at the table, and so you could learn and make mistakes together and build a sense of collective trust as you went forward."[42] Though Bloomberg and Klein would make their education reform reputation by remaking a dysfunctional urban education system, when it came to high schools, they jumped on a train that had left the station—and they held the throttle down.

BUILDING A SYSTEM THAT WORKS FOR KIDS

Eventually, Cahill and her colleagues would draft a Secondary Education Reform Plan that would, besides creating the two hundred new small high schools and closing thirty large ones, start literacy programs, introduce "small learning communities" into larger schools, and provide the administrative support necessary to ensure success. But Cahill, who also hit the ground running, quickly realized that there were several tracks to the high school turnaround gauntlet, and that she didn't have enough data to be sure exactly what kind of system to build.

"We knew what made effective schools," she recalls. "Leadership, high-quality teaching, coherence, mission, youth development. . . . But we didn't know how many of what kind of kid was actually in the system."[43]

Cahill coaxed her longtime collaborator JoEllen Lynch into joining the effort. Lynch had worked in the trenches of inner city education for nearly twenty years, helping a nonprofit organization called Good Shepherd Services create education alternatives for the city's most disenfranchised children, eventually called "transfer" schools. "Michele visited my school in the mid-80s," recalls Lynch, "and asked me to get more involved nationally, in creating a field of youth development. Mind you, I was a young person then, working in a small high school in the basement of a public housing project in Red Hook, Brooklyn. Okay?" But she had made it work, helping Good Shepherd create a model for schools who would take in "kids who were sixteen and had entered high school reading at fifth- and sixth-grade level and [with] very little numeracy background and in a short period of time bring them to a point where they could pass the Regents."[44]

Cahill and Lynch reached out to the Parthenon Group, a data analysis and research firm from Boston, to find out how many of which kind of student was out there, which students fell behind, how they progressed through the system, what the outcomes were, and how those outcomes differed by program.[45] "We picked Parthenon because they had experience in analyzing transfer schools," says Lynch. "They had done work for us at Good Shepherd Services in 2000. We didn't have to tell them what a transfer school was."[46]

Parthenon began gathering data on every student who entered New York City high schools in 1999, nearly a quarter million of them, and by 2005, as education journalist Sarah Garland reported, had accumulated data that was "shocking": "Nearly 140,000 high school-age youth in the city were at least two years behind where they needed to be to graduate on time. They had failed one or more grades in elementary or middle school and were way behind in accumulating the forty-four high school credits they needed to graduate."[47]

Cahill asked Parthenon to find out the exact role played by school size in student outcomes. "So many people were saying to me," she recalls, "'If size is the problem, why isn't it the problem for Stuyvesant?'"[48] One of eight specialized public "exam" schools in New York, Stuyvesant had 3,200 students and a 98.4 percent four-year graduation rate.[49]

Parthenon discovered that school size mattered much less (it explained 9 percent of the variation in outcomes) than did concentrations of low performers in the schools (which explained 22 percent of the variation). And with another statistical flourish, Parthenon determined that together, school size and concentrations of low performers explained 41 percent of the variation in the outcomes.

Just those two variables, concluded the Parthenon researchers, were "a powerful predictor of an individual school's ability to prevent Level 1 and Low Level 2 students from falling behind." (Level 1 and Level 2 were New York State score categories on standardized state math and English language arts (ELA) tests, where Level 1 was not proficient and Level 2 was below proficient. Thus Level 1 (L1) and Low Level 2 (LL2) scores on eighth-grade exams, though not a perfect metric, suggested that a student was one to three grade levels behind when entering high school.)[50]

Together with the significance of school size, the predictive power of the concentrations of L1 and LL2 students represented something like the keys to the kingdom. The researchers could then measure a high school's "preventive power"—its capacity to *prevent* students from becoming "over-age and under-credited" (the perfect candidates for dropping out).

The report put fourteen sample high schools on a chart to illustrate the point. The Manhattan Village Academy, with just 359 students—52 percent of them L1/LL2—had a preventive power score of 86. This meant that just 14 percent of its low-performing students would become over-age and under-credited with a high probability of dropping out before graduating. At the other end of the chart was Richmond Hill High School with 3,696 students, 58 percent of whom were L1/LL2. Parthenon determined that Richmond Hill had a preventive power score of just 55: 45 percent of its students would end up over-age and under-credited—in other words, a dropout factory.

In sum, the report provided Cahill and her team with powerful evidence that they were on the right track in their pursuit of a small schools strategy. But now they knew that not only would they need to create what Parthenon called "beat-the-odds" small schools, but they also had to dilute the con-centrations of low performance in those schools. In fact, Klein had given economist Alvin Roth the job of fixing what the *New York Times* called a "byzantine" process of distributing middle school students to high schools. And in 2004, the city unveiled a new system of choice for those students.

But it would prove a tough nut to crack. Though Roth's work for New York City would help earn a him a Nobel Prize in economics in 2012, a study by New York University's (NYU) Research Alliance showed that most low-income students still chose to attend schools in their neighborhoods—and those neighborhood schools had high concentrations of low-performing students:

NYC's low-achieving students were poorer, more likely to be black or Hispanic, and more likely to be male, compared with other students. As a group, they faced significant educational challenges. One third of low-achieving students had been absent 20 or more days in 7th grade and nearly as many had been late to school for 30 or more days. They were much more apt to have limited English proficiency and special education needs than were other students. Finally, they were highly concentrated in certain neighborhoods.

Indeed, while the new school choice system did "provide an avenue for students to enroll in schools citywide," the NYU researchers concluded, "in practice, students are constrained by familiarity with a school and their willingness to travel. All students appear to prefer higher-performing schools and schools that are close to home." And in choosing between higher-performing schools versus less travel, the early returns suggested, less travel won. As the NYU researchers suggested, the city would have to continue to improve neighborhood schools if they were to deflect the impact of high concentrations of low performers.[51]

THE REAL MIRACLE: TRANSFER SCHOOLS

But Cahill came back to the over-age and under-credited challenge again and again, appreciating not only how large the group was, but also how amenable it was to being educated if understood. Parthenon discovered, for instance, that twenty-seven thousand of the 1999 freshmen cohort who ended up in the over-age and under-credited category had actually managed to get twenty to twenty-five credits and pass two of the six Regents exams before dropping out.

That was encouraging. "That meant that they *could* pass high school," concluded Cahill, who began pulling transcripts and conducting focus group interviews to find out what else happened to these kids. "They were missing things all over the place. . . . They had life challenges, they were in single-parent families and the parent died, they were part of an immigrant family and had to move all the time and get a job. They would miss three weeks of a semester because of some crisis and then when they came back they couldn't make it up and then when the next semester came they couldn't get the same course because of scheduling problems. They weren't progressing toward their diplomas—and they were getting older."[52]

This kind of data would lead Cahill and Lynch to create young adult borough centers, located in the schools but offering classes in the late afternoon and evening. "We scheduled for every 200 kids," she explains. "We determined what courses they needed for graduation and also offered intensive counseling."[53]

Altogether there were some seventy thousand in the Parthenon cohort who needed, as Cahill puts it "recuperative education," which she defined as "an additional incentive for kids who were about two years behind in terms of high school credit for their age, who had usually failed ninth grade, who weren't getting anywhere in high school, and who had poor attendance—and by poor attendance I mean between missing 20 to 50 percent of their classes. . . . For them we developed the transfer schools, young adult borough centers, and a program called 'learning-to-work,' which we integrated with some transfer schools and adult borough centers."[54]

Cahill and Parthenon developed another metric, called "recuperative power," and asked another question: Are there any schools that have such power and know how to put even these students back on track to graduation?[55]

The answer was a qualified Yes. The city had a modest alternative school program that was meant to take care of these students—but few schools did. "They all beat the city average for getting these kinds of kids to graduation, which was 19 percent," explains Cahill. But one transfer school stood out: South Brooklyn Community High School, the school that JoEllen Lynch had started in Red Hook, one of the most impoverished and dangerous sections of the city. South Brooklyn was getting 69 percent of its over-age under-credited students to graduation. Said Cahill: "That beat the city average for *all* students!"[56]

Cahill convinced Klein to "ramp up" the South Brooklyn model and put Lynch in charge of a newly created Office of Multiple Pathways to Gradua-tion (OMPG) since, said Cahill, "she knew more than anyone in the country about how to graduate kids who had already dropped out or were very discon-nected."[57] Bloomberg and Klein "weren't so much interested in dropouts," recalls Lynch, "as they were in the population that would become chronically under- and unemployed, the people who never finish high school, use up so many of the city's resources, and have no clear avenue back to the workforce or life."[58]

The OMPG would come to include fifty-one "transfer schools" like South Brooklyn, twenty-three young adult learning centers, community-based orga-nizations that partnered with these programs, learning-to-work programs, as well as the city's career and technical education programs.[59]

"These were multiple pathways to the same diploma," Cahill emphasizes, "not alternative routes to a different diploma. . . . Everyone had different roles and not all the kids were the same, but everyone had the same goal: a Regents diploma."[60] Everyone who graduated from South Brooklyn passed the same history, math, English, and science Regents examinations that the students from Scarsdale passed. "The transfer schools had the same design principles as the new small schools, but much more intensive."[61]

Lynch emphasizes the importance of design in creating any school. "Small schools started long before we had the data from Parthenon," she says. "But in NYC it wasn't *small* that was the key. Gates funded schools outside of New York that had no design criteria [other than being small], and they failed. We made the decision from the very beginning; we had an intensive design criteria for these schools. Every element—mission, vision, culture, leadership, curriculum—it was all there."

In talking to Vanda Belusic-Vollor, principal at South Brooklyn from 2003 to 2011, one might think the kinds of graduation statistics achieved at South Brooklyn were easy. "Academic rigor and youth development" were the keys, she says. "And they are intertwined. Good teaching is actually good youth development."[62]

"The new small schools are in the preventive bucket," explains Lynch:

The assumption was that students were transitioning from eighth grade and schools would have the power to get them to graduate in four years—to prevent them from becoming over-age and under-credited. The assumption in the recuperative models is that students have not yet met the standards of eighth grade. They come into ninth grade way behind and the school, in the traditional setting, teaches them as if they were on grade level. But the student can't engage with the instruction.[63]

In the either/or world that modern education had become, the notion of "embedding" youth development into the academic program was something of a radical proposition. Students engaged with the instruction or they didn't. When the system worked, most students had ample opportunities to engage as they passed through elementary school—and were at grade level by high school. When it didn't work, as was the case with many urban districts, the failure to engage occurred early, continued through eighth grade, and landed thousands of students in high school disengaged and behind. The small high schools were designed to facilitate engagement—or even reengagement—by virtue of the personalization opportunities. The transfer schools, as Cahill said, worked on such reengagement with more intensity and more tools.

Belusic-Vollor had six DOE teachers for her 120 students' academic program and six staff from Good Shepherd Services, four of whom were "advocate counselors" (see following discussion). The two staffs were completely integrated. "You couldn't tell who worked for whom," says Belusic-Vollor. The school was ungraded; competence and mastery were the watchwords. A student graduated when he or she was ready. The school took new students in throughout the year and had three graduations a year. "The prerequisites for a transfer school," Belusic-Vollor laughs, "is failure in another school, as silly as that sounds. So you had to have gone to a high school and *not* been successful. You had to be two years off track to be eligible for a transfer school."[64]

Joel Klein got it. "Imagine starting a job as a ninth-grade teacher with five sections of freshman biology," he writes in his new memoir, *Lessons of Hope,* "in which half the students cannot read the textbook."[65] That was the fate of dozens of ninth-grade teachers and tens of thousands of their students, most of whom would never make it to graduation.

South Brooklyn was, essentially, providing a four-year education in two years—or less—to *bad* students, and making it stick for nearly 70 percent of them.[66] And very few students fell through the cracks at South Brooklyn. "In large comprehensive high schools you have things like 'I lost my Metrocard to get on the trains, so I'm going to sit in this office for three hours until I get one and not go to class,'" says Belusic-Vollor.[67] That didn't happen at South Brooklyn.

What follows is a summary of some of the secrets to South Brooklyn's success, as explained by Vanda Belusic-Vollor.

• Every student in South Brooklyn was assigned an *Advocate Counselor,* who was part of the Good Shepherd staff. "That Advocate Counselor's job was to be that young person's touch point and that family's touch point so every morning, when the kid walked in, the attendance was taken by the Advocate Counselor. What that looked like was six or seven adults in the lobby greeting young people and just very quietly taking attendance, making sure that they had a good night, they were ready for school, they went up to their classes. If an issue had emerged—like the lost Metrocard—the role of the Advocate Counselor was to work with the young person to make sure they could focus on school. So if I was a young person and my father got arrested the night before, rather than let that crisis stand in the way of school, the relationship was such that the Advocate Counselor would say, "Okay, I need you here and I need your head here for the next six hours. Let me figure this out with you, for you, and with your family," essentially whatever it took. Whether they got kicked out of their homes, they were arrested themselves, their families were arrested, they got thrown out by their parents, it was: "Okay, tell me what the issue is and now you need to trust me. You need to understand that I'm going to help you figure this out." The Advocate Counselors were not teachers because "teachers aren't trained to have these kinds of conversations and they have other things to worry about. This is a huge reason that we were successful."

• The rigorous academic part of the program featured *literacy across the curriculum* and practicing "metacognition." The latter meant "thinking out loud. You have to train teachers to pause and model [the thinking] process, out loud. We take for granted, as adults and teachers, what we do naturally as good learners." So that means a teacher would say, "I saw this and I read this and when I looked at them together, it meant this. Therefore, I believe this." Literacy across the curriculum meant doing what one of South Brooklyn's US history teachers did. "He only taught history through this reenactment kind of court drama. But the passing rate for his students on the Regent's exam was always between 88 percent and 100 percent."

- Realistic thinking through *constant benchmarking*. As a reaction to the standard college-and-career counseling in high school—"You want to be a lawyer? But you haven't passed English. You want to be a doctor? But you haven't passed biology"—South Brooklyn did benchmark assessments every two weeks. "This way, when the actual credit-bearing grade came out, there were no surprises. Every two weeks, a kid and his family knew exactly where he stood in every one of his classes. Those benchmarks were broken up into very specific categories. Kids could focus on an area of concentration if they needed to do better so if homework was a category and I got a 40 in the homework category and my overall grade was a 60, then I knew I needed to get my act together and do my homework with more seriousness and regularity." And it wasn't the teacher that had the conversation with the parent and student. It was the Advocate Counselor.

These practices, inaugurated by Lynch, were refined by Belusic-Vollor. "My first year I had fifty-six graduates, which was something like a 70 percent graduation rate," recalls Belusic-Vollor. "And I only remember it because Gates was breathing down our necks to replicate and we kept saying, 'We don't even know if this works.'"[68]

It did. And the transfer school system has grown smarter and larger. "There are a lot of new schools," says Belusic-Vollor, who is now Senior Executive Director of the Office of Secondary Readiness (the successor to the OMPG), "and they are getting numbers that make my numbers look bad."[69]

CONCLUSION

After jumpstarting small school creation in New York City and in districts throughout the country, the Gates Foundation has since turned its attention away from small schools. "Foundation president Bill Gates concluded that small schools did not have the effect on college readiness and graduation rates that he expected and the foundation moved on to other things," explained researchers from Duke and MIT.[70]

New York City would prove that the foundation perhaps gave up too soon. Though no one at Gates believed that school size was a silver bullet, New York showed how important *all* the other "attributes" were: academic rigor *and* personalization, as well as the layers of implementation requiring administrative expertise, management finesse, and political savvy.

"Personalization," for instance, didn't just mean making eye contact. It meant giving teachers and students a focus to their school mission, giving them a personal stake in creating and running the school, and creating a system that would ensure accountability for results. As Deborah Meier, says, "there are enough obstacles without size standing in the way."

But *size* was no magic wand. "The new small schools actually only worked because we were making systemic changes," says Michele Cahill, who cites the principal training efforts at the district's new Leadership Academy and the "cross-functional team" at headquarters to ensure "that teaching and learning, human resources, finance, facilities, accountability, procurement, partnerships would be coordinated and problems solved rather than going into the black hole of bureaucracy."[71]

"In summary," concluded the 2012 Manpower Demonstration Research Corporation report that first gave evidence to the stunning success of New York's small high schools program, "the present findings provide highly credible evidence that in a relatively short period of time, with sufficient organization and resources, an existing school district can implement a complex high school reform that markedly improves graduation rates for a large population of low-income, disadvantaged students of color."[72]

And, perhaps needless to say, it came as a surprise to many when MDRC issued its 2014 follow-up report finding that "these graduation benefits do not come at the cost of higher expenditures per graduate." Why? Because Cahill and her team worked smarter and, by getting so many more kids to graduation a year earlier, cheaper. In fact, said the MDRC researchers, *the cost per high school graduate is substantially lower for the small-school enrollees than for their control group counterparts* in the larger, comprehensive high schools.[73]

The costs of the programs run by the Office of Multiple Pathways, such as transfer schools, were not part of this MDRC analysis, but Parthenon offered some reassuring numbers based on the $37.5 million that the Bloomberg administration devoted to the OMPG projects, including thirty transfer schools. The cost "per seat" in a traditional high school was $7,200, reported Parthenon, and in a transfer school, $10,600.

But the traditional schools enjoy a sizable "cost avoidance" by not having to educate transfer students—or the many dropouts. And, of course, the value of a high school diploma would, in another analysis have to be considered. In fact, by Parthenon's estimate, each percentage point of graduation rate increase for the two hundred new small schools cost $23 million; each percentage point increase at thirty transfer schools cost $18 million.[74]

"One of Joel's major reforms was understanding where the money was," says Lynch. "Keep in mind that this is a $16 billion operation—now up to $20 billion or more. Think about that and how much waste there is in that. Joel unpacked the money. He found out where it was coming from and where it was going. And he made it work for kids."[75]

New York proved that high school reform is possible; that boosting graduation rates of the poor and unprepared, even if the effort is begun in high school, is possible; that *small* alone is not enough, that *choice* alone is not enough. The package of elements that make for successful schools, identified by educators for several generations, is what is needed. And, by following the money and making sure that it is targeted toward student achievement, it is a package that is affordable.

In the end, everyone who has been part of this dramatic high school makeover is proud that they have proven the skeptics—not to mention decades of flat-line trends—wrong. "Many, many people did not think that you could do something with high school students," says Cahill. "I think we have shown incontrovertibly that you can—that you can make tremendous progress."[76]

"When people say to me, 'The kids are so smart,'" says Vanda Belusic-Vollor, "I want to both pounce on them and jump for joy because . . . the issue was never that they weren't smart. The issue was that they didn't have the right supports to be able to shine."[77]

But it took more than just a belief in these students' abilities. It took hard work and hard thinking, as Michele Cahill says, to remake the schools that would make the kids shine.

NOTES

1. Joel Klein, *Lessons of Hope: How to Fix Our Schools* (New York: Harper Collins, 2014), xiii.

2. Author's interview with Iris Zucker, September 8, 2014.

3. Elissa Gootman, "Metal Detectors and Pep Rallies: Revival of a Bronx High School," *New York Times,* February 4, 2004; Editorial Board, "Reinventing High School," *New York Times,* February 1, 2005.

4. New York City Department of Education, "Progress Report Overview 2012–2013," links as follows: MHHS: http://marblehillschool.org/PDF/Progress_Report_Overview_2013_HS_X477.pdf; BETA: http://schools.nyc.gov/OA/SchoolReports/2012-13/Progress_Report_Overview_2013_HS_X213.pdf; BSLF: http://schools.nyc.gov/OA/SchoolReports/2012-13/Progress_Report_Overview_2013_HS_X284.pdf; ELLIS (now a "transfer" school): http://schools.nyc.gov/SchoolPortals/10/X397/AboutUs/Statistics/default.htm; NVAMS (first graduating class 2015): http://schools.nyc.gov/OA/SchoolReports/2013-14/School_Quality_Snapshot_2014_HS_X539.pdf; BTHS: http://schools.nyc.gov/OA/SchoolReports/2012-13/Progress_Report_Overview_2013_HS_X546.pdf; NVH (first graduating class 2015): http://www.newvisions.org/schools/entry/Humanities. See also the Wikipedia page

describing John F. Kennedy High School, http://en.wikipedia.org/wiki/John_F._Kennedy_High_School_(New_York_City).

5. Howard Bloom and Rebecca Unterman, "Sustained Positive Effects on Graduation Rates Produced by New York City's Small Public High Schools of Choice," *MDRC Policy Brief,* January 2012, http://www.mdrc.org/sites/default/files/policy-brief_34.pdf.

6. Rebecca Unterman, "Headed to College: The Effects of New York City's Small High Schools of Choice on Postsecondary Enrollment," *MDRC Policy Brief,* October 2014, http://www.mdrc.org/publication/headed-college; Robert Bifulco, Rebecca Unterman, and Howard S. Bloom, "The Relative Costs of New York City's New Small Public High Schools of Choice," *MDRC Policy Brief,* October 2014, http://www.mdrc.org/publication/relative-costs-new-york-city-s-new-small-public-high-schools-choice.

7. Editorial Board, "Small Schools Work in NYC," *New York Times,* October 18, 2014.

8. Author's interview with Michele Cahill, August 12, 2014, and September 25, 2014.

9. Atila Abdulkadiroʻglu, Weiwei Hu, and Parag Pathak, "Small High Schools and Student Achievement: Lottery-Based Evidence from New York City," Working Paper No. 19576, National Bureau of Economic Research, October 19, 2013.

10. National Commission on Excellence in Education, "Findings," in *A Nation at Risk: The Imperative for Educational Reform,* April 1983, http://www2.ed.gov/pubs/NatAtRisk/index.html and http://www2.ed.gov/pubs/NatAtRisk/findings.html.

11. "The Plan is New, The Ideal is Old," *Life,* December 14, 1953, 142.

12. Abdulkadiroʻglu, Hu, and Pathak, "Small High Schools and Student Achievement."

13. William A. Proefriedt, "Revisiting James Bryant Conant: Realism, Then and Now," *Education Week,* May 18, 2005; "The American High School Today," *Hispania* 42, no. 1 (March 1959): 155–57.

14. Theodore Sizer, *Horace's Compromise: The Dilemma of the American High School* (New York: Houghton Mifflin Harcourt, 1984).

15. Wikipedia, "The Coalition of Essential Schools," http://en.wikipedia.org/wiki/Coalition_of_Essential_Schools.

16. The New School of Northern Virginia, "Ten Common Principles," http://www.newschoolva.com/common_principles.php; and Seymour Fliegel, "Debbie Meier and the Dawn of Central Park East: When Teachers Take Charge of Schooling," *City Journal,* Winter 1994.

17. E-mail from Deborah Meier to the author, October 30, 2014.

18. Becky Smerdon and Kathryn Borman, eds., *Saving America's High Schools* (Washington, DC: The Urban Institute, 2009), 3.

19. "The Annenberg Challenge," http://annenberginstitute.org/challenge/about/about.html; William Celis, "Clinton Hails Annenberg's $500 Million Education Gift," *New York Times,* December 18, 1993.

20. Lief was president of New Vision for eleven years, helping make the nonprofit the largest educational reform organization in New York City devoted to improving

its public schools. During her tenure, New Visions worked in more than seven hundred NYC public schools.

21. Michael Melcher, "New Century High Schools and the Small Schools Movement in New York City" (New York: New Visions for Public Schools, 2005); Smerdon and Borman, *Saving America's High Schools,* 85.

22. Smerdon and Borman, *Saving America's High Schools,* 10.

23. Aimee Evan et al., *Evaluation of the Bill & Melinda Gates Foundation's High School Grants Initiative: 2001–2005 Final Report* (Washington, DC: American Institutes for Research, August 2006).

24. Ibid.

25. Ibid., 141.

26. Ibid., 31

27. Ibid.

28. Smerdon and Borman, *Saving America's High Schools,* 2.

29. "Even though Gates has largely abandoned its old strategy, those results are now pouring in," commented Jay Greene, head of the Department of Education Reform at the University of Arkansas, in August 2013. On his blog, Greene called attention to several new studies: Jay Greene, "It's a Blowout: Tom Vander Ark 4, New Gates PLDD Strategy 0" (blog post), August 29, 2013, http://jaypgreene.com/2013/08/29/its-a-blowout-tom-vander-ark-4-new-gates-pldd-strategy-0/; Jay Greene, "Why is the Man with the Goatee Smiling?" (blog post), October 16, 2014, http://jaypgreene.com/2014/10/16/why-is-this-man-with-the-goatee-smiling/.

30. Author's interview with Robert Hughes, September 8, 2014.

31. Greg J. Duncan and Richard J. Murnane, *Restoring Opportunity: The Crisis of Inequality and the Challenge for American Education* Cambridge, MA: Harvard Education Press, and New York: Russell Sage Foundation, 2014), 88.

32. Sarah Garland, "Big Gains in the Big Apple: A Special Report," *Washington Monthly,* July/August 2010; Klein, *Lessons of Hope,* 30.

33. New York State Higher Education Services Corporation, "Regents Requirements," http://www.hesc.ny.gov/prepare-for-college/your-high-school-path-to-college/regents-requirements.html; New York State Education Department, "General Education and Diploma Requirements," http://www.p12.nysed.gov/ciai/gradreq/revisedgradreq3column.pdf.

34. The requirements were modified in the fall of 2014 to allow for a vocational/technical subject to be counted toward graduation. See Sarah Moses, "State Regents Board Approves New Options for Students to Meet Graduation Requirements," Syracuse.com, October 20, 2014.

35. Author's interview with Cahill.

36. Author's interview with Leah Hamilton, October 10, 2014.

37. Author's interview with Hughes.

38. Ibid.

39. Author's interview with Kirsten Larson, September 8, 2014.

40. David M. Herszenhorn, "The Decline and Uplifting Fall of Morris High," *New York Times,* June 30, 2005.

41. Author's interview with Larson; Melcher, "New Century High Schools"; Smerdon and Borman, *Saving America's High Schools,* 88.

42. Author's interview with Hughes.

43. Author's interview with Cahill.

44. Author's interview with JoEllen Lynch, November 11, 2014.

45. Parthenon Group, "New York City Secondary Reform Selected Analysis," New York Department of Education, 2005.

46. Author's interview with Lynch.

47. Garland, "Big Gains in the Big Apple."

48. Author's interview with Cahill.

49. New York City Department of Education, "Progress Report Overview 2012–2013," Stuyvesant High School, http://schools.nyc.gov/OA/SchoolReports/2012-13/Progress_Report_Overview_2013_HS_M475.pdf.

50. Parthenon Group, "New York City Secondary Reform."

51. Lori Nathanson, Sean Corcoran, and Christine Baker-Smith, "High School Choice in New York City: A Report on the School Choices and Placements of Low-Achieving Students," New York University, The Research Alliance for New York City Schools, April 2013. See also, Tracy Tullis, "Cracking the School Choice Code," *New York Times,* December 7, 2014.

52. Author's interview with Cahill.

53. Ibid.

54. Ibid.

55. Parthenon Group, "New York City Secondary Reform."

56. Author's interview with Cahill.

57. E-mail from Cahill to the author, November 7, 2014.

58. Author's interview with Lynch.

59. Author's interview with Vanda Belusic-Vollor, October 3, 2014.

60. E-mail from Cahill to the author.

61. Ibid.

62. Author's interview with Belusic-Vollor.

63. Author's interview with Lynch.

64. Author's interview with Belusic-Vollor.

65. Klein, *Lessons of Hope,* 79.

66. Author's interview with Lynch. Because there are no grades (i.e., grades 9, 10, 11, etc.) in transfer schools and students took only those courses needed for graduation, as JoEllen Lynch points out, some students graduated in six months and some in eighteen months. It was not uncommon for a transfer school to have three graduation ceremonies in a school year.

67. Author's interview with Belusic-Vollor.

68. Ibid.

69. Ibid.

70. Atila Abdulkadiroˇglu, Hu, and Pathak, "Small High Schools and Student Achievement."

71. E-mail from Cahill to the author.

72. Bloom and Unterman, "Sustained Positive Effects on Graduation Rates."

73. Bifulco, Unterman, and Bloom, "The Relative Costs of New York City's New Small Public High Schools of Choice."

74. Parthenon Group, "New York City DOE Multiple Pathways Strategy: Summary Findings," Michele Cahill, JoEllen Lynch, Leah Hamilton. The Parthenon Group, Kosmo Kalliarekos, Robert Lytle, Tammy Battaglino, Lisa Cloitre, Beth Danaher, Christopher Librizzi, Bill & Melinda Gates Foundation, July 20, 2006. "CONFIDENTIAL. DRAFT WORK PRODUCT FOR DISCUSSION ONLY," 51.

75. Author's interview with Lynch.

76. Author's interview with Cahill.

77. Author's interview with Belusic-Vollor.

Chapter Six

College-Prep High Schools for the Poor

Joanne Jacobs

In a Texas border town along a curve of the Rio Grande, everyone takes college classes in high school. Half of the class of 2014 earned an associate's degree, a vocational certificate, or a year's worth of college credits, as well as a Hidalgo Early College High School diploma. For Mexican American students in a minimum-wage town, it's better to aim too high than to take the easy path, says Superintendent Ed Blaha.

At a San Jose charter high school, Latino students (and a few blacks, Asians, and whites) struggle to get on the college track and stay there. *Ganas* (Spanish for "desire," "determination," or—yes—"grit") is essential for Downtown College Prep's (DCP) students.

"Find a way or make one" is the motto of Providence St. Mel (PSM), an all-black private school, formerly Catholic, on Chicago's West Side. Every year, all graduates are accepted at four-year colleges and universities, and more than half go to selective "tier 1" colleges.

President Obama wants the United States to lead the world in college graduates, but college dreams usually don't come true for the children of poorly educated, low-income parents. Two-thirds of high school graduates enroll in college each fall,[1] yet only 51 percent of low-income (bottom quintile) students go to college, compared to 65 percent of middle-income and 81 percent of upper-income (top quintile) students.

Enrolling is just the first step in a long journey.

Nationwide, only 59 percent of students who enrolled in a four-year school in fall 2006 had earned a bachelor's degree six years later. Success rates are much lower at open-access and less selective institutions, where low-income students are likely to enroll.[2] Although half of all people from high-income families earn a bachelor's degree by age twenty-five, just one in ten people from low-income families do.[3]

116

Some blame "undermatching": half of students from lower-income or less educated families go to less selective colleges than they're qualified to attend, studies show.[4] "Nationwide, low-income minority students are disproportionately steered toward colleges not where they're most likely to succeed, but where they're most likely to fail," write Ben Miller and Phuong Ly in the *Washington Monthly*.[5]

Many attend what they call "college dropout factories," such as Chicago State University, where the six-year graduation rate is 13 percent, or Southern University in New Orleans, where the six-year graduation rate is 5 percent. Even more choose community colleges and for-profit colleges with low success rates. President Obama's recent proposal for "free" community college tuition would encourage needy students to enroll in the two-year public sector. Federal grants-in-aid could be used for rent, food, and other living expenses, not just for textbooks.

Only about one in three top-performing students from low- and moderate-income families attends a college with a six-year graduation rate of at least 70 percent, according to a new coalition led by Bloomberg Philanthropies.[6] The initiative hopes to raise that number by funding counselors to help students apply to selective colleges and maximize their financial aid. "Using video chat, email, telephone and text, they will mimic the support network—composed of guidance counselors, teachers, parents and friends—that more affluent high-school students take for granted," writes David Leonhardt in the *New York Times*.[7]

Most disadvantaged students, however, are not high achievers. Low-income students are less likely to take a strong college-prep curriculum, reports ACT, and most leave high school without the skills they need to succeed in college.[8]

College testing service ACT has developed readiness benchmarks predicting whether students have a 50 percent chance of earning a B or a 75 percent chance of earning a C in first-year courses such as writing, algebra, social science, or biology. Among 2012 graduates who took the ACT, only 10 percent of those from families with less than $36,000 in income met readiness benchmarks in all four areas (writing, math, reading, and science), and another 10 percent met benchmarks in three subjects. Forty-six percent of lower-income students met no benchmarks. That means nearly half were not prepared to pass any first-year college course.[9]

In 2014, only 18 percent of black students and 23 percent of Latinos met three or four benchmarks, ACT reported.[10] The achievement gap between wealthy and poor students is widening, according to Sean Reardon, a Stanford education professor.[11] Federal programs to help disadvantaged students prepare for college have shown little success, concludes a Brookings analysis, though there are "hints" that summer programs, mentoring, tutoring, and parent involvement "have sometimes been associated with higher college enrollment."[12]

Low-income achievers often lose ground in high school, an Education Trust study found. "They enter strong and leave less so," says Kati Haycock, the group's president. "Something is going seriously wrong." Education Trust looks for schools that are "beating the odds" for disadvantaged students. Few are high schools, says Haycock. "We've seen how not easy this is."

It's not easy, but it's not impossible either. This chapter introduces three high schools—a district-run public school, a charter school, and a private school—that work relentlessly to help disadvantaged students get to and through college. It will look at what's working, what's still a work in progress, and how policymakers and philanthropists can support and create odds-beating high schools in their communities.

FIND A WAY OR MAKE ONE

"It's easy to get kids into college," says Paul Adams, founder of PSM's and now its executive chairman. Qualifying them for top schools—not just unselective universities and community colleges—is more difficult.

The greatest challenge, even for the best college-prep high schools, is inculcating the academic and character strengths that will enable low-income, first-generation students to get through college. Strong academic skills are necessary, but students also need to be industrious, resilient, and determined to overcome obstacles and complete a degree.[13]

High schools that make a difference for disadvantaged students share some common approaches.

They Start Early

Hidalgo's "early college for all" program starts in elementary school, where teachers introduce college expectations, and intensifies in middle school, with career planning and preparation for the placement exam that will enable students to start taking college classes in high school. Ninth graders take a University Success course that teaches study skills, note taking, and time management.

Once a high school, PSM now starts in prekindergarten, though many students enroll later. Those who start in ninth or tenth grade have to work very hard to catch up academically and to learn the school culture. "I'm not sure pre-K is early enough," says Adams. "Maybe we need to start before they're born."

Downtown College Prep, where 80 percent of new students are two or more years behind, began as a high school in 2000. The average ninth grader started with fifth- to sixth-grade reading and math skills and the belief that homework was optional. To have any chance at college success, some students were put on "the five-year plan."

In 2010, DCP opened a middle school in East San Jose. Sixth graders typically start with fourth-grade skills. By ninth grade, the average student is working at or above grade level. That's enabled the East San Jose high school to offer two engineering courses and plan for Advanced Placement (AP) courses in a wide range of subjects. The flagship high school opened a feeder middle school this year. Jennifer Andaluz, DCP's cofounder and executive director, plans to redesign the high school to serve prepared students. "No more ninth graders who can't read!"

They Create a Safe, Supportive, "College-Going Culture"

Students must believe they can improve if they work hard enough. They must go to college with academic skills and the ability to handle fear, frustration, and failure. No guts, no glory. DCP's lore includes the story of the boys' basketball team's first season. It should have been a crushing defeat, but the Lobos were uncrushable. The *San Jose Mercury News* ran a front-page story:

> Sammy Garcia is one basketball player who can see progress in a 98-10 loss. "What do you mean? This was much better than the first game," he said Thursday.
>
> Downtown College Prep High School, where grade-point averages mean more than scoring percentages, lost its opener the day before, 110-6.
>
> . . . Jennifer Andaluz, the school's co-founder and executive director, doesn't worry that the routs will harm the psyches of her students. "These kids have all lost before," she said.
>
> Years later, Mac Dickerson proudly recalls playing in that lopsided game. He played basketball in a summer church league to improve. By senior year, he was captain of the team. "We had some solid wins," he recalls. "We proved we could grow. We could get better." [14]

They Plan

"Successful schools really work hard on consistency in academic expectations and discipline standards," says Haycock. "Support isn't just offered. They make sure kids get help." Groups of teachers "analyze data to see what's working and what isn't." Daniel King, who brought early college for all to Hidalgo, doesn't believe in dreams. "Instead of just dreaming and then waking up at age twenty-five . . . there's a difference between a dream and a plan of work."

That echoes PSM's mission statement: "Work, plan, build, and dream—in that order."

They Use a Longer School Day or Summer School

PSM has a long school day, and students with less than a 2.0 grade point average stay even later each day and attend summer school. DCP also has a long day, including a mandatory study period and heavy use of summer school. At Hidalgo High, taking college classes in the summer is cool, says Superintendent Blaha. Students say, "You're not taking college classes? Why not?"

They Reach Out to Parents and the Larger Community

Downtown College Prep, PSM, and Hidalgo Early College High are deeply embedded in their communities. Downtown College Prep and PSM raise millions of dollars for college scholarships and special programs. They also look to local businesses for internships. Hidalgo works closely with University of Texas–Pan American, South Texas College, and Texas State Technical College.

DCP offers evening and weekend workshops for parents—in both Spanish and English—to explain college options. That includes how to pay for it without heavy loans. Going to college is "a rite of passage for whole family," a DCP study concluded. Senior photos aren't of the student alone. Seniors pose with their mothers, fathers, and often grandparents, brothers, and sisters. Hidalgo schools have little staff turnover. "Principals know the parents"—and sometimes the grandparents, says Blaha. "There's a sense of trust."

They Introduce Students to the Larger World They Hope to Enter

Classes on college campuses, internships at businesses, summer camps, and wilderness adventures can be preparation for going to a college where classmates will be more affluent and a lot whiter than their neighborhood friends. Downtown College Prep teaches the school culture to incoming sixth graders in a summer College Corps at nearby Santa Clara University, a Jesuit school that has provided scholarships to DCP graduates. Students sleep in the dorms for a first taste of college life.

Santa Clara University also hosts a five-week summer session for DCP's high school students. The students take college classes in ceramics and writing taught by "real professors," who are asked to grade them as though they were college students. Providence St. Mel donors fund Summer of a Lifetime, which gives Chicago kids the kind of enriching experiences their parents couldn't afford. Sheila Foster, now a teacher at the school, remembers learn-ing archery, horseback riding, canoeing, and kayaking at a Minnesota camp.

Twelfth-grader Jessica Bailey studied theater and classical civilization at Oxford. "My drama teacher was an actor. She called in a dramaturge to work on the script we were doing. We did a workshop at the Globe Theatre." Jes-sica made friends from Lebanon, the United Arab Republics, the Philippines, and Cambodia. Her classmate, Ebonee Offord, went to a summer session at Brown and keeps in touch with one of her professors and a girl from Thailand.

They're Usually Small

Hidalgo High is small for a comprehensive high school, with 962 students. Downtown College Prep's high school has 420 students. Providence St. Mel's high school enrollment is 225. "It's possible to get very strong results in a large school, but it's not clear it can be done if kids are way, way behind," says Haycock.

Small schools have "the Cheers effect." They're places where "everybody knows your name."

They Don't Have to Be Selective

As a private school, PSM can reject students who don't meet its academic or behavioral standards. Parents who aren't willing or able to pay tuition—a minimum of one hundred dollars a month for low-income families—will send their children elsewhere. Downtown College Prep's model is designed for underachievers. Hidalgo has a small alternative school, but everyone else in town goes to the same high school. "Low-income strivers are vastly more likely to succeed at a low-poverty or selective exam school," says Haycock. As an individual, "always go to the highest-quality, most selective place."

But systemwide, exam schools and high-performing charters "bleed off" the high achievers, she says. The challenge is to create high schools that provide a path to college for all students. "The only way out of poverty for low-income kids is a college education now."

They Align Curriculum to College Expectations

In the college-for-all era, many high schools place all or almost all students on what's supposed to be a college-prep track. If students aren't prepared to pass a real algebra, biology, or English course, teachers are pressured to pass them along anyhow. Even A and B students may find themselves tak-ing remedial courses in college. College-prep high schools for disadvantaged students must understand what students need to succeed in college.

Taking college courses in eleventh and twelfth grade gives Hidalgo students a sense of what they'll need if they go on to a university or to the community college to learn a trade. University-bound students often take AP courses in addition to dual-enrollment courses. Providence St. Mel has aligned its curriculum to Illinois and Common Core standards and AP curriculum strands, says DiBella. Teachers engage students in discussion and debate to ensure they understand what they're learning. Remediation happens after school, not during classes. "We don't dummy down" the curriculum, says the principal. Forty-five percent of students take AP courses.

Rigor has been a challenge for DCP, which was designed for underachievers. "Blended learning"—self-paced programs using adaptive software—has transformed math instruction. "If you walk into a math class, you'll see every student working at their own level on a Chromebook with the teacher moving to various small groups," says Andaluz.

In English classes, students used to read six or seven books as a class. Now, the whole class reads two or three books, and each student reads fifteen to twenty books at his or her level. "They're doing lots more reading and writing," says Andaluz. The high school offers AP Spanish and US history classes. Andaluz hopes to expand enrollment to six hundred students to support more advanced and AP courses.

EARLY COLLEGE IN THE RIO GRANDE VALLEY

Hidalgo, Texas, is one of the poorest and least-educated towns in the state—and in the United States. Unemployment is high, and wages are low. Proclaimed the "killer bee capital of the world" in 1992—there's a giant bee statue in front of City Hall—Hidalgo also is the early college capital of the United States. Nearly all students at Hidalgo's only comprehensive high school come from low-income Mexican American families. Half are not fluent in English. Some are the first in their families to attend high school. Many of their parents speak only Spanish.

Yet 83 percent of Hidalgo Early College High School students pass at least one college class. Twenty-two percent complete an associate's degree, and 25 percent earn a certificate. Others earn enough credits to get a head start on a vocational certificate or a degree. "Early college," also known as "dual enrollment," is spreading across the country. The idea is not aimed at honors students. Early college is meant to motivate students who aren't on the college track, raising their aspirations as well as their academic competence.

In 2005, University of Texas–Pan American proposed that Hidalgo start an early college program within its high school. The Gates Foundation funded the experiment. "Why not do it for everyone?" thought Daniel King, who was Hidalgo Independent School District's superintendent at the time. It was a crazy idea. The district had raised its graduation rate, but many high school students were working below grade level. However, King believed students needed to make "the connection" between high school, college, and the rest of their lives.

The district aligned classes to prepare students to take college courses in eleventh and twelfth grade, writes Thad Nodine in *Hidalgo Sets Sail*: "Since 2005, the district's efforts have transformed its elementary and middle schools as well as its high school. The district has driven college expectations, more rigorous course sequencing and student support systems into all of its schools."[15]

Middle school students begin preparing to pass the state exam that qualifies them to take college-level courses. "They need tenacity, a commitment to work and study," says King. "We can impart that." Early college changed the culture at Hidalgo High. Taking college classes—sometimes on a community college or university campus, sometimes at the high school—became the cool thing. "Their friends are doing it. They want to do it."

Ed Blaha, Hidalgo's current superintendent, was principal of Hidalgo High when the early college program started. It took time to get buy-in from teachers and students, he recalls. "We created freshman and sophomore classes to build students' confidence." For example, everyone takes a course called University Success that teaches study skills, note taking, and time management. The summer before junior year, all rising juniors took six college credits in speech and computer information systems. "That was an eye opener for the kids," says Blaha. Professors were told not to water down the courses. Yet "a vast majority" earned the six college credits. "Students said, 'I can do this.'"

Forty-eight rising seniors took philosophy at UT–PanAm over the summer. Their classmates were college-age students. "They thought our kids must be little geniuses," recalls Blaha. Forty-four Hidalgo students passed; forty earned a B or an A.

Career planning starts in sixth grade and "goes a little deeper" in seventh and eighth. "They need exposure to what's out there," says Blaha. "There's a big world beyond the Rio Grande Valley. The opportunities are immense." By high school, students have chosen an area of interest, though they may change their minds as they go along.

Hidalgo tries to get students to pass the state's college readiness exam, which will qualify them for college courses, as soon as possible. However, even those who never pass the exam can take four college courses: speech, computer science, Spanish, and art appreciation. About 20 percent of students choose a vocational pathway, taking courses at a nearby community or technical college.

When Hidalgo started the early college program, it had grant money to pay university professors to teach at the high school, with a high school teacher serving as an aide, tutor, and study group leader. Teachers learned about college expectations. Now that the grant has run out, Hidalgo is paying teachers a small bonus to earn a master's degree in their subject area so they can be hired as adjunct professors. This has made early college—including the extra tutoring required—financially feasible.

The high school's low pass rate on the state exams turned up in 2007 but remains below the state average. The graduation rate, 98.8 percent, is much higher than the state average. By eleventh grade, Hidalgo High students score close to the state average in reading, math, and science and slightly above in social studies. However, only 58 percent of the district's 2013 graduates were college-ready in all areas: 77 percent in math, 69 percent in reading, and 64 percent in writing, reports the Texas Higher Education Coordinating Board.[16]

Fifty-four percent of 2013 graduates enrolled in a Texas college or university, with 55 percent at a four-year institution and 45 percent at community college. Those who went out of state aren't counted, but most stay close to home.

Undocumented students aren't eligible for financial aid, but some manage to go to college anyhow. "You'll find kids who will fight their way to it," says Blaha. Many Hidalgo parents grew up in Mexico, where mandatory schooling ends at sixth grade. At first, some didn't see what good it would do to earn college credits. But that's changed, says Blaha. Parents' expectations are rising on the border—and across the country.

In a 2009 Pew Hispanic Center survey, 88 percent of Latinos aged sixteen and older agreed that a college degree is necessary to get ahead in life today, compared to 74 percent of the general population.[17] Latino college enrollment has surged. Sixty-nine percent of Latino high school graduates in 2012 enrolled in college, compared to 67 percent of whites.[18]

However, young Latinos are less likely than their white classmates to enroll in a four-year college, less likely to attend a selective college, less likely to be enrolled in college full time, and less likely to complete a bachelor's degree. Many go to community colleges, take remedial courses, and drop out before earning a credential of any kind. Raising aspirations isn't enough: Students need to be prepared to succeed.

Nationwide, the average early college student graduates from high school with a year of college credit, says Joel Vargas of Jobs for the Future, which coordinates the Early College High School Initiative. Early college students are more likely to enroll in college, and persistence rates appear to be higher, too. However, the programs are so new that it's hard to track graduation rates.

An American Institutes for Research study completed in 2014 compared early college students at ten high schools to students who'd applied for early college but lost the lottery. The early college students earned higher English scores and were more likely to earn a high school diploma (86 percent to 81 percent) and enroll immediately in college (81 percent to 72 percent.)[19]

Early college students were just as likely as the control group to go to four-year colleges, but were much more likely to enroll in two-year colleges. The impact was stronger for minority students than non-minority students, stronger for lower-income students than higher-income students, and stronger for students with higher achievement in middle school than students with lower achievement in middle school. Early college students earned higher scores on state exams and had better attendance rates, according to a 2011 SRI study on the Texas High School Project.[20]

Early college high school students in North Carolina are more likely to be on track for college than similar students in traditional high schools, according to Julie Edmunds, a University of North Carolina researcher. In some cases, the early college model is closing the achievement gap between advantaged and disadvantaged students.[21]

Early college high school students have higher attendance and fewer suspensions, reports Edmunds. They report "more positive school experiences than students in the control group, including better relationships, higher expectations, more rigorous and relevant instruction, and more academic and social support." In her study, 86 percent of early college students enrolled in college, compared to 65 percent of the control group.

North Carolina has the most early college programs, including some five-year programs designed to include the first two years of college. A federal Investing in Innovation grant to North Carolina New Schools[22] is funding early college high schools in rural areas of the state. Texas is number two in early college programs and is expanding its programs rapidly. Denver wants to offer early college for all, reports Vargas. Brownsville, Texas, and Bridgeport, Connecticut, also are looking at the Hidalgo model.

DOWNTOWN COLLEGE PREP: TO AND THROUGH

Berenice Cervantes's parents—Dad has a third-grade education, Mom made it to fifth grade—left their small town in Mexico when their daughter was a baby. The town had an elementary school, but no middle school or high school. They wanted better opportunities for their kids.

They picked crops in California's Central Valley and then they found work in San Jose, California. Her father was a driver, her mother a janitor. "I saw their sacrifice, how hard they worked," recalls Cervantes. "I had to excel to pay them back. My grades were my paychecks to them." A Mount Holyoke graduate, Cervantes is college access and success coordinator for Summer

Search, a nonprofit that provides mentoring, summer enrichment experiences, and counseling to disadvantaged students from tenth grade through college.

McKinley "Mac" Dickerson spent several years in a homeless shelter when he was in elementary school. In middle school, his emotional issues led to a special-education diagnosis. As an agent and trainer for Transamerica, Dickerson helps families plan their finances, including how to save money for college. He earned an economics degree from University of California at Santa Cruz. His goal is to be "DCP's first millionaire alumni," he says.

Both are 2005 graduates of DCP, a scrappy charter school in San Jose. The city's first charter, it opened its doors—the doors of an old church and a former YWCA blocks apart—in 2000. Two young teachers, Greg Lippman and Jennifer Andaluz, targeted underachievers from Mexican immigrant families, kids who were "failing but not in jail," as Lippman put it. With a longer school day and a relentless focus on college prep, they believed their charter could put C, D, and F students on the college track.

In the early years, 85 percent of its students were Latino, and nearly all were from low-income and working-class families. Some came with special-ed labels: learning disabled, developmentally delayed, emotionally and be-haviorally disordered. Others weren't fluent in English. Psychologist Carol Dweck hadn't yet popularized the importance of the "growth mindset," the belief that hard work will lead to success. The Knowledge Is Power Program hadn't yet concluded that disadvantaged students need "grit" to make it through college.

Downtown College Prep was all about grit, known as *ganas,* before it was fashionable. "We're not good now but we can get better" was the unofficial motto, as I wrote in my book, *Our School,* about DCP's early years:

> At DCP, low achievers aren't told they're doing well; they're told they can do better, if they work hard. The school doesn't boost self-esteem with empty praise. Instead Lippman and his teachers encourage what's known as "effica-cious thinking," the belief that what a person does has an effect. If you study, you'll do better on the test than if you goof off. Work hard in school, and you can get to college. You have control over your future. So, stop making excuses and start getting your act together.[23]

At one assembly, teachers acted out the fable of the tortoise and the hare. A math teacher bragged about how he didn't need to work, while the Mexican-American "college readiness" teacher kept on going and won the race.

Lippman and Andaluz had overestimated their students' skills, they real-ized. "They can't read," Andaluz said. They'd overestimated the power of a college-going culture. Students quickly adopted the goal of going to college. It took much longer to learn the work habits of serious students and even longer to develop the reading, writing, and math skills. As principal, Lippman was quick to say, "I made a mistake. We need to do this differently." The founders realized some students needed English as a second language courses or remedial math ("math reasoning") or remedial English ("verbal reasoning") in addition to Algebra I and English I. Downtown College Prep struggled—and it got better.

These days, with two middle schools and a second high school, 90 percent of DCP students come from low-income families; 96 percent are Latino. Forty-one percent of parents did not complete high school. Many of the immigrant parents didn't start high school. Only 4 percent of parents and 13 percent of older siblings have a college degree. Of the school's enrollees, 80 percent of enrollees are below grade level by at least two years in English, math, or both.

In San Jose's Mexican immigrant neighborhoods, DCP has made college-going the "new normal," said Andaluz at the 2014 graduation, which also celebrated the tenth anniversary of the first commencement. The difference between people who "reach their full potential" and those who don't is "how they deal with adversity," said the keynote speaker, Salman Khan, creator of Khan Academy. Brain scans show that "the time when the brain grows is when you get questions wrong, when you fail at something but you power through it and keep on going." It was a very DCP message.

Honesty remains the policy, says Edgar Chavez, who monitors college readiness as college success director. It's OK to make mistakes, as long as you learn from them. "Who you are isn't who you're going to be," adds Prisilla Lerza, who works with donors, alumni, and parents as community engagement director.

Even if graduates need remedial coursework in college, they're "emotionally ready" for the challenges, says Andaluz. "We work to build their self-efficacy," the belief that they are capable of achieving their goals if they work hard enough. Graduates "are ready to fail, to take risks and to persist in college," she says. Some students take double math and double English in ninth grade. If they fall behind, they go to summer school to stay on track. The attrition rate—once very high—has come down dramatically in recent years thanks to self-paced learning and a new discipline policy.

To be eligible for a University of California or California State University school, students must pass the A–G college-prep sequence with Cs or better. Ninety-one percent succeed. The median grade-point average is a 3.07, but the median ACT is only 17. Of the school's graduates, 95 percent of graduates enroll in college: 18 percent start at the University of California, and 35 percent start at a California State University campus. In all, 84 percent are accepted at four-year schools.[24] By comparison, 53 percent of California's high school graduates—34 percent of California Latinos—enroll in college. State-wide, 15 percent of Latino high school graduates enroll at a four-year school. About 20 percent of DCP students are undocumented, which means they're not eligible for state or federal student aid. Most start at community colleges, which cost very little. DCP raises scholarship funds to help them transfer to a university after two years. The school also works with nonprofits to help students set up college savings accounts. For every dollar the student puts in, the nonprofit will provide two dollars from the federal government. Undocumented students are eligible. That's helped DCP students avoid or minimize college loans, says Lerza, who used to be the financial aid counselor.

"To and through" is DCP's motto. Counselors don't just help seniors apply to college and figure out how to pay for it. Using social media, Skype, and email, they work with graduates to help them cope with academic, personal, and financial problems in college—and out. Graduates can use the Alumni Success Center at the downtown high school campus to study or apply for jobs. Dropouts come by for advice on making a new college plan. "We say we're not grade six to twelve, we're grade six to sixteen," says Lerza. "Really, we're grade six to age thirty."

Downtown College Prep's graduates—often the children of gardeners, janitors, and construction workers—don't have connections in the professional world. Downtown College Prep counselors and alumni "serve as a career network for our students," she says. In addition, the school has partnered with Beyond 12, a nonprofit that monitors students' college progress and provides online coaching, quizzes, and other tools to keep students on track to a degree.[25]

Counselors encourage students to choose the most selective "right-fit" college, says Andaluz. The two-year college retention rate is 90 percent. The class of 2012 had a 98 percent retention rate, double the state average for all college students. Graduates who start at community college are transferring to state universities after two years, often with help from the Puente Project, which provides academic and personal counseling.

However, the path to college graduation "is not a linear journey," states *I Am the First,* a study of DCP's impact.[26] There are many stumbles and side trips for first-generation students. By 2012, only 49 percent of the class of 2004 had earned a degree. Another 18 percent were enrolled in a college or alternative program. Of the class of 2005, 30 percent of the class of 2005 had completed college and 27 percent were enrolled. Six years later, 21 percent of the class of 2006 were college graduates six years later and 58 percent were enrolled.

Overall, 58 percent of DCP graduates have earned a degree or are working toward one, says Chavez. His job is to improve those numbers.

Luis Falcon started in DCP's first class, but had to repeat eleventh grade. He earned his diploma in 2005 and got into a California State University. But his plans were derailed when he was stabbed—and nearly killed—by gang members. He spent a week in a coma and nine months in rehab. (As a victim of a violent crime, he qualified for a green card.) He tried community college, dropped out, and took a factory job. He tightened screws for three years. Eventually, he reenrolled in community college. He volunteered as a tutor at DCP and finally transferred to University of California at Santa Cruz. Nine years after he finished high school, Falcon earned a history degree. A Teach for America corps member, he's now a social studies teacher at a DCP middle school.

Dickerson, Falcon's classmate in the class of 2005, also took nine years to complete a UC–Santa Cruz degree. "I did the ugliest amount of growth in college," he says. "I needed to do it, but it wasn't pretty growth." In 2010, one course short of graduation, he ran out of money, but made up the missing credit in 2014.

Berenice Cervantes was an academic star at DCP. She'd always wanted to go to college, but claims she "didn't know how to go about it."

"If I hadn't gone to DCP, I probably would have stayed local," says Cervantes. "I might have gone to community college and tried to transfer." Instead, DCP's college counselor pushed her to apply to Mount Holyoke, which gave her a full scholarship. She almost turned it down. The college counselor set up a trip to western Massachusetts for Cervantes and her mother. "I needed my mother to see it and say OK."

The first year, Cervantes struggled with writing. She learned to ask for help. She used office hours to talk to her professors and took advantage of the tutoring center. "I knew I had to earn my spot there." She improved, earning a degree in international relations. After two years as DCP's college counselor, she moved on to Summer Search. As college access and success coordinator, she passes on the skills she learned at Mount Holyoke: how to find help and build a "team" of supporters. "It's so key to know they belong on campus," says Cervantes.

She works with students from seventeen Silicon Valley high schools. All complete a wilderness trip that puts them in a different environment, a chance to "connect with others who don't look like them." A second trip takes them abroad for academics or community service. A third trip is a college trip.

PROVIDENCE ST. MEL: THE HARD WORK SCHOOL

Boys in sagging pants step off the Chicago Transit bus. As they approach a large, brick building, they pull up their khakis and tuck in their shirts.

Providence St. Mel doesn't allow street fashions or street values. "You can recognize a Providence St. Mel student," says senior Greg Magee. "There's a certain esteem. We're proud of what we have going on here."

Founded by the merger of two Catholic schools, PSM nearly closed in 1978. The Archdiocese didn't want to cover the budget deficit or repair the 1929-era building. Principal Paul J. Adams III raised money to turn PSM into an independent school dedicated to preparing African American students for college success. PSM's supporters now include some of the largest foundations and corporations in Chicago.

Ninety-nine percent of students are black and 80 percent come from families who qualify for a free- or reduced-price lunch. All PSM students are accepted at four-year colleges and universities. Most go to selective universities. Seventy-three percent earn a bachelor's degree, according to a 2004 study. Principal Jeanette DiBella thinks it's even higher now. She's trying to persuade a university to update the study.

The average family pays $300 a month in tuition for the ten-month school year, but some pay as little as $100 a month, a small fraction of the $14,200 annual cost per student. Everyone pays something. It's increasingly difficult to persuade parents to pay tuition when charters are free, says Adams, who is now the executive chairman. PSM's median ACT score is 24, compared to 14–16 for nearby high schools and 17.6 for Chicago public schools. But many parents don't realize how important that is, he says. "It's a miracle we get some of our kids," he says. "After four generations of miseducation. . . ."

The school starts with pre-K, but most ninth graders are new to PSM. Among top students, "we get what's left" after the selective-enrollment high schools take their pick and high-quality charters run their lotteries, says DiBella. At the secondary level, applicants who are two years or more below grade level must attend summer school to show they can "follow our behavioral expectations and make it academically," says DiBella. A few are rejected every year.

Low-performing students get lots of extra help to catch up. Teachers monitor their progress closely. All students with less than a 2.0 grade-point average must stay after school for an extra study period and attend summer school. By the end of junior year, all students need at least a 2.0 grade-point average to meet their "junior contract." A few fall short and transfer out.

As a teacher of emotionally and behaviorally disordered students in her Chicago Public Schools career, "I'm good at reshaping behavior," says DiBella. She expels 1–2 percent of students. But there are rules. If a student becomes pregnant—or gets a girl pregnant—"you lose the privilege of being in our school," says DiBella. Students understand the consequences, she says. "We're very strict on discipline, very structured." Students aren't suspended:

They're assigned to clean the nearly hundred-year-old building, assisting "our somewhat grumpy maintenance staff." Consistency is key. Grades, homework policy, discipline—everything must be consistent. Students need to know what to expect.

DiBella came to PSM in 1996. The average teacher has been there for twelve years. That stability is an asset. "We recruit and retain teachers who will stick. They have to be content specialists who are very smart and passionate about their subject." Teachers need to empathize with students but not pity them, says DiBella. She won't hire "missionaries."

"I'm not into feeling sorry for poor students on the West Side," she says. "It's not 'you poor pitiful child, your mother's in jail, your grandmother's sick.'" Her message is, "You can do it. We have a ticket to get out of poverty." Some parents complain that their children have to stay too late and work too hard, says Adams. "We have a formula that works. I'm not going to change it."

"We teach our students to value education more than the streets," says DiBella. That requires a "warm and supportive atmosphere that makes students feel valued in class and believe in themselves," she stresses. "I believe in you. You can and will succeed."

PSM teaches discipline, says Owens Shelby of the class of 2000, an assistant state's attorney in Cook County. "You have to be organized. You have to be prepared for class. If you don't complete a homework assignment, you stay after class to finish it and still get half off."

PSM is stricter than public schools, as Tim Ervin discovered when he started in ninth grade. The academic standards are higher and there is much more homework. "I bought in right away. If I knew what the rules were, I followed them." PSM made him "dream bigger," says Ervin, who was the valedictorian in 1991. He was graduated from Purdue and worked in business for seventeen years. He volunteered as a basketball coach and was ordained as a minister. After a corporate layoff, he returned to PSM to coach basketball and teach Christian Morality. Both subjects focus on developing character, says Ervin. Tough love works, he says. "We work you because we love you. If kids feel you care, they'll do whatever you want."

PSM was a lot harder than her neighborhood public school, says Sheila Foster, who transferred in third grade. She'd been a shy student, an average achiever. Her PSM teachers wouldn't "let me fade into the background."

"The expectations are through the roof—but not unattainable," says Foster. "They help you develop a work ethic." When she made the quarterly honor roll, she was awarded a share of stock in McDonald's. "Nobody in my neighborhood owned stock. I was a third grader and an owner of stock. Nobody my age had heard of the stock market." She kept making the honor roll and saw her stock accumulate. Students can sell their shares when they graduate and go to college—or continue to build their portfolio. "I learned early on that hard work will pay off," says Foster. A University of Illinois graduate, she went on to earn a master's degree and now teaches PSM's kindergarten class.

PSM is "an island that excludes gangs, substance abuse and other criminal behaviors," concluded a 2004 Michigan State study.[27] "This is a place where students can work and learn without having to be concerned about their safety."

Violence has worsened in Chicago in the last ten years, but PSM has a large security guard and a metal detector at the door to keep the chaos out. That's important to parents, who choose the school for safety as well as academics. "Some boys change out of their uniforms when they leave," says DiBella. "They need to blend in" as they travel back to their homes. When a student was badly beaten by someone trying to steal his sneakers, PSM started requiring students to wear black shoes. Nobody wants to steal "church shoes."

Inside, the school is orderly and purposeful. Visit any classroom, starting in prekindergarten, and a student will shake hands, introduce him or herself, and explain what the class is studying at the moment. Outside, neighborhood teens "expect us to be condescending and patronizing," says Greg Magee. "Of course, I'm humble and down to earth," he adds, to the laughter of his classmates.

"My friends don't understand why I'm so serious about school," says Ebonee Offord, also a twelfth grader. "Everything we do is about getting ready to go to the next level." Senior Mbahgwie Mudoh's parents came from Cameroon to attend college in the United States. "With my family, coming to America from Africa, education, education, education . . . it's very important to them," he says. Students use the word "love" to describe science, writing, history, theater, and an internship at a consulting firm.

Jessica Bailey's mother told her, "You're too smart for public school." In PSM's elementary school, she planned to be a biologist. Then, "I fell in love with theater," inspired by the school musical. A twelfth grader, she hopes to major in theater at Northwestern, but she also loves history. Jessica is wearing a black polo shirt advertising a past school musical, *Fiddler on the Roof.* An all-black high school did *Fiddler*? "We thought it was a little odd at first, but it came out great!" says Jessica. "I was Fruma!"

Her friend Ebonee was "determined to be neurologist" in first grade. "I was seven, and I was planning to go to Stanford." Now she wants to be a novelist or actress. She's aiming at Columbia, Brown, and the University of Michigan. Mbahgwie hopes to major in business at DePaul and then work at Deloitte, an accounting firm where he was an intern. "I fell in love with what they do," he says. Greg is eyeing the University of Iowa's writing program. He hopes to write for television.

In PSM classes, teachers "expect us to talk, not just regurgitate information," says Jessica. "Greg is notorious for never agreeing with the teacher. But you have to come up with evidence to support your argument." In AP classes, starting in eleventh grade, teachers "treated us like college students," says Ebonee. "They say, 'It's your responsibility to do the work.'"

Seniors take a class that gives them time to explore college options, write essays, and apply for the financial aid that will make college possible. Everyone takes the ACT at least three times. It's not enough to get in. They need scores high enough to qualify for scholarships. Figuring out how to pay for college is the most stressful part, says Jessica. But it's all stressful. "You're standing on the edge of a cliff, and you're about to jump!"

There are other college-prep models for disadvantaged students. Brooklyn's P-TECH, designed with help from IBM, takes students through high school and the first two years of community college. Students can earn an associate's degree and a job offer from IBM. It's expected some will go on to earn a bachelor's degree, but that's not their only path to the middle class. President Obama praised the school in his 2013 State of the Union speech and visited later that year.

There are many high-performing "no excuses" charter schools that specialize in educating lower-income black and Latino students. In Boston, the MATCH charter, which provides intensive tutoring, gets very strong academic results.

Cristo Rey, a network of Catholic schools, has a longer school day four days a week. On the fifth day, students work in a professional workplace, learning job skills, building a network, and contributing their pay to the school to defray the costs of their education. A new Cristo Rey school in San Jose is piloting self-paced, personalized, blended learning. In an intensive summer math program, students gained 1.5 to 2 years of proficiency in a few months.[28]

St. Benedict's Prep in Newark, an all-boys Catholic school run by Benedictine monks, used to educate the children of working-class Irish and German immigrants. Now it prepares young black males to be mature, responsible, educated adults.[29]

To make upward mobility a reality, college must be more than a dream for low-income students. It needs to be, as Daniel King puts it, "a plan of work." College and career counseling is especially critical for students whose parents aren't college educated. Counseling needs to start in middle school at the latest and continue—in some form—through college. Students need to be introduced to potential careers and told what they need to be doing in school to reach their goals. Is a C average good enough to make it at a university? No. Will it prepare the student to train for a skilled job at a community college? Probably not. Are there high-paying jobs for people who "just can't do math?" Not really.

Once students are thinking about their goals, they need a choice of schools that will help them get there. Urban Catholic and other private schools can be very effective—if donors keep them alive. Charter caps or a lack of facility funding may limit the number of "no excuses" charter options. High-quality magnet schools can't take everyone who applies. And comprehensive high schools may not offer challenging courses. (Letting unprepared students take AP-in-name-only courses, with no hope of passing the exam, doesn't really help.)

Students who choose a career pathway need rigorous courses, too—but not necessarily the same ones required for a bachelor's degree. As Hidalgo illustrates, career-minded students can use dual-enrollment to earn vocational certificates.

Some states pay tuition and book costs for "early college" students, making it possible for low-income students to participate. Many are aligning community college and state university courses so that students can transfer credits easily. Philanthropists can fund summer and after-school enrichment and job programs to motivate disadvantaged students and expand their horizons. It's especially important to make it possible for beating-the-odds schools to track their graduates, understand their struggles, and help them overcome personal and academic challenges. After all, there's a lot to learn.

NOTES

1. "Immediate Transition to College," National Center for Education Statistics, http://nces.ed.gov/programs/coe/indicator_cpa.asp.

2. National Center for Education Statistics, http://nces.ed.gov/programs/coe/indicator_cpa.asp.

3. *White House Report on Increasing Opportunity for Low-Income Students: Promising Models and a Call to Action* (Washington, DC: The Executive Office of the President, 2014), http://www.whitehouse.gov/sites/default/files/docs/white_house_report_on_increasing_college_opportunity_for_low-income_students_1-16-2014_final.pdf.

4. Jonathan I. Smith, Matea Pender, and Jessica S. Howell, "The Full Extent of Academic Undermatch," *Economics of Education Review*, 32 (2013): 247–61, doi: 10.1016/j.econedurev.2012.11.001.

5. Ben Miller and Phuong Ly, "College Dropout Factories," *College Guide* (blog), *Washington Monthly*, August 10, 2010, http://www.washingtonmonthly.com/college_guide/feature/college_dropout_factories.php.

6. Caroline Hoxby and Christopher Avery, *The Missing One-Offs: The Hidden Supply of High-Achieving, Low-Income Students* (Washington, DC:

Brookings Institute, 2013), http://www.brookings.edu/~/media/projects/bpea/spring%202013/2013a_hoxby.pdf.

7. David Leonhardt, "A New Push to Get Low-Income Students through College," *The Upshot, New York Times,* October 28, 2014, http://www.nytimes.com/2014/10/28/upshot/a-new-push-to-get-low-income-students-through-college.html.

8. *The Condition of College and Career Readiness: Low-Income Students Class of 2012,* ACT, 2013, http://www.act.org/newsroom/data/2012/states/pdf/LowIncomeStudents.pdf.

9. Ibid.

10. "The Condition of College & Career Readiness 2014: Key Findings," ACT, accessed November 22, 2014, http://www.act.org/research/policymakers/cccr14/findings.html.

11. Sean F. Reardon, "The Widening Academic Achievement Gap between the Rich and the Poor: New Evidence and Possible Explanations," in *Whither Opportunity? Rising Inequality and the Uncertain Life Changes of Low-Income Children,* ed. Greg J. Duncan and Richard J. Murnane (New York: Russell Sage Foundation Press, 2011).

12. Ron Haskins and Cecelia Elena Rouse, *Time for Change: A New Federal Strategy to Prepare Disadvantaged Students for College,* Policy Brief, Spring 2013 (Washington, DC: Future of Children, 2013), http://www.brookings.edu/~/media/multimedia/interactives/2013/college_roi/college_prep_low_income_students_haskins.pdf.

13. Richard V. Reeves, Joanna Venator, and Kimberly Howard, *The Character Factor: Measures and Impact of Drive and Prudence* (Washington, DC: Center on Children & Families at Brookings, 2014), http://www.brookings.edu/~/media/research/files/papers/2014/10/22%20character%20factor%20opportunity%20reeves/22_character_factor_opportunity_reeves.pdf.

14. Clay Lambert, "Uncommon Hoop Dreams," *San Jose Mercury News,* December 5, 2002.

15. Thad R. Nodine, "Hidalgo Sets Sail: A School District Supports All Students in Earning College Credits," *American Educator* 35, no. 3, (2011): 21–27, https://www.aft.org//sites/default/files/periodicals/Nodine.pdf.

16. "Tracking Postsecondary Outcomes Dashboard—Texas High School Graduates," Texas Higher Education Coordinating Board, accessed November 22, 2014, http://reports.thecb.state.tx.us/approot/hs_college/hs_college_main_launch.htm.

17. *Between Two Worlds: How Young Latinos Come of Age in America* (Washington, DC: Pew Hispanic Center, 2009), http://www.pewhispanic.org/2009/12/11/between-two-worlds-how-young-latinos-come-of-age-in-america.

18. *High School Drop-out Rate at Record Low: Hispanic High School Graduates Pass Whites in Rate of College Enrollment* (Washington, DC: Pew Hispanic Center, 2013), http://www.pewhispanic.org/files/2013/05/PHC_college_enrollment_2013-05.pdf.

19. Andrea Berger, et al., *Early College, Continued Success: Early College High School Initiative Impact Study* (Washington, DC: American Institutes for Research, 2014), http://www.air.org/sites/default/files/downloads/report/AIR%20ECHSI%20Impact%20Study%20Report-%20NSC%20Update%2001-14-14.pdf.

20. "Project: Evaluation of the Texas High School Project," SRI Education, http://www.sri.com/work/projects/evaluation-texas-high-school-project (accessed November 22, 2014).

21. Julie Edmunds, et al., "Mandated Engagement: The Impact of Early College High Schools," *Teachers College Record* 115, no. 7 (2013): 1–31, http://www.tcrecord.org/content.asp?contentid=17044.

22. *Changing the Future through Early College High Schools* (Raleigh, NC: North Carolina New Schools, August 2013), http://ncnewschools.org/wp-content/uploads/2014/08/Early-College-overview.pdf.

23. Joanne Jacobs, *Our School: The Inspiring Story of Two Teachers, One Big Idea, and the School That Beat the Odds* (New York: Palgrave Macmillan, 2005).

24. "Key Performance Indicators," DCP Impact Report, Downtown College Prep, http://www.dcp.org/discover-our-impact/results/key-performance-indicators/ (accessed November 22, 2014).

25. "Mission," Beyond 12, http://beyond12.org/mission.html (accessed November 22, 2014).

26. "I Am the First," DCP College Success Report, Downtown College Prep, http://www.dcp.org/discover-our-impact/results/college-success-report/.

27. Michael Pressley, Lisa Raphael, J. David Gallagher, et al., "Providence-St. Mel School: How a School That Works for African American Students Works," *Journal of Educational Psychology* 96, no. 2 (2004): 216–35.

28. Ashley Bateman, *The Cristo Rey Network: Serving Sustainable Success* (Arlington, VA: Lexington Institute, 2014), http://www.lexingtoninstitute.org/the-cristo-rey-network-serving-sustainable-success/.

29. Steven Malanga, "It's Hard to be Saints in the City," *City Journal,* September 2, 2014, http://www.city-journal.org/2014/bc0902sm.html.

Chapter Seven

High-Quality Career and Technical Education

Bob Schwartz and Nancy Hoffman

Americans historically have had a hard time coming to grips with the realities of class. Many of our great-grandparents and grandparents came here to escape a world in which their opportunities for liberty and economic mobility were almost entirely constrained by the circumstances of their birth. The enduring belief of each successive generation of Americans has been that demography need not be destiny.

From Ben Franklin to Barack Obama, every generation of Americans has been able to point to inspiring examples of people who have risen from modest origins to the very pinnacle of success in one or another spheres of American life. We tell ourselves that America is the only country in which such extraordinary life stories could happen—for unlike the European countries many of our forefathers fled, we have no rigid class system limiting the ability of ambitious and hardworking young people to realize their potential.

Central to this cultural narrative is our belief in education as the principal engine of economic and social mobility. One of the great public policy success stories in the past century was our decision to greatly expand access to higher education in the period following World War II. We achieved this both through massive investments by states such as California and New York in building world class public universities and comprehensive higher education systems, and through the federal government's investment in providing student financial aid, most notably with the GI bill. Again, we enjoyed noting the contrast with Old World countries, where higher education continued to be seen primarily as the province of the wealthy.

Where in this narrative does vocational education fit? In a world in which most jobs required no more than a high school education and only a relative handful of young Americans went on to college, education that prepared people to work in the traditional trades and crafts was a perfectly respectable

137

option. Not only was there little social stigma attached to vocational education, in mid-twentieth-century America this was actually a mainstream path to help high school students make their way into the labor market.

But with the gradual decline of manufacturing and the rapid expansion of the service sector in the second half of the twentieth century, college became the preferred route to good jobs that paid a family-supporting wage. Consequently, not only did vocational education lose market share in the economy of high schools, but too often, vocational programs also became "dumping grounds"—places to send students deemed unfit for rigorous academic work.

While there have always been examples of highly successful vocational programs and schools in urban as well as rural America, there have unfortunately also been notorious examples of vocational schools serving predominantly low-income and minority youth that led only to dead-end jobs.

In 2008 one of us (Schwartz) and two Harvard colleagues began to discuss the possibility of developing a report on education and employment. We were mindful that twenty years earlier, a commission established by the W. T. Grant Foundation published a powerful report entitled *The Forgotten Half: Non-College Youth in America.* The big take-home message from that report was that on virtually all indicators of social and economic well-being, those young people not in college were less well-off than their college-going counterparts. Yet as a society we seemed to have no serious strategy to help these adolescents make a successful transition into the workforce and, more generally, into adulthood.

By 2008, the phrase "non-college youth" no longer was in use, for over the preceding twenty years high schools had, for the most part, ended the practice of dividing their students into the "college-bound" and the "work-bound." This is not to suggest that tracking had disappeared—but rather to observe that as the movement to raise academic expectations and standards for all students had grown over this period, so had the notion that the central purpose of high school was to prepare all young people for college.

Americans were bombarded with a steady barrage of media stories showing the growing differential in lifetime earnings between those with a college degree and those without, and about the disappearance of manufacturing and the accompanying loss of well-paying jobs that did not require a college degree. Economists kept warning of the "hollowing out" of the US economy, telling us we were heading into a world in which there would only be two kinds of jobs: high-skill, high-wage jobs requiring at least a four-year degree, and low-skill, low-wage jobs for everyone else.

Given these messages, it should be no surprise that by 2008 "college for all" had become the new mantra, accepted by parents and by young people themselves. "College Begins in Kindergarten" was the message on the Education Trust T-shirts, and university banners had become ubiquitous in primary grade classrooms in urban America. In surveys of high school seniors asking about plans after high school, over 90 percent said they were going to college. The following October, over two-thirds of graduates were in fact enrolled in some form of postsecondary education.

But when we looked at the college attainment data for young people in their mid-twenties, we found that less than 30 percent had a four-year degree. Ten percent had a two-year degree, and another 10 percent or so had a one-year, postsecondary certificate with value in the labor market. This raised for us the question of whether we still in fact had a "forgotten half," and whether we had made any progress over these two decades in developing a national strategy to help our young people make a successful transition into an increasingly challenging and demanding labor market. It was this question that led to the development of the report we released in 2011, *Pathways to Prosperity: Meeting the Challenge of Preparing Young Americans for the 21st Century.*[1]

THE RESPONSE TO THE *PATHWAYS* REPORT

The argument of the *Pathways* report was at one level quite simple. It was organized around three questions: First, if fewer than one young person in three is successfully completing a four-year college degree by age twenty-five, does it really make sense to organize high schools as if this should be the goal for all students?

Second, if respected economists are now telling us that at least 30 percent of the jobs projected over the next decade will be in the "middle skills" category—technician-level jobs requiring some education beyond high school but not necessarily a four-year degree—shouldn't we start building more pathways from high school to community colleges to prepare students to fill the best of those jobs, especially in high-growth, high-demand fields such as information technology and health care?[2]

Finally, if countries like Austria, Germany, the Netherlands, Norway, and Switzerland have built vocational systems that prepare between 40 and 70 percent of young people to enter the workforce by age twenty with skills and credentials valued by employers—and if these countries have healthy economies and much lower youth unemployment rates than the United States—shouldn't we study their vocational policies and practices to see if there are lessons we can adapt to our own setting?[3]

Over the next year, we had speaking invitations from organizations in over thirty states and five countries to talk about the implications of the report. Generally speaking, people in these meetings bought the argument of the report. Their question was: How do we address the questions and challenges it raised?

Our response was: We do not have a detailed set of recommendations in our back pocket, but we would be happy to work with you collaboratively to figure out a strategy customized to your state or region. These conversations led to the creation of the Pathways to Prosperity Network in 2012. The Network is a partnership between Jobs for the Future, Harvard Graduate School of Education, and now ten states. It focuses on helping participating states build career pathways that span grades 9–14 and are designed to help young people attain postsecondary degrees and credentials that can launch them into careers in high-growth, high-demand fields—while keeping open the option of further education.[4]

THE CASE FOR CAREER PATHWAYS

In the three years since the *Pathways* report was released, several developments have given significant impetus to the career pathways movement. On the research side, the Georgetown Center on Education and the Workforce has released several reports providing further evidence that the returns to education are not simply a function of how much you have had, but what skills you have acquired. According to the Center's studies, there are now very significant overlaps between the earnings of those with licenses and one-year, postsecondary certificates and those with two- and four-year degrees. Most striking, nearly one-third of those with two-year degrees are out-earning the average four-year-degree holder.[5]

In Florida, for example, those who graduated in 2009 with a two-year technical degree (an associate of applied science [AAS] degree) were, within two years, out-earning the average young four-year-degree holder by about $10,000.[6] More recent research from the Federal Reserve Board of New York has documented the struggles of young four-year-degree holders more generally, reporting that over 40 percent of them are working in jobs that historically did not require a college degree.[7] Given the rising costs of college—plus the average debt burden of $26,000 young graduates are carrying—these numbers are causing many parents to question the assumption that an investment in a four-year degree is a guarantee of economic security for their children.

More relevant to the topic of this chapter has been a series of international studies of economic mobility showing that, contrary to our view of ourselves, the United States is no longer the country where those born into poverty have the greatest chance of moving up in the world. As these studies have made their way into the mainstream press (see, for example, the January 4, 2012 front-page *New York Times* story, "Harder for Americans to Rise from the Lower Rungs"), Americans have had to face the fact that such Old World countries as Denmark, Finland, Germany, and Norway—and our New World neighbor, Canada—all have significantly higher rates of economic mobility than we do.

In one study, 42 percent of American men whose fathers were in the bottom fifth of the income distribution remained in the bottom fifth, while in Denmark, Finland, and Norway the numbers were between 25 and 28 percent. Even more difficult for Americans to accept is that even in the United Kingdom, the quintessential class-bound society we love to compare ourselves with, only 30 percent of men with fathers in the bottom quintile remained there.[8]

Except for the United Kingdom, virtually all the European countries that have higher economic mobility rates than we do have much stronger vocational systems than ours, and send a significantly smaller percentage of young people off to four-year colleges or universities. Given the no-longer-assured returns to a four-year degree in the United States—and the evidence from other countries that a high-quality vocational education system designed to serve at least 40 percent of the youth population can be an important contributor to both economic prosperity and mobility—the stage may finally be set for a more serious policy focus on revitalizing career and technical education (CTE) in the United States.

THE PATHWAYS NETWORK AND THE NEW, IMPROVED CTE SYSTEM

In the two years since we launched the Pathways Network, a consensus has begun to emerge about the contours of a revitalized CTE system—one that might begin to reflect some of the lessons from the strongest European systems. This consensus has been reflected in the policies and new funding opportunities created in some of the states we are working in, most notably California, Delaware, Ohio, and Tennessee, as well as in the Obama administration's "Blueprint" for the reauthorization of the Perkins Act, the principal federal program supporting CTE.[9]

The first core principle in the emerging consensus is that we must build career pathways that span secondary and postsecondary education. The response to the "college for all" mantra cannot be to return to an earlier era in which some young people are prepared for college while others are prepared for work. Rather, the new mantra must be that all young people will need some form of postsecondary education or training to be able to thrive in this increasingly demanding economy. Therefore, we must build a set of career-focused pathways leading to postsecondary technical education that sit alongside the strictly academic pathway that leads to a four-year college or university.

The strongest European programs enroll students at age sixteen in a three- or four-year, full-time program that combines three or four days a week of learning at the workplace with a day or two of continued academic class work. Those students emerge from their program with at least the equivalent of one year of postsecondary training—if not the equivalent of an associate's degree. No US high school vocational program provides that degree of intensive training in an occupational area.

The second core principle is that CTE programs need to be much more demand-driven than they currently are. This means two things. First, programs must be designed based on a careful analysis of regional labor market trends, and especially focused on those industries and occupations that are not only rapidly growing but require people with a solid foundation of core academic as well as technical skills. In other words, the focus should be on fields with good jobs that pay good wages and have the potential to get young people onto a career ladder that leads to the middle class.

Second, employers from the target occupational sectors need to be at the table from the beginning. They not only help ensure that the programs are designed to equip young people with the knowledge and skills required for success in that sector, but also provide internships and other forms of workplace learning for participating students throughout the duration of the program.

A third core principle is that all students need to be provided much greater access to career information, awareness, and exposure beginning at least as early as the middle grades. This puts them and their parents in a position to make informed choices among an array of career pathways at some point in their high school years. We believe *all* students would benefit from a much more systematic exposure to the world of careers while in middle and high school, even those who know they are headed for a four-year university. The fact that so many young university graduates are floundering in the labor market tells us that too many students arrive at college with no career plan, choose majors based solely on interest with no reference to the job market, and then find out only upon graduation that they have few marketable skills.

It is these core principles that have guided the development of the Pathways Network. Our work with states is in large measure helping them design grades 9–14 pathways focused on high-demand occupations; build early and sustained career information, awareness, and exposure programs; and develop strategies to engage employers in much more meaningful ways.

In our view, this latter challenge requires the presence of strong intermediary organizations that sit between the employer community and schools and colleges and are staffed to design and manage internships and other forms of workplace learning. In some regions, workforce investment boards or chambers of commerce take on this role, but these regions are the exceptions, not the rule. Without some organization that takes responsibility for managing the logistics of placing and supporting young people in workplaces, small and medium-size employers are unlikely to participate—which means that we are unlikely to get to scale.

While the real work of building career pathways happens at the regional labor market level, some of the major challenges and barriers to success can only be addressed at the state level. By design, career pathways programs cut across the education and workforce systems, and across K–12 and postsecondary education. Each of these systems has its own governance arrangements, funding streams, governmental bureaucracies, and political constituencies.

Absent a strong state leadership group committed to addressing regulatory and funding barriers and running political interference, each region is forced to wrestle on its own with such questions as who pays for dual enrollment, or how to address employer concerns about liability for sixteen-year-olds in the workplace.

These principles and strategies can best be seen at work in California, where they undergird the design of the California Career Pathways Trust (CCPT). Launched in 2013 with a $250 million appropriation, it is arguably the largest investment any state has ever made in a competitive grants program for career-related education. The Trust is administered by the California Department of Education but developed collaboratively with the Community College Chancellor's Office and the Workforce Investment Board. It focuses on building regional consortia that bring together high schools, community colleges, and employer associations to build grades 9–14 career pathways in high-skill, high-growth fields designed not only to enable more young people to successfully transition from high school to community college to work, but also to fuel regional economic growth.

In May 2014, the state awarded thirty-nine grants to such consortia. Demand for these competitive grants was so intense that in June, the legislature decided to appropriate an additional $250 million for a second round this year. On the federal level, in 2014 the Obama administration distributed $100 million in a grants program called Youth CareerConnect based on similar principles.

GETTING FROM HERE TO THERE

It is one thing to articulate a set of principles to guide the revitalization and redesign of CTE in our big, diverse country. It is quite another thing to figure out how to build on the strengths of the current system to move us, over time, to a world in which at least 40 percent of young Americans are enrolled in programs built upon those principles.

The first step is to acknowledge that there is no single program model upon which to build the new system. Within the states in our Pathways Network, and in others we have visited, we have seen highly effective CTE programs in stand-alone vocational high schools, regional vocational centers, career academies nestled inside larger high schools, and early college high schools (ECHSs) operated in partnership with colleges or universities. We are consequently agnostic about form. We advise the states and regions we collaborate with to build on what works.

It would be nice if a "what works" discussion could be grounded in evidence, but this is a field in which the evidentiary base is very weak. The one study that advocates consistently invoke is a random assignment study of career academies published in 2006 by the Manpower Demonstration Research Corporation. The study showed virtually no impact on education outcomes—but a significant impact on earnings over an eight-year period for male participants.[10] Beyond that study, there is little data that would enable anyone to privilege one CTE-related program model over another.

Following are short profiles of five exemplary schools or programs representing five different career education models. Each serves a substantial proportion of low-income students. Most have impressive high school graduation and postsecondary enrollment rates (others are too new). Some represent models that have already been scaled; the others, models that could be.

Model 1: Worcester Technical High School, Worcester, Massachusetts (*Stand-alone Urban CTE High School*)[11]

In June 2014, President Obama gave his only high school commencement address of the year at Worcester Technical High School, on the outskirts of Worcester, Massachusetts. With 181,000 people, Worcester is the second-largest city in New England. Sheila Harrity, then the National Association of Secondary School Principals–winning principal of the school, evinced surprise, but Worcester Tech is one of the state's highest performers despite being declared a failing school in 2006. While Massachusetts schools are known for high academic achievement, few know that its twenty-six regional vocational high schools and three agricultural schools have waiting lists, strong results on the Massachusetts Comprehensive Assessment System (the state assessment), and higher high school completion rates than the state average. For over forty years, the schools have followed a unique schedule—the first four months of ninth grade, students circulate among career areas offered. Then, with advising, they pick their area of concentration. From then on, the schedule alternates—a week of academics, a week of "shop." Even with higher-than-state-average low-income and special ed populations, 82 percent of Worcester Tech's class of 2014 graduates are bound for a two- or four-year college. Others get good jobs right out of high school since they have industry-recognized credentials, and often dual-enrollment college credit. Along with the full array of vocational programs, the school offers Advanced Placement courses and many internship opportunities.

A US Department of Education Blue Ribbon School, housed in a $90 million state-of-the-art building on a four-hundred-thousand-square-foot campus, Worcester Tech represents the best of the full-time vocational high school models. Perhaps most impressive is the work experience students gain at Worcester Tech. Students work in profit-making enterprises, both inside the school and externally. The student-run, 125-seat restaurant serves meals to the public at reasonable prices. Also operating at the school: a L'Oreal Redken salon and day spa, a sixteen-bay automotive service center, a full-service bank with ATM, and a state-approved preschool.

In partnership with Tufts University, one of the highest-ranked veterinary schools in the country, Tufts at Tech provides subsidized animal care to low-income families in the Worcester region; students participate in treatment of over 250 animals per month. The carpentry, plumbing, and electrical students built the veterinary clinic. The graphic students created the name and designed the logo and brochures, and the painting and design students created the signage.

Model 2: Center for Advanced Research and Technology, Clovis, California (*Regional CTE Center*)[12]

"This is my second year as a student in the Economics and Finance Lab," writes graduating senior Sam Hodorowski, in her blog on the homepage of the Center for Advanced Research and Technology (CART). "During these two years, I have put together financial portfolios, gone on two internships, created a non-profit and am currently creating a for-profit business. None of these are things I would be able to do, especially not with such skill and precision like I have been able to, if not for CART." A part-time regional career center located in Clovis, California (near Fresno), CART provides half-day programs for 1,300 eleventh and twelfth graders from fifteen high schools. While CART uses CTE funds and has some programs that are standard in California's Regional Occupational Programs, nothing is standard about a CART education—starting with the CART facility and the CART approach to learning.

The seventy-five-thousand-square-foot CART building, designed to replicate a high-performance business atmosphere, is organized around four career clusters: professional sciences, engineering, advanced communications, and global economics. Teachers, business partners, and invited experts work not in classrooms but in large open spaces filled with equipment, work stations, and student work—spaces similar to those at a high-tech startup or science lab.

Within each cluster are several career-specific laboratories in which students complete industry-based projects and receive academic credit for advanced English, science, math, and technology. Boundaries between disciplines don't exist since students are problem solving and learning as one would in the real world. Students do everything from testing water in the Sierra to making industry-standard films to trying out aviation careers by actually flying planes. Teaching teams include business and science partners, and as bios of teachers indicate, many teachers have extensive professional experience.

There are no grade or test requirements for admission; CART students must make the case for themselves as appropriate CART students. Through learning plans, individualized attention, and collaboration with business partners, teachers, and parents, students design programs of study that qualify them to pursue the postsecondary path of their choice—from entry-level positions to industry certification to university admission. According to a 2009 transcript study using data from the California Partnership for Achieving Student Success, researchers found that in the prior seven years, CART students matriculated to postsecondary institutions at a higher rate than a matched sample of similar students from the area's high schools.

Model 3: Wake Early College of Health and Sciences, Raleigh, NC (*STEM-focused Early College High School*)[13]

Wake Early College of Health and Sciences and WakeMed, one of Raleigh, North Carolina's, major hospitals, is helping lead the way to the kind of work-linked learning that equips students with solid skills for careers and postsecondary education. WakeMed helped to found Wake Early College of Health and Sciences in 2006 and remains a key partner, along with Wake Technical Community College.

When students in the class of 2013 received their high school diplomas, more than half also earned associate's degrees. Several earned certifications as nursing assistants and emergency medical technicians. The school's graduation rate has remained well above 90 percent for its first four classes, and the class of 2013 achieved a 100 percent graduation rate.

Every student learns not only in the classroom, but also on Wake Tech's health sciences campus and in WakeMed's main hospital. Students participate in job shadowing, internships, and other activities that put them in direct contact with practicing medical professionals. They get firsthand exposure to health care careers and learn from people in those jobs about the skills—hard and soft—necessary for success. They see science, technology, engineering, and mathematics (STEM) in action every day.

Several new STEM early colleges are sponsored by major companies. New York City's Pathways in Technology Early College High School (P-TECH) is sponsored by IBM and partners with the New York City Department of Education and the Early College Initiative at the City University of New York. Graduates of this six-year program should emerge with AAS degrees in computer systems technology or electromechanical engineering technology; the first class is in its fifth year. Governor Cuomo and the New York legislature have funded twenty-six P-TECH adaptations across the state. SAP, the German business solutions company, is sponsoring several early college programs: one just opened in New York City and another will open in Boston in 2015.

New York City also has schools opening sponsored by an advertising industry organization, Montefiore Hospital, and Con Edison. Paramount Farms, a major agricultural company in California's Central Valley, is sponsoring the development of five early colleges focused on agriculture business management, plant sciences, and agriculture mechanics needed for the Valley's agriculture industry.

Model 4: Southwire 12 for Life, Carrollton, Georgia
(*Employer-sponsored School in a Workplace*)[14]

Half of the world's copper rod for electric wires and cables is made with the patented Southwire Continuous Rod method of production in rural Carroll County, Georgia. A family-owned company, in the early 2000s, Southwire leaders became worried about filling the human capital pipeline. Only one-third of Carroll County high school students completed school, and even graduates seemed unprepared for jobs.

Southwire came up with a radical idea to build a factory that would be staffed by at-risk students. Students would work four-hour shifts and spend four hours in academics. Despite worries that ran from safety to coordinating school schedules, 12 for Life opened in 2007 with sixty-nine students, admitted preferentially because they had poor attendance and academic records, came from stressed and troubled families, and were likely to drop out.

At the start, 12 for Life students took their classes at the high school and then came to work. But in 2013, Southwire built six classrooms, including a science lab and a computer lab, inside the 12 for Life facility. As of 2013, about one-third of students took their academic classes in those classrooms, while the rest attended the county high school.

The Carroll County public school system staffs the facility with teachers and counselors and pays for transportation. Southwire covers all other costs, including wages, facilities, utilities, maintenance, and the salaries of ten Southwire supervisors. Student earn eight dollars per hour plus a fifty-cent-per-hour bonus during weeks of perfect attendance and another fifty-cent-per-hour bonus during weeks when they hit a production target. Each week, roughly half receive both bonuses and earn nine dollars per hour. (A full-time Southwire employee performing similar tasks would earn fourteen to fifteen dollars per hour plus benefits.)

Perhaps the most surprising part of this story is how well teenagers can perform: 12 for Life students are, on average, 30 to 40 percent more productive than adult employees on the same tasks. The students typically work in small teams, with operating lines laid out so that each team sees how others are performing—the competition is a great fuel for productivity. Student workers now generate over $1.7 million in profits, most of which is invested back into the program.

Not only has Southwire benefited, so have the district and the students. From 2007 to 2013, 12 for Life students graduated at a 78 percent rate, compared to 55 percent among demographically and academically similar Carroll County students. Some 40 percent of 12 for Life graduates went on to postsecondary education. Fifty graduates joined Southwire as regular employees. Southwire has added life skills workshops to the program, helping student learn how to file taxes and open bank accounts. School coordinators also provide optional mentoring, matching students with adults—most from within Southwire. As one observer noted, students wear their 12 for Life T-shirts like they're coming back from a rock concert.

Model 5: District-Wide Career Academies, Long Beach, California (*Wall-to-Wall Career Academies*)[15]

Arguably the highest quality career-focused high school reform strategy in the country, Linked Learning is an approach now deeply embedded in nine California districts and expanding elsewhere. A decade of support from the James Irvine Foundation to districts and a multitude of partners has provided technical assistance, capacity building, research, and resources to build out the Linked Learning approach.

Certified Linked Learning pathways are built around four elements: rigorous academics, real-world technical skills, work-based learning, and personalized support. California has passed legislation to expand Linked Learning, and more recently, appropriated $500 million for the CCPT, an initiative that draws in part on the Linked Learning approach.

Long Beach Unified School District (LBUSD) embraced Linked Learning as a districtwide structure for redesigning all its high schools, with almost all students across the district currently in career-themed pathways. LBUSD high schools are large, some with over four thousand students; prior to Linked Learning, they had been organized into smaller learning communities, but not with industry-connected themes. Today, high schools have pathways in architecture, construction, and engineering; media and communications; health science and medical technology; engineering and design; manufacturing and product development; and public service.

Because LBUSD committed to enabling students to experience the real-world applications of their classroom work, the district had to make substantial changes in the way it did business. Cal State–Long Beach established a Linked Learning teacher-training program and in-service workshops to support teachers in providing project-based, integrated academic and career-focused units of study. LBUSD also provided teacher externships in industries that enable teachers to design projects and assignments reflective of the demands of employers. And because of stable and trusted district leadership, and the close proximity of both Long Beach City College and Cal State–Long Beach, partnership agreements forged between these institutions mean that LBUSD graduate can matriculate into pathways aligned with their high school's Linked Learning theme; at City College, the first semester is free of charge.

MARRYING TWO MODELS

In our view, the two models that, if combined, would hold the most promise for achieving scale within comprehensive high schools are career academies and ECHSs. Career academies have come a long way since MDRC began its study in 1995. There are now several thousand academies operating all over the country, including nearly one thousand in California.

The National Academy Foundation (NAF), launched in 1985 by Sanford Weill, then CEO of American Express and later Citigroup, currently sponsors 565 academies across the country. These academies serve about eighty-two thousand students, two-thirds of whom are African American or Latino. National Academy Foundation academies operate in five career areas: finance, health care, preengineering, information technology, and hospitality and tourism. They have very high self-reported high school graduation and college-going rates. Over half of NAF graduates complete a four-year degree, and 90 percent report that NAF participation helped them in their career choice.[16]

Early college high schools are a more recent phenomenon, begun in 2002 by the Bill and Melinda Gates Foundation with grants to several organizations to expand existing schools or start new ones, and a grant to Jobs for the Future to provide technical assistance and coordination to the school developers. Thirteen years later there are approximately eighty thousand students in 280 early colleges; nearly three-fourths are students of color. The ECHS graduation rate is 90 percent, and the average ECHS student graduates high school with thirty-eight college credits. Roughly 30 percent graduate with an associate's degree or a postsecondary certificate.[17]

At its best, the academy model integrates rigorous academics with a sequence of technical courses, augmented with an aligned internship, in a particular career area. However, most academies have weak or nonexistent connections to postsecondary programs in the same field. They don't see building these relationships as part of their mission, for they are in the high school reform business, not the career preparation business.

Conversely, ECHSs came into being explicitly to blend high school and college, and they have definitively demonstrated that their acceleration model can help entire cohorts of low-income and minority kids seamlessly navigate the transition to college—and leave high school with a year or more of free college credit. While roughly one-third of early colleges have a STEM focus, there is relatively little focus in the ECHS model on careers, and little explicit effort to align high school and college technical courses into a career pathway for young people.

However, when the strengths of these two models are combined, as they are in the WakeMed example profiled previously and the growing network of P-TECH schools in New York, Chicago, and Connecticut, students have an opportunity to demonstrate that they are genuinely college- and career-ready. The early college movement has definitively demonstrated that the best predictor of college readiness is the successful completion of college courses, preferably taken on a college campus. We argue by analogy that the best predictor of career readiness is the successful completion of a workplace internship, something that is built into the WakeMed and P-TECH models.

GETTING TO SCALE: THE SWISS EXPERIENCE[18]

We have had the opportunity over the last several years to spend time visiting and studying vocational education systems in Australia, Denmark, Germany, the Netherlands, Norway, Singapore, Sweden, and Switzerland. While all of these systems have some admirable features from which the United States could learn, we believe the Swiss system has the most to teach us. For one thing, like the United States, it is a state-based system. Education is the responsibility of the cantons, not the national government—and Swiss cantons, like US states, are highly diverse. That said, there is a federal office that oversees vocational education and provides substantial leadership, quality control, and support.

Perhaps the most important feature of the Swiss vocational education and training (VET) system is that it is genuinely a mainstream system: 70 percent of Swiss youngsters enroll in vocational education programs at age sixteen. These typically last three or four years and combine learning at a workplace with continued academic study. When 70 percent—the largest percentage of any of the systems we visited—of a nation's young people are in vocational education, it becomes the norm, not the exception, so it is difficult to attach any sense of stigma.

Almost by definition the system is serving a broad range of students, and the range of occupations for which VET is the preferred preparation is equally broad. One of the great strengths of the Swiss system is that for those who start out in vocational education, there is not only a clear path leading to postsecondary vocational education—culminating in a network of Universities of Applied Sciences—but there are also crosswalks for those wanting to transfer over to the strictly academic pathway. Those wanting to leave the academic pathway and transfer to the vocational side, however, must first get a year's work experience, thereby signaling the value the Swiss attach to learning at the workplace.

If there is a single key to the success of the Swiss VET system, it is the deep engagement of employers and the leadership role played by the associations that represent them. Simply put, Swiss corporate leaders believe that their high-skill, high-wage economy can only be sustained by an early and continuing investment in the development of their future workforce. Swiss employer associations take the lead role in developing occupational standards for their industry sector, and work in partnership with educators in developing curriculum aligned with the requirements and expectations of the workplace.

They also participate in assessing the performance of students at the end of their apprenticeship in order to ensure that they meet national standards. Most important, they provide paid three- or four-year apprenticeship slots and assume the costs of providing training and coaching for their apprentices. It is hard to overstate just how different this is from the role that employers play in the American CTE system, where the norm for even the most engaged employers is participation on an advisory committee, some opportunities for job shadowing, and perhaps the provision of a few short-term, unpaid internships.

The informal conversations we had with students in vocational schools and a variety of work settings—banks, factory floors, a senior citizen residence, and many others—were as important as our conversations with employers. Almost everywhere we saw bright, engaged kids who were clear about what they were learning and why, and who radiated a sense of agency and self-confidence. The adults who surrounded them, especially their workplace supervisors and mentors, were full of praise for what their students had accomplished, and for what the students had contributed to the culture and climate of the workplace through their energy and openness to new learning.

We began our visits to Switzerland and other "dual system" countries with some skepticism about sixteen- and seventeen-year-olds in the workplace, but we have seen that under the right conditions work can be a powerful contributor to healthy youth development. We now understand what Swiss employers mean when they describe the system as being "win-win" for both the economy and young people.

One measure of that success is that the youth unemployment rate in Switzerland is the lowest in Europe, consistently between 3 and 7 percent. Another is that Swiss employers neither require nor receive any direct subsidy from the government for employing apprentices. Careful economic cost-benefit analyses have shown employers that over three years the contributions to bottom-line productivity by apprentices more than offset the investment in wages (approximately $700 a month, growing to $1,100 by year three) and associated training costs.

ADAPTING LESSONS FROM ABROAD

Americans are understandably skeptical about what can be learned from a country like Switzerland. It is small, wealthy, and looks relatively homogeneous. In the United States it would be a medium-size state, like Maryland. In reality it is quite diverse, with three different language groups and one-fourth of its population born outside of Switzerland. Its immigrants, however, are mostly internal to Europe, and it has nothing like our level of child poverty. Furthermore, it has had an apprenticeship system for many generations, and that system is deeply embedded in the country's social fabric and political culture. It would be foolhardy to pretend that one could simply pick up that system and transplant it in the United States.

That said, in our view it would be equally foolish to behave as if there is nothing we can learn from the Swiss VET system, and that the principles that undergird that system and the policies and practices that drive it cannot possibly be adapted in some form in our setting. As is probably apparent from some of our earlier references to the Pathways Network, the Network is at least in part organized around a set of ideas based on what we have seen in Switzerland and other high-performing vocational systems.

Of the many challenges we face in moving our secondary education system more in the direction of the Swiss system, let us focus on just two. The first concerns the quality of prior academic preparation young people would need in order to take advantage of the kind of rigorous career pathways we are advocating. One big advantage of the Swiss (and other European) education systems is that compulsory schooling ends at the end of "lower" secondary education, typically ninth grade.

This seems to have two big effects. It concentrates the attention of the system on ensuring that, to the extent possible, all young people get the academic underpinnings they will need during those years to make a successful transition to whatever comes next. And it says to young people who are bored with school that if they can hang on through ninth grade, there is an attractive option that will enable them to complete their high school education in a much more applied-learning mode, spending most of their time learning and working alongside adults in a workplace rather than only with age mates in classrooms. Switzerland's impressive math performance on the Program for International Student Assessment (PISA), taken when students are in ninth grade, suggests that these incentives work for both the system and the students.[19]

In the United States, the best evidence that offering young people the opportunity to get started on college and career early can strengthen the development of core academic skills comes from the ECHS data cited previously. They suggest that if students in the middle grades can see a way to accelerate their path through school and into the workplace, it might motivate them to get the academic foundation they need.

The challenge for the system is to deliver on the promise of the Common Core: to provide all kids at least through tenth grade with a solid floor of literacy, quantitative reasoning, and critical thinking skills. The jury is very much out on whether we have the capacity or the will to do this, but one constituency whose voice will be crucial is employers—which brings us to the second big challenge.

American employers and their associations typically do not play a significant role in education and workforce preparation. While they may participate on advisory committees for vocational schools and centers, they play virtually no role in the comprehensive high schools most students attend. However, many employers do have close working relationships with community colleges, often turning to them for customized training to upgrade the skills of incumbent workers. Rather than asking employers to get entangled with high schools, an alternative strategy is to bring employers and community college leaders together—first to set the standards and specifications for the career pathways, and then to map backward to connect the high schools.

We know it will not be possible to build a Swiss style "dual system" in the United States, in which high school students are spending three days a week at a workplace. But we do think it is possible to build a system in which over a three- or four-year period, spanning grades 11 to 13 or 14 and including summers, students get six months of workplace learning built into a career pathway program.

CAREER PATHWAYS AND ECONOMIC MOBILITY

Given the historically low status of vocational education in the United States—and especially the understandable skepticism of African American and Latino parents that anything labeled "vocational" can be a route into the middle class for their children—it is no wonder that advocates for the new CTE (ourselves included) emphasize that career pathways represent an alternative route *into* postsecondary education, not an alternative *to* college.

It should also be no surprise that for messaging reasons we lead with programs with a strong STEM foundation in fields such as health care and information technology, rather than the more traditional trades such as carpentry, automotive repair, and plumbing. The reality, of course, is that these jobs today also typically require a strong mathematical foundation and some computing skills, and pay a family-supporting wage.

If the new, improved CTE is to gain sufficient political momentum to become a significant engine of economic mobility, several things would have to happen. First, well-structured partnerships need to be built among high schools, postsecondary institutions, and employers. This would give parents and students visible evidence that career pathways that begin in high school can lead seamlessly into postsecondary education and employment. Second, exposure to myriad careers—and the education and training requirements for entering those careers—must begin early and become a much more systematic component of the middle school and high school experience.

The third issue that must be addressed is the question of which students participate in CTE. The challenge is embodied in the saying, "Vocational education is a wonderful thing—for other people's children." If CTE continues to be seen primarily for at-risk youth and for students who can't be expected to do serious academic work, it will never gain the resources and political support it needs to be fully effective. Most important, it will never gain the serious engagement of the employer community. Employers may be persuaded to participate out of a sense of corporate social responsibility, but unless and until CTE becomes a mainstream system, serving a very broad range of young people, employers will not see investing in CTE as a way of building their own future workforce.

Many years ago, sociologist William Julius Wilson argued that social programs directly focused on the poor were less likely to gain political traction than programs that were targeted especially to help the poor but were embedded within a more universal design (e.g., Medicare and Social Security).[20] The career pathways movement needs to be designed and marketed as a strategy to improve the economic prospects of a broad range of students, not just the poor.

Given the statistics cited earlier about the underemployment of young college and university graduates, the rising student debt burden, and the growing evidence about the returns to two-year technical degrees, middle-class parents are beginning to reexamine the notion that the only successful outcome of a high school education is enrollment in a four-year college.

As two educators with advanced degrees in the liberal arts, we certainly don't want to argue that the only purpose of postsecondary education is to prepare people for the workforce—more education is always a good thing. But take the evidence from *Academically Adrift*, a 2010 sociological study of the learning gains of a sample of students in a broad cross-section of four-year institutions: It appears that far too many students simply drift into college with no clear plan, get caught up in the pressures of peer culture and social life, and leave college with little evidence of growth in such foundational skills as analytic reasoning and writing, let alone with preparation for a career.[21] Only six students in ten who start a four-year college graduate within six years, and new evidence tells us that those with "some college" are no better off in the labor market than those with only a high school diploma.

Yes, a four-year degree, especially for low-income youth and students of color, remains a prize worth pursuing—and given the abysmally low attainment rates among those groups, we should be focused on increasing their access, retention, and completion at four-year institutions. But two-year degrees and one-year postsecondary certificates also pay off. And we must strengthen and expand the pathways leading to these options in order to launch more young people into careers that can, in turn, propel them into the middle class.

NOTES

1. Ronald Ferguson, Robert Schwartz, and William Symonds, *Pathways to Prosperity: Meeting the Challenge of Preparing Young Americans for the 21st Century* (Cambridge, MA: Harvard University Graduate School of Education, February 2011), http://dash.harvard.edu/bitstream/handle/1/4740480/Pathways_to_Prosperity_Feb2011-1.pdf?sequence=1.

2. Anthony P. Carnevale, Nicole Smith, and Jeff Strohl, *Recovery: Job Growth and Education Requirements through 2020* (Washington, DC: Georgetown University Center on Education and the Workforce, 2013).

3. Organization for Economic Cooperation and Development, *Learning for Jobs* (Paris: OECD).

4. For a progress report on the first two years of the Pathways Network, see *The Pathways to Prosperity Network: A State Progress Report, 2012–2014* (Boston, MA: Jobs for the Future, June 2014), http://www.jff.org/publications/pathways-prosperity-network-state-progress-report-2012-2014.

5. Anthony P. Carnevale, Stephen J. Rose, and Andrew R. Hanson, *Certificates: Gateway to Gainful Employment and College Degrees* (Washington, DC: Georgetown Center on Education and the Workforce, 2012), 4.

6. Grace Chen, "Community Colleges vs. State Schools: Which One Results in Higher Salaries?" Community College Review, http://www.communitycollegereview.com/articles/315.

7. Jaison R. Abel, Richard Deitz, and Yaquin Su, "Are Recent College Graduates Finding Good Jobs?" *Current Issues in Economics and Finance,* Federal Reserve Bank of New York 20, no. 1, 2014.

8. For a review of these studies, see Julian B. Isaacs, "International Comparisons of Economic Mobility," in Ron Haskins, Julia B. Isaacs, and Isabel V. Sawhill, *Getting Ahead or Losing Ground: Economic Mobility in America* (Washington, DC: Brookings Institution, 2008).

9. See *Investing in America's Future: A Blueprint for Transforming Career and Technical Education* (Washington, DC: US Department of Education, April 2012), https://www2.ed.gov/about/offices/list/ovae/pi/cte/transforming-career-technical-education.pdf.

10. James J. Kemple, *Career Academies: Long-Term Impacts on Labor Market Outcomes, Educational Attainment, and Transitions to Adulthood* (New York: MDRC, June 2008), http://www.mdrc.org/publication/career-academies-long-term-impacts-work-education-and-transitions-adulthood.

11. See http://portal.techhigh.us/Pages/default.aspx and *Boston Globe,* http://www.bostonglobe.com/metro/2014/06/11/obama-arrives-speak-worcester-technical-high-school-commencement/KXjgLx35Ggax7oANjZpWmO/story.html.

12. Adapted from "What is CART?" (see http://cart.org/what-is-cart/) and *A Model for Success: CART's Linked Learning Program Increases College Enrollment* (Clovis, CA: Center for Advanced Research and Technology, January 2011), http://irvine.org/images/stories/pdf/grantmaking/cart%20findings%20report%20final.pdf.

13. Adapted from Wake Early College, "Work-Linked Learning Creates Opportunities," http://ncnewschools.org/testimonials/profiles/work-linked-learning-creates-opportunities/. Also see school website: http://healthscienceec.wcpss.net.

14. Adapted from Jan Rivkin and Ryan Lee, "Southwire and 12 for Life: Scaling Up?" Harvard Business School Case 714-434, October 2013, http://www.hbs.edu/faculty/Pages/item.aspx?num=45785.

15. Adapted from Joel Knudson, "Meeting 17 Summary—College and Career Readiness for All: Linked Learning in Long Beach," The California Collaborative On District Reform, November 7–8, 2011, http://www.cacollaborative.org/sites/default/files/CCDR_Meeting_17_Summary_Final.pdf.

16. National Academy Foundation, "Statistics and Research, 2013–14," www.naf.org/statistics-and-research.

17. Michael Webb and Carol Gerwin, *Early College Expansion: Propelling Students to Success at a School Near You* (Boston: Jobs for the Future, 2014), 12, http://www.jff.org/sites/default/files/publications/materials/Early-College-Expansion-Ex-Summ_031414.pdf.

18. Nancy Hoffman and Robert Schwartz, "The Swiss Vocational Education System" (Washington, DC: National Center on Education and the Economy, 2014).

19. In 2012 Switzerland outperformed every European country except neighboring Lichtenstein on the PISA mathematics assessment.

20. William Julius Wilson, *The Truly Disadvantaged: The Inner City, the Underclass, and Public Policy* (Chicago: University of Chicago Press, 1987).

21. Richard Arum and Josipa Roska, *Academically Adrift: Limited Learning on College Campuses* (Chicago: University of Chicago Press, 2011).

Part III

THE EARLY YEARS

Chapter Eight

Starting at Five Is Too Late: Early Childhood Education and Upward Mobility

Elliot Regenstein, Bryce Marable, and Jelene Britten

If education is truly going to support upward mobility, it should start to do so at birth—because the first years of life are when a great education can make the biggest difference. Research is very clear that the time from when a child is born through age five is a critical period of brain development and provides the foundation for later learning. We also know that high-quality early learning can have a significant, long-term impact on children.

However, we don't yet have consensus on how best to scale those early learning experiences to reach high numbers of low-income children while maintaining quality. But because we know that low-income kids can't wait until kindergarten to start their education, it's time to take what we know about the learning and developmental needs of young low-income children and come up with policy solutions that meet those needs.

This chapter discusses how families and teachers can work together to help upward mobility get off to a great start in the years from birth through kindergarten entry. This work has no simple solutions or silver bullets, because it requires numerous connections that traditional education systems have not always fostered: between "academic" and "nonacademic" skills, between families and professionals, and—importantly—between early learning providers and the public schools. Best practices in the early years can put kids on a positive trajectory heading into kindergarten and, ideally, inform best practices in kindergarten and beyond.

PATHWAYS TO PROSPERITY BEGIN AT THE BEGINNING

Research shows that a language gap between low- and high-income children begins to open in the first year of life and can be measured when children are

159

as young as nine months old.[1] Early education can help close that gap, but only if it is high quality and fosters a language-rich environment and interactions.

Infants learn language from the environment around them and from the grownups in their lives, a fact that can lead to significant variation in how much language children pick up. A seminal Hart and Risley research study shows that children raised in a family of professionals hear eleven million words per year—compared to six million words per year in working-class families and three million words per year in families on welfare.[2]

Though the raw number of words to which a child is exposed matters, so too does the nature of that interaction. Research is also showing that the quality of the words and how they are used matters, not just the quantity.[3] In the early years, when the brain is still developing, responsive engagement with adults can actually have a long-term impact on the brain's architecture.[4] Similarly, stressful life experiences in childhood associated with living in poverty—including violence and lack of medical care, among other risk factors—can have an adverse effect on brain development, including the vital areas that enable a child to learn language.[5]

Because language acquisition is a dynamic process, getting off to a slow start impacts a child's ability to learn as he or she gets older.[6] If a child starts out behind, it can be hard to catch up; Hart and Risley found a connection between the number of words a child hears between birth and age three and academic success at ages nine and ten.[7] That draws a direct line between language development in the infant–toddler years and third-grade reading scores—and children who are behind in third grade are less likely to graduate from high school and are disproportionately in poverty.[8]

The bottom line: Children who enter kindergarten behind in school readiness tend to remain behind throughout their schooling.[9] But although low-income children are more likely to enter kindergarten less prepared than their peers, it doesn't have to be that way.

WHAT GREAT EARLY LEARNING LOOKS LIKE

A fundamental premise of all education-improvement efforts is that improving the quality of public education can influence long-term outcomes. That premise applies with even more force before the age of five. Quality early childhood programs can make a difference in helping low-income children reach kindergarten readiness and establish stronger academic trajectories. These programs can begin addressing the language gap even in the first few months of life, if they are properly designed and engage children for a sufficient duration.[10]

The best early learning programs—like the best K–12 schools—depend on effective teachers having the skills, knowledge, competencies, and supports to utilize well-designed standards and assessments to promote learning and development. However, developmentally appropriate best practices used in developing early language and literacy look a lot different than most K–12 teaching, and these practices are most effective when they engage adults in children's lives.

Early Learning Blurs Lines between Academic and Nonacademic Skills

Whereas teachers may talk about "academic" and "nonacademic" skills with regard to older children, in early learning the best programs and teachers focus on integrating both types of skills. Early learning programs recognize that children can only learn "academic" skills, such as reading, math, and science, if they have the social and emotional skills to thrive in the classroom. For many children, emotional and behavioral difficulties make it difficult to succeed in school. In a national survey of kindergarten teachers, the respondents reported that 16 percent of children entering kindergarten had a difficult transition and exhibited serious problems, such as difficulty following directions, difficulty working independently, difficulty working as part of a group, and problems with social skills.

The results of this study are consistent with the findings of existing research. Child Trends's analysis of the Early Childhood Longitudinal Survey Kindergarten Cohort identified that four out of five children entering kindergarten demonstrate developmentally appropriate learning-related social skills. The analysis also found that social–emotional skills vary depending on income levels: 71 percent of low-income children exhibited prosocial behaviors, compared with 84 percent of children from higher-income families.[11]

In the adult world, it is clear that academic skills alone do not fully explain a person's success. The same is true in all aspects of education, starting with early learning. There is evidence that low-income children are more likely to struggle in the nonacademic areas, a fact that can contribute to ongoing inequality. When early learning programs succeed at helping children develop academic and nonacademic skills, they do so using the same infrastructure that undergirds K–12 education: standards, curricula, and assessments that support great teaching. But how the best early learning programs strive to implement those standards, curricula, and assessments can look a lot different than what happens in many schools—and there is no question that, as in K–12, the impact of the teacher and supportive leadership is essential to the success of a classroom.

Great Teaching in Early Learning

As in K–12 education, superlative early learning requires superlative teachers. An effective teacher should possess knowledge on the principles of early childhood development and have the skills to engage with both children and parents in a caring and respectful manner.[12] Teachers who are successful in promoting academic gains for children in early learning settings are responsive to a child's individual needs and create language-rich learning environments.[13]

In quality early childhood programs, learning should be child-initiated. Practices that embody quality instruction in early learning environments include planned activities based on curriculum goals; individualized activities tailored to each child's unique developmental status; individual, small-group, and large-group activities; supportive classroom environments and learning materials; engaging with families to promote learning at home; developing and maintaining secure attachments between children and teachers; and using classroom data to determine children's progress toward curriculum goals.[14]

In all birth-to-five programs, addressing the language gap requires an interactive environment and proactive, meaningful engagement with children. This will look different across ages, and practitioners' approaches may vary with special populations. With the youngest children, a process called *joint attention* occurs when caregivers and infants focus on the same object or event and the adults put into words what the infant is observing or hearing.[15]

In later years, one common practice (used in Head Start) is for teachers to explain uncommon words before starting to read a book and flag the word again during and after the book.[16] Throughout these years, it is essential for adults to conduct conversations with children in which they maintain eye contact and respond thoughtfully to what a child has said; this is a key to language development.[17]

Language acquisition for dual language learners is complex and rich, as they may experience multiple languages and cultures in varying settings. Research and best practice indicate that children should be encouraged to retain and develop their home language as they learn English.[18] For these learners, early education programs must support and respect the child's home language and culture, and teachers should demonstrate an understanding of the child's family culture—and, whenever possible, speak the child's language and use linguistically and culturally appropriate assessments in both languages.[19]

There are important systemic choices that affect teachers' ability to impact children. The research base on small class sizes and low teacher/child ratios is particularly strong in the birth-to-five years group,[20] which is important for individualizing instruction. One benefit of smaller class sizes is the ability to conduct more effective assessments, because the teacher primarily administers the assessments in early learning. Unfortunately, systems of ongoing professional development in early learning are often inadequate,[21] which may also sound familiar to policymakers and practitioners focused on K–12.

SIDEBAR: AN EXAMPLE OF GREAT TEACHING

Jackie Green, who teaches infants and toddlers at Educare Seattle, applies many of the elements of great teaching to her daily interactions with young children. She creates a language-rich environment, even with infants, by verbalizing her actions and responding to babies' gestures and babbling as if they were in a conversation. She also makes sure to hold eye contact with the infants during their interactions.

Her effective teaching strategies extend beyond the individual relationships she develops with the infants and toddlers, as she aims to create a classroom environment that supports learning and social–emotional growth. She stocks her classroom with objects, like blocks and geometric shapes, with which children can explore and play. In these instances of child-directed learning, she lets the child decide what aspects of the classroom to explore and uses their interests to engage with them.

For example, a child may decide to play with a ball and tube. After seeing the child play by rolling the ball down the tube, she may take turns with the child in exploring different ways to play with those two objects. This activity also serves the purpose of promoting social–emotional growth, because the child explores in a safe environment and learns how to take turns.

Green balances child-directed learning with special, teacher-directed classroom activities. One such activity involves the children tasting the kiwi fruit. Extending the activity over the course of two days, Green has the children touch and play with kiwi on the first day and then try the kiwi on day two. On the day the children taste the kiwi, Green creates a visual chart that tracks whether the children like or dislike how the new fruit tastes. Over the course of the entire activity, she continues to nurture vocabulary development by offering new words that children can use to describe their experiences.

Through using all of these teaching approaches, Green says she hopes to "plant the seeds for future learning" by creating a solid foundation in a child's early years.[22]

Standards and Assessment

Learning standards are essential for scaling up high-quality early learning programs. All states now have learning standards for preschoolers, and almost all have them for infants and toddlers.[23] As in K–12, individual programs use those learning standards to choose a curriculum and, ideally, as the basis of formative assessments. When early learning standards cover the full range of developmental domains—both academic and nonacademic—early learning programs provide the kind of comprehensive developmental experience children need to be truly ready for kindergarten.

All states that have early learning and development standards have standards that cut across multiple domains. Even though different states give them somewhat different names, they generally include titles like *reading, language, math, science, social skills, behavioral control, motivation,* and *problem solving.* States have sought to put these into developmentally appropriate progressions, beginning at birth, and then align them with their state K–12 standards.[24]

Although great progress has been made in early learning standards, there is still a long way to go. States have claimed that their standards across early learning and K–12 are aligned,[25] but alignment is not universal—and where there is alignment, it may be primarily in the academic domains. Meanwhile, curriculum choices at the K–12 level are difficult enough in the Common Core subjects,[26] even before considering how to address multiple domains of learning.

As for choosing curriculum in early learning, research on specific curricula is still limited, particularly for dual language learners and children with disabilities. The creators of the major evidence-based early learning curricula—including the widely used *Creative Curriculum* and *HighScope*—have made efforts to align to Common Core standards. However, policies that allow for great local flexibility in developing and choosing curricula[27] make the early learning curriculum landscape perhaps even more varied than that of K–12.

The developmental state of early learning child assessment also lags significantly behind K–12. Leading researchers have found that it is developmentally inappropriate to use assessments on children under age eight for accountability purposes.[28] In early learning, teachers generally administer assessments, which are used to help inform instruction for children.[29]

A major trend in early learning assessment is kindergarten-entry assessments, which are administered individually by kindergarten teachers using a standardized rubric. These assessments can inform instruction, and they can also help provide a picture of how children are doing at kindergarten entry.[30] About half of all states have a statewide policy requiring kindergarten assessment.[31] The best practice in kindergarten-entry assessment is to assess the full range of developmental domains;[32] while eleven states implement assessments that address the full range of domains covered in their learning standards, others use assessments focused only on reading or a more limited set of domains.[33]

SIDEBAR: A GREAT PRESCHOOL AT WORK

John Kocher, a preschool teacher at Educare Milwaukee, finds ways to make learning playful for his three-year-old students, such as incorporating music and movement into lesson plans. "Music is fun," Kocher says. "If you can make learning concepts fun, it can help with children's memory and retention."

Kocher and his fellow teachers use a singing game called "Shape Shop." They give each child in a group a shape, such as a circle, heart, or diamond, made from felt. Then teachers and children sing the "Shape Shop" song, calling out a different child's name with each verse. When a child hears his name in the song, he stands up and places his shape on a felt board. The children practice listening skills, taking turns, and shape recognition, all while singing.

Modeling positive relationships and behaviors in the classroom is critical to helping young children develop strong social–emotional skills. For instance, if one child takes a toy from another, Kocher will intervene and ask each child to consider the feelings of the other. He asks the child who grabbed the toy how she would feel if someone grabbed her toy. And he asks the child who originally had the toy if she would give it to the other child when she is finished. Kocher helps the children find the words to express their feelings and come to an agreement about the toy. And, before long, he'll see one child giving the toy to the other. "It's important to show them how to look at the situation from their friend's perspective," Kocher says. "That's not always easy for young children."

Kocher and other teachers at Educare Milwaukee are also trained in the Wisconsin Pyramid Model for Social and Emotional Competence. The teachers learn strategies on how to help children manage emotions and maintain positive relationships with their peers and teachers.

Engaging parents in the classroom is also key to helping young children succeed. Teachers at Educare Milwaukee have take-home activity folders in the classrooms for parents. The activities are linked to classroom lesson plans and are projects parents can easily do at home with their child. "The activities help the parent build a relationship with the child and give the child extra education at home," Kocher says.

Through these and other intentional teaching methods, Kocher says he "gives children and families the tools to help them succeed in the future."[34]

Family Engagement in Early Learning Programs

The best early learning programs partner actively with families to facilitate both child and parent success. Many low-income parents[35] lack access to information about child development, which means that early learning programs often focus on partnering with families about how they can be most effective in supporting their children. Early learning providers can take important steps to engage families—and, indeed, federal and state program requirements often require them to do so.

The best early learning teachers think of parents as essential partners in supporting child development. Teachers should regularly solicit information from parents about their children and their home experience and invite parents to spend time in the classroom.[36] Staff should focus on building trust with parents through interactions that are respectful of the family's background and culture and, in particular, are sensitive to the dynamics of the community the school serves.[37] This includes not only asking parents about the child but sharing data about the child—and then working with parents to develop effective strategies for meeting a child's needs.[38]

This kind of ongoing engagement takes time and requires that center-based programs and schools have sufficient staffing to allow for regular attention to engaging with families.[39] Parental advisory councils and support groups provide time for leadership development and networking among parents, which gives parents a stronger sense of connectedness.[40]

Early learning providers can also help train parents to advocate for their children. Parents can be advocates at home, in their children's schools, and in their communities.[41] Parents who are involved in such advocacy not only experience personal growth but also can serve as important role models for their children.[42] The benefits of this type of family engagement are far reaching, and schools that provide opportunities for leadership and input from families are better able to meet the needs of their students.[43]

However, low-income families often face daily pressures and economic barriers that can limit their time, energy, and access to critical information and connections that support their engagement in their child's school.[44] And schools and districts, too, often lack the staff, resources, and strategies to effectively engage parents. Early learning can be an opportunity for preparing parents to engage and advocate for their children throughout their children's K–12 schooling and a model for how schools can effectively engage parents.[45]

Having early learning programs prepare parents to advocate on behalf of their children takes on particular relevance in communities that have school options or choice. Parents of all socioeconomic backgrounds seek to utilize school choice, but research shows that less-educated parents may be more likely to identify lack of knowledge about the choice process as a barrier to getting their children to the right school.[46] One support that early learning programs can provide is helping parents understand and navigate their choice options. For example, Educare Schools initiate transition planning meetings with parents and a multidisciplinary team of staff at least six months before the child moves on to a new school.[47]

Two-generation strategies that offer supports for children and their parents are emerging and have shown positive results for entire families.[48] Beyond sharing knowledge, family engagement can help parents connect to health and nutrition services, work and housing supports, and mental health services—all of which can help improve children's home environments.[49]

Strategies such as providing job training or linking families to additional income supports that increase family income during the early childhood years can improve children's academic success in both the short and long term.[50] Home-visiting programs that include case management support connecting parents to community-based resources, including mental health treatment, can improve the child's socioemotional and cognitive development[51] and reduce maternal stress.[52] Center-based early childhood programs that are combined with job training programs have improved children's attendance and socioemotional health, while also increasing maternal well-being.[53]

SIDEBAR: HOW CENTERS ENGAGE FAMILIES

Supporting the parent–child relationship is central to the family engagement and support philosophy at Educare Schools across the country. "My role is to help parents understand their child and what they need to do to continue to help their child grow," says Nena Cunningham, a family services coordinator at Educare Central Maine. Cunningham begins building a strong relationship with parents by coordinating with classroom teachers to share information about how their children are doing at school.

For example, Cunningham and classroom teachers noticed that a two-year-old boy at the school struggled with articulation in his speech development. At first, his mother declined to have her son evaluated. But as the staff continued to share their observations with her, she finally acknowledged that she had trouble understanding what he said and that she wanted help. "She really had to feel comfortable with us to admit that, and she had to want to make that decision on her own," Cunningham says. Cunningham set up an evaluation for the boy, who is now receiving speech therapy for articulation. The mother later sent an email to classroom teachers thanking them for looking out for her son and being a second family.

Cunningham is confident that by giving parents tools to ensure their children's healthy development and advocate for their children's education, parents will carry those skills with them beyond Educare. She sees this happen when parents whose children attended Educare and are now in elementary school come back to visit. They update her on their children's development and ask for advice on how to address any challenges their children are facing at school.

"You can't build a house without a solid foundation," Cunningham says. "That's what our program prides itself on: helping build that base so that families have the tools they need to be successful later on in whatever they do."[54]

THE PROGRAMS SERVING EARLY LEARNERS

Scientific research makes clear that the first five years of life are incredibly important to brain development and long-term outcomes and that the interactions children have with adults in those five years have an enormous impact on their development—even permanently influencing the architecture of their brains. Though these developmental concepts are widely accepted, what is much more actively debated is whether the large-scale programs currently serving young children are having a positive impact. There are, in fact, numerous and varied programs serving young children, each of which is designed and funded to accomplish different goals. The research on these programs largely reflects their different purposes.

Major Early Childhood Education Funding Supports

Home Visiting

Because so much of children's language development occurs in the home, a major support for early literacy is a parent-coaching program known as home visiting. In home visiting, trained professionals work with parents in the home environment to provide information on child development and parenting practices, which include child language development.[55] Though there are multiple program models and curricula for home visiting, there are commonalities in the different programs' approaches.

Models generally start with a coach and parents setting goals together, covering a range of outcomes. From then on, the home visitor sets a regular schedule of visits with the family to help build parental understanding of key child development concepts and to enhance parent–child connections. Home visitors also serve as key referral points, helping parents find and connect with community-based resources of which they may not have been aware.[56] These programs can help parents improve their skills and can be particularly useful for low-income parents, who face obstacles that may impact their ability to support their children's language development during these critical years.[57]

SIDEBAR: THE TWO-GENERATION IMPACT OF HOME VISITING

A home visitor's job—providing support services in the homes of families—requires successful family engagement. Some home visitors go above and beyond in order to connect with and engage parents and their children. In addition to offering information on child development topics and positive parenting strategies, home visitors can cultivate strong connections with families by addressing their unique needs. Home visitors who make intentional efforts to tailor curricula to families' circumstances have been more successful at creating lasting relationships with the parents and children.[58]

A Nurse Family Partnership home visitor working in Dallas shows how a flexible approach to home visiting and family engagement can produce results for both the children and parents. She responded to the family's specific needs by accompanying the parents to get health insurance, working to find stable transportation and employment, and even meeting at a different location that was more convenient on certain days. All of these extra efforts paid off. The parents, now graduated from the program, have found jobs and are making plans to get college degrees, while the child is enrolled in child care.[59] By providing these concrete supports along with the standard curriculum, home visitors can develop better relationships with the families, increasing the likelihood that the family will remain enrolled in the program and receive its full benefit.

Early Head Start (Birth through Age 3)

For children who receive center-based care, Early Head Start—which serves children in poverty under the age of three—is a model that has shown an impact on language development. Compared to children who had not participated in the program, Early Head Start children scored higher in an assessment of cognitive development and were less likely to fall in the "at-risk" range for developmental functioning and for language development. Early Head Start produced more positive impacts for minority children and helped to reduce the gap in developmental outcomes.

The impact of Early Head Start is enhanced through longer involvement in the program, as children of parents who enrolled in the program while pregnant showed better outcomes. Further, parents of children in Early Head Start programs are more likely to enroll their children in other child care programs, such as Head Start or state pre-K.[60]

Head Start and State Pre-K (Ages Three through Five)

Head Start and state-funded pre-K serve low-income children who are three and four years old:

- According to 2013 data, Head Start enrolls 529,774 four-year-olds and 390,814 three-year-olds[61]—about 38.7 percent and 3.5 percent of the eligible populations, respectively. Head Start eligibility is restricted to children who are in poverty or have other special needs, but state pre-K programs have a wide range of eligibility requirements. Head Start does not require bachelor-certified teachers, although 66 percent of teachers currently have a bachelor's degree.[62] Head Start costs vary substantially from site to site, but overall the program in 2013 spent $7,573,095,000 to fund 903,679 enrollment slots for children, an average of $8,380 per child.[63]
- Nationally, 1,100,000 four-year-olds and 238,737 three-year-olds are served by state pre-K programs. The sizes of state programs vary considerably, with the largest program for four-year-olds in Florida (serving 78 percent of children) and the largest program for three-year-olds in Vermont (serving 80 percent of children). Ten states have no state pre-K program at all, and fourteen states that serve four-year-olds do not serve any three-year-olds.[64] The quality of state pre-K varies considerably from state to state.[65] State-funded preschool is delivered in both school- and community-based settings.[66]

While some local school districts fund preschool locally, federal and state accountability systems may actually discourage them from doing so. These systems judge district and school performance on test results in third grade and up.[67] Districts seeking immediate improvement on these systems frequently focus their energy on short-term strategies in the tested years rather than on longer-term strategies like early learning.[68] Given that the average superintendent lasts less than four years on the job,[69] they may make the reasonable calculation that an investment in early learning simply will not help them demonstrate improved performance during their likely tenure; the children born at the beginning of their superintendency will not take accountability tests for more than eight years, and even the four-year-olds are five years away from taking standardized tests.[70]

The problem is exacerbated further in communities with high mobility rates, where early learners have a good chance of moving out of the district before third grade.[71] As long as these incentives are in place, it is unlikely that districts will make early learning a focus of discretionary spending (including Title I federal funds and local property tax dollars).

Child Care

Although Head Start and state pre-K intentionally focus on education, many parents of children younger than school age rely heavily on subsidized child care as a work support—including for children enrolled in Head Start and pre-K, which frequently do not provide custodial care for the duration of parental work days.[72] The federal government supports child care through the recently reauthorized Child Care and Development Block Grant, which requires that states add their own funding; in total, the program serves roughly a million children from birth to age six nationwide.[73] Child care subsidies are generally provided on a sliding scale, with parent copays increasing at higher income levels.[74] Child care can be extremely expensive, and in many states is more expensive than tuition at public universities.[75]

Although many child care providers seek to provide educational content, states generally do not fund child care at a level that allows providers to retain a high-quality workforce and provide standards-based education.[76] According to a study of child care centers, those programs that paid wages above the median wage were able to hire a workforce where 51 percent of the employees had a bachelor's degree, while centers paying below the median wage hired a staff with less educational background—only 27 percent had a bachelor's degree.[77]

The Impact of Early Education

It is generally acknowledged that high-quality early learning can have a meaningful long-term impact. The work of Nobel Prize–winning economist James Heckman has focused on the long-term benefits to society that early learning can provide, based in significant part on the landmark Perry Preschool study.[78] Although more recent studies, by definition, have not produced results spanning a similar duration, evaluations of Educare schools (a high-quality model focused on at-risk children) have shown a significant impact on kindergarten readiness.[79]

There are also positive research results from programs of a larger scale. Early Head Start has shown positive impacts in social and emotional development, parental engagement, and language development; the program has helped reduce the development gap for minority children, and greater dosage of the program increases its impact.[80] Head Start has shown positive impacts on kindergarten readiness[81] and long-term outcomes,[82] although famously its most recent impact study did not show an increase in third-grade test scores.[83] Evidence-based home visiting has shown a positive impact for participating families.[84] Also, increasingly, a large body of evidence positions providing early learning experiences as an essential strategy for mitigating the effects of poverty on children's health.[85] Participation in high-quality early education programs has been linked to a variety of short-term and long-term health benefits, including improved physical, oral, and behavioral health in adulthood.[86]

As noted, state preschool programs vary in quality, but some of the better ones have exhibited promising research results. The Early Childhood Longitudinal Study finds that children from low-income families who attend preschool show persistent gains.[87] New Jersey's well-regarded Abbott preschool program showed an impact on its graduates in elementary school language arts and literacy and math.[88] Oklahoma's state pre-K program has shown an impact on vocabulary scores and print awareness, with low-income children particularly benefiting from preschool attendance.[89]

Researchers have differed on the methodologies used in these studies. The regression discontinuity design used to analyze preschool programs in New Jersey and Oklahoma has been attacked for not being a randomized design and for not appropriately accounting for attrition, which some argue produces bias in results and overestimates effects.[90] And the methodology of the Head Start Impact Study that showed no benefits in third grade has been criticized for not adequately accounting for the number of children in the control group who may have actually gotten the treatment.[91]

A major challenge in the field is that while both supporters and critics of early learning investment agree that long-term outcomes are relevant to the impact of early learning, existing data systems are generally inadequate to determine exactly what happens to children between when they leave early learning programs and when they take accountability tests in later years. And even though advocates and detractors will both point to accountability test scores to make a point,[92] early learning supporters point to research—including Dr. Heckman's—showing impacts beyond test scores.[93]

There is still a great deal that is unknown about which children stand to benefit the most from which programs, allowing for increased efficiency in early learning investment; there is also a great deal that isn't yet known about early learning participants' subsequent learning experiences between kindergarten entry and third grade,[94] making it difficult to isolate the impacts of early learning. These questions ultimately need better answers. For the moment, though, what is clear is that the achievement gap begins opening long before kindergarten, that high-quality early learning can make a positive difference for low-income children, and that early learning done cheaply does not make the same kind of positive impact.

Strengthening the Impact of Early Learning

Fundamentally, the most critical difference between early learning and K–12 is that children have an obligation to attend K–12 schools and those schools are obligated to enroll them—neither of which is true in early learning. All early learning programs are voluntary, and the vast majority are not designed to be universal. Both K–12 and early learning schools face difficult choices about how to provide a high-quality education with limited resources, but early learning faces the additional challenge of trying to expand access.

This is one of the major reasons that debates about the early learning research base take on such a sharp edge. In K–12, research about effectiveness doesn't seriously threaten the underlying idea that children are entitled to a public education, so the whole reform conversation is about how good that education is going to be. In early learning, debates over research tend to be about whether children will have access to any early learning at all. But even analysts seen as critical of early learning generally concede that high-quality early learning can have a positive impact for the most at-risk children.[95]

Therefore, it is important to frame the early learning research debates correctly. The issue is not whether the early years matter (they do) or whether program quality can affect long-term outcomes (it can). Rather, the issues are whether government can deliver high quality at scale and which children should be the beneficiaries of government spending.

The research on early learning may reflect the reality that we know what works but that governments sometimes fund programs at a level of quality lower than what we know works. Existing programs have had some positive impacts on children, but they can do more. The Head Start of today is a better program than the Head Start of a decade ago studied in the Impact Study, but it will be better still if ongoing efforts to improve quality are successful. In state pre-K programs, pressure to increase enrollment can mean that new dollars are used for expansion at the expense of quality improvement, which can reduce the impact on the children who need help the most. Sound design and execution of early learning programs takes resources, and too many scaled programs have simply not been adequately funded to produce results for young children.[96]

Take teacher quality, which is widely accepted as a central part of achieving better long-term outcomes. In K–12, there may be a vigorous debate about the quality of teacher-preparation programs,[97] but there is no serious suggestion that someone without a bachelor's degree of some kind could conduct the work of K–12 teaching. By contrast, some of the largest early learning programs in the country—including Head Start and state pre-K programs in California and Florida—do not require bachelor's degrees for all teachers,[98] although many teachers in those programs have bachelor's degrees anyway (including 66 percent in Head Start[99]). But even for teachers with bachelor's degrees, salaries in early learning lag well behind K–12 salaries.[100] This means that the best teaching prospects are unlikely to enter the field and are unlikely to remain in it if they do; financially, they would be much better off teaching older children.

Skeptics of the early learning research base are often justified in accusing elected officials of bait and switch: politicians use impressive research results to justify early learning investment and then fund programs that look nothing like those that produced the impressive research results. These skeptics also correctly point out that universal preschool is not actually a strategy for closing the achievement gap.[101]

Universal preschool has benefits that these skeptics may undersell,[102] and given emerging research on child development, it may be time to revisit the societal compact that calls for public education to begin with kindergarten. But at this point, one of the best strategies for states and communities focused on closing the achievement gap—or preventing it before it occurs—is to provide high-quality early learning to the children with the highest needs, starting at birth and with sufficient quality and dosage to make a difference.

PROVIDING CONTINUITY FOR YOUNG CHILDREN

If education begins before the age of five, there must be an intentional approach to connecting prekindergarten education with the education children receive in kindergarten and beyond. Transitions can be tough on young children and their families—but though early learning practitioners frequently seek to make a child's transitional experience as seamless as possible, federal and state policies can make it difficult to give children the continuity they need in the first five years.

Given the fractured nature of early childhood funding and the fact that all children will at some point transition into K–12 schools, the ability to manage transitions for young children is critical. Entry into kindergarten presents its own set of challenges, but there are best practices schools and early learning providers can use to increase the likelihood of children succeeding in their kindergarten year.

Continuity within Early Learning

Research shows that continuity of care benefits both children and parents. It benefits children because it gives them more time to form trusting relationships with adult teachers and staff, which is critical to their early development.[103] It benefits parents by providing them with a steady point of contact who understands their child's needs.[104] Unfortunately, due to economic, job, and housing instability, families in low-income communities face complex challenges and also are often mobile,[105] which means that children may experience multiple environments in their early years.

Early education funding alone can't reduce child mobility, but unfortunately, policies governing early learning programs often exacerbate the problem by increasing the number of transitions children encounter before kindergarten entry.

- Although subsidized child care funding is generally insufficient to fund standards-based early education, many providers of standards-based early education rely on child care funds to keep children enrolled, because pre-K and Head Start funding on its own is insufficient to provide the full-workday coverage that parents need. But state policies regarding eligibility for subsidized child care often require that parents whose incomes increase lose access to the subsidy, which may mean that they can no longer afford child care.[106] Parents whose incomes fluctuate may find themselves in and out of eligibility, making it difficult to provide consistent early care and education services for their children. Setting policies that allow for continuous eligibility through income fluctuations would create greater stability for parents and children.
- For low-income children, two years of preschool (at ages three and four) generally leads to better results than just one year.[107] But fourteen states with preschool for four-year-olds do not fund preschool for three-year-olds.[108] Not only does this mean that low-income children will have less access to early learning services, but it also likely means that they will be in different settings as three-year-olds and four-year-olds—adding at least one significant transition to their early education.

Even children who remain in the same program may have trouble establishing trusting relationships when staff turnover is high. Because of a variety of factors—low wages in the early childhood workforce, lack of professional supports, negative school climate, and teacher stress[109]—staff turnover in many programs is indeed quite substantial. The turnover rate for child care staff is 29.5 percent per year, much higher than the 9.8 percent rate of turnover for elementary school teachers.[110]

Where possible, early learning programs provide stable environments with consistent relationships, including practices like looping, where children have the same preschool teacher as three-year-olds and four-year-olds (a practice that can also be used for children from birth through age three).[111] But funding structures can make that difficult and can lead to children having to change settings many times before they enter kindergarten.

Best Practices for Kindergarten Transition

Managing a successful transition to kindergarten requires cooperation from lots of sources. District leaders, school leaders,[112] teachers, parents, and partners in the community can all contribute toward helping children make a smooth adjustment to kindergarten.

District-level leaders can support school-level personnel by ensuring that the district has a clear and shared definition of kindergarten readiness. State learning standards that actually align between early learning and kindergarten help but are not enough on their own; local leaders need to make sure that there is a definition of kindergarten readiness that is clearly understood by parents, principals, teachers, and early learning providers other than the school district. To that end, the definition should be developed with all of those stakeholders so that they all feel ownership of it.

With that framework in place, school-level leaders and teachers in elementary schools can ensure that they are reaching out to early learning providers, and the leaders and teachers in early learning settings can reach out to their school colleagues. This can be challenging, because early learning providers typically do not use school district attendance boundaries—meaning that a receiving school may be bringing in children from dozens of places and an early learning program may be sending children to multiple schools. In these situations a community-level strategy may be more successful, particularly one focused on developing a shared communitywide definition of kindergarten readiness that all early learning and K–12 schools can work from.

A real challenge in these conversations is the difference in qualifications between early learning teachers and leaders and their K–12 counterparts. Frequently the K–12 leaders have much more extensive academic qualifications; some early learning teachers and leaders are sensitive about the disparity, and some K–12 leaders have a hard time taking seriously the work of less-qualified early learning teachers. The right mindset is needed in both camps for the collaborative work of managing transition to be successful, and there are numerous examples of successful partnerships between early learning and K–12 that can inform efforts in communities that have struggled to build ties.

Despite the many potential obstacles, there is a lot schools can do to work with early learning providers to help get kids ready for their new environment and new expectations. Planning for the transition should start months before kindergarten entry and should engage parents.[113] Aligned professional development and professional learning communities for early learning and early elementary staff in the same districts, when possible, supports alignment of standards and curricula and can help provide aligned experiences for children and families across this transition. Data sharing across early learning and early elementary informs planning for instruction.

Families, too, should be provided with opportunities to engage with educators from both the early learning setting and the school. Schools can engage in "bridging activities" that bolster the connections between home and school environments, which requires both intentional outreach from schools and parental involvement.[114] Bridging activities can include parents attending the new school during the first days or weeks of class or teachers making home visits to the family.[115] Some schools offer specialized programs for families and children during the summer before the kindergarten transition.

These programs, two to three weeks in duration, provide time for children to meet their new teachers, make new friends, and learn about kindergarten routines and allow parents to learn more about kindergarten and ways they can be involved to promote their children's learning.[116] Studies analyzing the impact of transition practices show that these activities can have a positive impact on student outcomes and that the effect is greater for children from low- or middle-socioeconomic backgrounds.[117]

Community leaders outside of schools can help facilitate connections among schools, parents, and early learning providers by hosting events and support groups. Not only can these help connect parents to education professionals, but these can also help parents connect with each other—and those connections can provide parents with more confidence in their dealings with schools. For example, community organizations have hosted panel discussions on kindergarten registration that create an opportunity for parents to ask questions, voice concerns, and learn about school processes.[118] And it can reinforce to school officials the importance of partnering with communities they serve as well as engaging in transition activities.

In some cities, charter schools provide an opportunity to reduce the number of transitions for children. Washington, DC, has been at the vanguard of this movement, which is not surprising: as a "state," the District of Columbia ranks second behind Arizona for having the highest percentage of students enrolled in charter schools[119] and ranks ahead of all states for the percentage of its students enrolled in preschool (both three-year-olds and four-year-olds).[120] Unlike in some other jurisdictions, charter schools in the District of Columbia can enroll three- and four-year-olds and receive full funding for them. This allows charter schools to add three- and four-year-olds to their program, which many of them have done.[121] It has also led to successful charter schools focused on early learning, most notably the schools administered by the AppleTree Institute.[122]

SIDEBAR: AN EXAMPLE OF SUCCESSFUL TRANSITION

Teachers at Earl Boyles Elementary in Portland, Oregon, facilitate successful transitions through the Kindergarten Counts Early Kindergarten Transition Program, a two-week summer class for children and families. Children with an increased risk of struggling during the transition to kindergarten participate in daily half-day classes, and parents join five of those classes. During the two-week session, teachers like Andreina Velasco lead group activities that serve the joint purposes of helping children become familiar with the kindergarten environment and teaching parents ways to support their children in the new school year. In one group activity, Velasco, children, and parents join to form a human knot and then work together to untie themselves. After completing the human knot activity, Velasco then talks with the children and parents about what they learned.[123] These fun group activities ease children's anxiety around the new school year by creating a space for them to develop friendships with their future classmates.[124]

Both children and parents benefit from participating in the program. Children exhibit growth at home and in the classroom: parents report that their children are better behaved, and teachers describe how these students become leaders for their classmates. Parents are better able to help their children because they gain knowledge on child development and learn strategies they can use to support their children throughout the kindergarten school year and beyond.[125]

KEY PUBLIC POLICIES SUPPORTING BEST-PRACTICE INSTRUCTION AND FAMILY ENGAGEMENT

The first five years are a critical period for child development and are potentially a launching point for upward mobility. But to realize that potential, policymakers must take a number of important steps.

- *Keep family needs front and center in policymaking.* Policymakers have significant influence on how local educators engage with families. Do state education accountability policies require educators to engage families? Do state child care funding policies allow families to remain in programs consistently and allow providers to combine child care funds with other sources to meet child educational needs, while supporting the low-income workforce? Are early learning programs designed and funded to serve as gateways for parents to supports they may need—like health care and job supports—that help create a better home environment for children?
- *Act before kids turn three.* There's no question that the period before a child turns three—including pregnancy—is an incredibly important time developmentally. Prenatal health supports, home visiting, and quality center-based education can all play a role in supporting low-income parents as they nurture their children through these critical years.
- *Keep acting when kids turn three.* Many low-income children would benefit from two years of preschool, but a lot of states fund only one. Although universal preschool for four-year-olds can be a good thing developmentally (and politically), it's not actually a long-term strategy for closing the achievement gap; that comes from investing earlier in the kids who need it most—which includes three-year-olds, forgotten in many states.
- *Put in place a framework for quality.* In early learning, as in K–12, standards, assessments, and accountability play an important role in shaping local practice and decision making. And as in K–12, doing those things well at the state level doesn't guarantee success at the local level—but it can go a long way toward supporting local educators. States already have in place standards and accountability policies, and many are moving toward having early learning assessments; getting these policies right is an important step toward improved programs at the local level.
- *Fund programs to deliver quality.* Great standards and assessments only come to life in the hands of effective teachers, and historically, early learning providers haven't been funded to hire and retain those great teachers. States can structure their preschool and child care funding to deliver quality—and, importantly, quality in the first five years doesn't mean putting kids at desks. Great teachers in the early years keep it fun and help kids learn through play, and in all likelihood many K–12 teachers would be better off doing the same. State programs typically get what they pay for, and programs that don't pay for educational outcomes generally won't get them. And if providers are paid to provide educational outcomes and still can't deliver, then funding should be moved to other providers.
- *Engage schools.* Too many superintendents and principals think of early learning as "other"—they don't see it as connected to their educational mission. Even when there are preschools in school buildings, they ignore them.

There's a lot that more states could do to help K–12 leaders engage success-fully with early learning, potentially starting with making sure that K–12 leaders actually understand child development.[126] There are great examples of districts that have shown tremendous leadership on early learning issues,[127] and state accountability and support policies can help stimulate more.

- *Engage community providers.* Even in states with primarily school-based preschool programs, the percentage of time children spend in school settings prior to kindergarten entry is quite small. Community-based preschool programs, child care settings, and Head Start are all essential parts of the early childhood system, and policymakers should utilize them thoughtfully. Many state preschool programs already ensure a place for them and encourage them to collaborate with school districts.[128]
- *Partner with philanthropies.* Many states have philanthropic communities that contribute significantly to the early learning system. In some states, there are formal public–private partnerships.[129] In many states, philanthropies have played a key role in supporting advocacy and research that has helped create the right conditions for state government success. State governments and philanthropies are both limited in what they can achieve, but working together is the best way for each to maximize their impact.
- *Prioritize.* Public resources will always be limited. What the research tells us is that if our goal is to use early learning to break the cycle of poverty, we need to focus on the children with the greatest need, invest in children as young as possible, and make sure investments are of high quality. Some early learning investments have other goals, and may be specifically designed to serve those different purposes. But a serious focus on using early learning to eliminate the achievement gap requires actions that match the strategy to the goal. While some families can afford to provide high-quality early learning for their children, many cannot, and thus public support is crucial to preventing the achievement gap before it starts.

Early childhood education alone can't break the cycle of poverty, but it can play a critical role in helping to do so at the starting point. It can help ensure that schools serving primarily children in poverty aren't playing catch-up from when children first walk in the door. Starting early is key, as is being thoughtful about the actual needs of children and families and then really striving to meet them. Education doesn't begin in kindergarten, and neither should policy efforts to unlock the potential of children.

NOTES

1. Tamara Halle, et al., *Disparities in Early Learning and Development: Lessons from the Early Childhood Longitudinal Study–Birth Cohort (ECLS-B)* (Washington, DC: Child Trends, 2009).

2. Betty Hart and Todd R. Risley, *Meaningful Differences in the Everyday Experiences of Young Children* (Baltimore, MD: Brookes Publishing, 1995); see also Katie Dealy, Debra Pacchiano, and Priya Shimpi, *The Language of Babies, Toddlers, and Preschoolers: Connecting Research to Practice* (Chicago: Ounce of Prevention Fund, 2007), accessed September 14, 2014, http://www.ounceofprevention.org/languageofbabies/index.html#/7/zoomed.

3. Douglas Quenqua, "Quality of Words, Not Quantity, Is Crucial to Language Skills, Study Finds," *New York Times*, October 16, 2014, http://www.nytimes.com/2014/10/17/us/quality-of-words-not-quantity-is-crucial-to-language-skills-study-finds.html?_r=0; Adriana Weisleder and Anne Fernald, "Talking to Children Matters: Early Language Experience Strengthens Processing and Builds Vocabulary," *Psychological Science* 24, no. 11 (2013): 2143–52, doi: 10.1177/0956797613488145.

4. Jack P. Shonkoff and Deborah A. Phillips, eds., *From Neurons to Neighborhoods: The Science of Early Childhood Development* (Washington, DC: National Academies Press, 2000).

5. *The Science of Early Childhood Development: Closing the Gap Between What We Know and What We Do* (Cambridge, MA: National Scientific Council on the Developing Child, 2007); see also *It's Possible: Closing the Achievement Gap in Academic Performance* (Chicago: Ounce of Prevention Fund), accessed September 14, 2014, http://www.ounceofprevention.org/news/pdfs/ClosingTheAchievementGap.pdf.

6. Catherine E. Snow, M. Susan Burns, and Peg Griffin, eds., *Preventing Reading Difficulties in Young Children* (Washington, DC: National Academies Press, 1998).

7. Hart and Risley, *Meaningful Differences in the Everyday Experiences of Young Children*.

8. Donald J. Hernandez, *Double Jeopardy: How Third-Grade Reading Skills and Poverty Influence High School Graduation* (Baltimore: Annie E. Casey Foundation, 2011), http://files.eric.ed.gov/fulltext/ED518818.pdf (accessed August 15, 2014).

9. Sean F. Reardon, "The Widening Academic Achievement Gap between the Rich and the Poor: New Evidence and Possible Explanations," in *Whither Opportunity? Rising Inequality and the Uncertain Life Changes of Low-Income Children*, ed. Greg J. Duncan and Richard J. Murnane (New York: Russell Sage Foundation Press, 2011); see also Kathryn Tout, et al., *The Research Base for a Birth through Age Eight State Policy Framework* (Bethesda, MD: The Alliance for Early Success and Child Trends, 2013).

10. A. Martin, et al., *Early Head Start Impacts Over Time and by Level of Participation* (Washington, DC: Mathematica Policy Research, 2008); Martha Zaslow, et al., *Quality Dosage, Thresholds, and Features in Early Childhood Settings: A Review of the Literature* (Washington, DC: Office of Planning, Research and Evaluation, Administration for Children and Families, US Department of Health and Human Services, 2010); see also Tout, et al., *The Research Base for a Birth through Age Eight State Policy Framework*.

11. *Kindergartners' Social Interaction Skills* (Bethesda, MD: Child Trends), accessed September 20, 2015, http://www.childtrends.org/?indicators=kindergartners-social-interaction-skills.

12. Karen M. La Paro, et al., "Quality in Kindergarten Classrooms: Observational Evidence for the Need to Increase Children's Learning Opportunities in Early Education Classrooms," *Early Education and Development* 20, no. 4 (2007): 657–92; Martha Zaslow et al., *Toward the Identification of Features of Effective Professional Development for Early Childhood Educators: Literature Review* (Washington, DC: US Department of Education, Office of Planning, Evaluation and Policy Development, Policy and Program Studies Service, 2010); see also Dealy, Pacchiano, and Shimpi, *The Language of Babies, Toddlers, and Preschoolers: Connecting Research to Practice.*

13. Dale Walker, et al., "Prediction of School Outcomes Based on Early Language Production and Socioeconomic Factors," *Child Development* 65, no. 2: 606–21; see also Nugent, Yazejian, and Bryant, *The Research Foundation of the Educare Intervention Model.*

14. Kathy Hirsh-Pasek, et al. *A Mandate for Playful Learning in Preschool: Presenting the Evidence* (New York: Oxford University Press, 2008); Karen M. La Paro, et al., "Quality in Kindergarten Classrooms: Observational Evidence for the Need to Increase Children's Learning Opportunities in Early Education Classrooms," *Early Education and Development* 20, no. 4 (2009): 657–92; Julia L. Mendez, "How Can Parents Get Involved in Preschool? Barriers and Engagement in Education by Ethnic Minority Parents of Children Attending Head Start," *Cultural Diversity and Ethnic Minority Psychology* 16, no. 1: 26–36; Eboni C. Howard, *Moving Forward with Kindergarten Readiness Assessment Efforts: A Position Paper of the Early Childhood Education State Collaborative on Assessment and Student Standards* (Washington, DC: Council for Chief State School Officers, 2011), accessed August 29, 2014, http://www.ccsso.org/Documents/CCSSO_K-Assessment_Final_7-12-11.pdf; Bridget K. Hamre and Robert C. Pianta, "Early Teacher–Child Relationships and the Trajectory of Children's School Outcomes through Eighth Grade," *Child Development* 72, no. 2: 625–38; Francisco Palermo, et al., "Preschoolers' Academic Readiness: What Role Does the Teacher-Child Relationship Play?" *Early Childhood Research Quarterly* 22, no. 4: 407–22.

15. Malinda Carpenter, Katherine Nagell, and Michael Tomasello, "Social Cognition, Joint Attention, and Communicative Competence from 9 to 15 Months of Age," *Monographs of the Society for Research in Child Development* 63, no. 4: serial no. 225; see also Dealy, Pacchiano, and Shimpi, *The Language of Babies, Toddlers, and Preschoolers: Connecting Research to Practice.*

16. "Domain 1: Language Development," Head Start, Administration for Children and Families, Early Childhood Learning & Knowledge Center, last modified September 5, 2014, http://eclkc.ohs.acf.hhs.gov/hslc/tta-system/teaching/eecd/Domains%20of%20Child%20Development/Language%20Development%20and%20Communication/edudev_art_00011_061405.html (accessed September 14, 2014).

17. Shonkoff and Phillips, eds., *From Neurons to Neighborhoods: The Science of Early Childhood Development.*

18. *Dual Language Learning: What Does It Take? Head Start Dual Language Report* (Washington, DC: Office of Head Start, Administration for Children and Families, US Department of Health and Human Services, 2008), http://eclkc.ohs.acf.hhs.

gov/hslc/tta-system/teaching/eecd/Individualization/Learning%20in%20Two%20 Languages/DLANA_final_2009%5B1%5D.pdf (accessed September 12, 2014).

19. *Linguistic Diversity and Early Literacy: Serving Culturally Diverse Families in Early Head Start,* EHS NRC Technical Assistance Paper No. 5 (Washington, DC: Early Head Start National Resource Center at ZERO TO THREE and the Head Start Bureau, 2001), https://eclkc.ohs.acf.hhs.gov/hslc/hs/resources/ECLKC_Bookstore/ pdfs/ta5%5B1%5D.pdf (accessed September 12, 2014).

20. Shonkoff and Phillips, eds., *From Neurons to Neighborhoods: The Science of Early Childhood Development*; J. Ronald Lally, *The Science and Psychology of Infant–Toddler Care: How an Understanding of Early Learning Has Transformed Child Care* (Washington, DC: ZERO TO THREE, 2009), http://main.zerotothree. org/site/DocServer/Lally_30-2.pdf?docID=10641 (accessed August 28, 2014). As Nugent et al. explain: "Higher teacher child ratios are a structural indicator of quality because of the associated teacher behaviors observed in these settings. Teachers working in a classroom with a higher staff–child ratio are more positive and sensitive and less detached and harsh in their interactions with the children. This is especially true for infant early learning environments. Higher staff–child ratios can also bring about improved child outcomes, as a 2002 study found connections between high staff–child ratios and higher child cognitive and social ability. Low group size is another structural quality indicator. Teachers working with a smaller group are better able to devote their attention to interacting with children in a positive and responsive manner. Smaller group size increases the number of interactions between teacher and student and most directly predicts positive care giving. As with teacher child ratios, smaller class size is most impactful for infants." Nugent, Yazejian, and Bryant, *The Research Foundation of the Educare Intervention Model.*

21. Marcy Whitebook and Sharon Ryan, *Degrees in Context: Asking the Right Questions about Preparing Skilled and Effective Teachers of Young Children,* NIEER Preschool Policy Brief no. 22 (Berkeley, CA: Center for the Study of Child Care Employment and the National Institute for Early Education Research, 2011).

22. Jackie Green, interview by Jelene Britten, October 2014, over the telephone, Chicago, IL.

23. Elliot Regenstein, *Considering a Multistate Approach to Early Learning Standards,* Policy Conversations no. 2 (Chicago: The Ounce of Prevention Fund, 2013), http://www.ounceofprevention.org/national-policy/conversations/Early-Learning-Multistate-Standards.v1.080513.pdf (accessed September 2, 2014).

24. Kristie Kauerz, *Ladders of Learning* (Washington, DC: New America Foundation, 2006); see also Tout et al., *The Research Base for a Birth through Age Eight State Policy Framework.*

25. Regenstein, *Considering a Multistate Approach to Early Learning Standards,* appendix.

26. Matthew M. Chingos and Grover J. "Russ" Whitehurst, *Choosing Blindly: Instructional Materials, Teacher Effectiveness, and the Common Core* (Washington, DC: The Brown Center on Education Policy at Brookings, 2012), http://www.brook ings.edu/~/media/research/files/reports/2012/4/10%20curriculum%20chingos%20 whitehurst/0410_curriculum_chingos_whitehurst.pdf (accessed September 2, 2014).

27. Helen H. Taylor, "Curriculum in Head Start, Head Start Bulletin #67," Head Start, Administration for Children and Families, Early Childhood Learning & Knowledge Center, last modified August 27, 2014, http://eclkc.ohs.acf.hhs.gov/hslc/tta-system/teaching/eecd/Curriculum/Teaching%20Strategies/CurriculuminHea.htm#curr (accessed September 12, 2014).

28. Samuel J. Meisels, *Accountability in Early Childhood: No Easy Answers,* Occasional Paper no. 6 (Chicago: Erikson Institute, Herr Research Center for Children and Social Policy, 2006); Lorrie Shepard, Sharon Lynn Kagan, and Emily Wurtz, eds., *Principles and Recommendations for Early Childhood Assessments* (Washington, DC: Goal 1 Early Childhood Assessments Resource Group and National Education Goals Panel, 1998), http://govinfo.library.unt.edu/negp/reports/prinrec.pdf (accessed September 2, 2014).

29. Shannon Riley-Ayers, *Formative Assessment: Guidance for Early Childhood Policymakers,* CEELO Policy Report (New Brunswick, NJ: Center on Enhancing Early Learning Outcomes, 2014).

30. Kyle Snow, *Developing Kindergarten Readiness and Other Large-Scale Assessment Systems: Necessary Considerations in the Assessment of Young Children* (Washington, DC: National Association for the Education of Young Children, 2011), http://www.naeyc.org/files/naeyc/file/research/Assessment_Systems.pdf (accessed September 2, 2014).

31. Diane Schilder and Megan Carolan, *State of the States Policy Snapshot: State Early Childhood Assessment Policies* (New Brunswick, NJ: Center on Enhancing Early Learning Outcomes, 2014), http://ceelo.org/wp-content/uploads/2014/03/CEELO_policy_snapshot_child_assessment_march_2014.pdf (accessed September 2, 2014).

32. *Kindergarten Entry Assessment: Practices and Policies* (Washington, DC: Hanover Research, 2013), http://www.hanoverresearch.com/media/Kindergarten-Entry-Assessments-Practices-and-Policies.pdf (accessed September 2, 2014); Howard, *Moving Forward with Kindergarten Readiness Assessment Efforts: A Position Paper of the Early Childhood Education State Collaborative on Assessment and Student Standards.*

33. Schilder and Carolan, *State of the States Policy Snapshot: State Early Childhood Assessment Policies;* Jennifer M. Stedron and Alexander Berger, *NCSL Technical Report: State Approaches to School Readiness Assessment* (Washington, DC: National Conference of State Legislatures, 2010), http://www.ncsl.org/documents/Educ/KindergartenAssessment.pdf (accessed August 29, 2014).

34. John Kocher, interview by Jelene Britten, October 2014, over the telephone, Chicago, IL.

35. Christina Walker, *Head Start Participants, Programs, and Staff in 2013* (Washington, DC: CLASP, 2014), http://www.clasp.org/resources-and-publications/publication-1/HSpreschool-PIR-2013-Fact-Sheet.pdf (accessed on August 29, 2014). The term *parents* is used even though in many early learning programs serving low-income children, a high percentage of children live with a single parent or nonparental custodian. For example, 59 percent of children enrolled in Head Start nationally live with a single parent.

36. Elise Trumbull, Carrie Rothstein-Fisch, and Patricia M. Greenfield, *Bridging Cultures in Our Schools: New Approaches that Work* (San Francisco: WestEd, 2000); *Positive Parent–Child Relationships,* Understanding Family Engagement Outcomes: Research to Practice Series (Washington, DC: National Center on Parent, Family, and Community Engagement), http://eclkc.ohs.acf.hhs.gov/hslc/tta-system/family/docs/parent-child-relationships.pdf.

37. Felipe González Castro, Manuel Barrera, Jr., and Lori K. Holleran Steiker, "Issues and Challenges in the Design of Culturally Adapted Evidence-Based Interventions," *Annual Review of Clinical Psychology* 6: 213–39, doi: 10.1146/annurev-clinpsy-033109-132032; Genevieve Benedetti, *Innovations in the Field of Child Abuse and Neglect Prevention: A Review of the Literature* (Chicago: Chapin Hall at the University of Chicago, 2012).

38. Martha Blue-Banning, et al., "Dimensions of Family and Professional Partnerships: Constructive Guidelines for Collaboration," *Exceptional Children* 70, no. 2 (2004): 167–84.

39. Carl J. Dunst, Carol M. Trivette, and Deborah W. Hamby, "Meta-analysis of Family-Centered Helpgiving Practices Research," *Mental Retardation and Developmental Disabilities Research Reviews* 13, no. 4 (2007): 370–78.

40. Jeffry A. Simpson and W. Steven Rholes, "Attachment, Perceived Support, and the Transition to Parenthood: Social Policy and Health Implications," *Social Issues and Policy Review* 2, no. 1 (2008): 37–63, doi: 10.1111/j.1751-2409.2008.00010.x.

41. Judy Langford and Bernice Weissbourd, "New Directions for Parent Leadership in a Family-Support Context," in *Leadership in Early Care and Education,* ed. Sharon Kagan and Barbara T. Bowman (Washington, DC: National Association for the Education of Young Children, 1997), 147–53.

42. Shayna D. Cunningham, Holly Kreider, and Jenny Ocón, "Influence of a Parent Leadership Program on Participants' Leadership Capacity and Actions," *School Community Journal* 22, no. 1 (2012): 111–24.

43. Susan Auerbach, "Beyond Coffee with the Principal: Toward Leadership for Authentic School–Family Partnerships," *Journal of School Leadership* 20, no. 6 (2010): 728–57; Concha Delgado-Gaitan, "Involving Parents in the Schools: A Process of Empowerment," *American Journal of Education* 100, no. 1 (1991): 20–46.

44. Suzanne M. Bianchi, "Changing Families, Changing Workplaces," *Future of Children* 21, no. 2 (2011): 15–36; Vonnie C. McLoyd, "The Impact of Economic Hardship on Black Families and Children: Psychological Distress, Parenting, and Socioemotional Development," *Child Development* 61, no. 2 (2008): 311–46; W. Jean Yeung, Miriam R. Linver, and Jeanne Brooks-Gunn, "How Money Matters for Young Children's Development: Parental Investment and Family Processes," *Child Development* 73, no. 6 (2002): 1861–79.

45. Audrey A. Trainor, "Diverse Approaches to Parent Advocacy During Special Education Home-School Interactions: Identification and Use of Cultural and Social Capital," *Remedial and Special Education* 31, no. 1 (2008): 34–47.

46. Michael DeArmond, Ashley Jochim, and Robin Lake, *Making School Choice Work* (Seattle, WA: Center on Reinventing Public Education, 2014).

47. "Educare Model Framework Description, Final Version May 30, 2014."

48. P. Lindsay Chase-Lansdale and Jeanne Brooks-Gunn, "Two-Generation Programs in the Twenty-First Century," *Future of Children* 24, no.1 (2014): 13–39.

49. Mary Jane England and Leslie J. Sim, eds., *Depression in Parents, Parenting, and Children: Opportunities to Improve Identification, Treatment, and Prevention Efforts* (Washington, DC: National Academies Press, 2009); Nicole Forry, et al., *Family–Provider Relationships: A Multidisciplinary Review of High Quality Practices and Associations with Family, Child, and Provider Outcomes*, Issue Brief OPRE 2011-26a (Washington, DC: Office of Planning, Research, and Evaluation, Administration for Children and Families, US Department of Health and Human Services, 2011).

50. Greg J. Duncan and Katherine Magnuson, "The Long Reach of Early Childhood Poverty," *Pathways* (2011): 22–27.

51. John M. Love, et al., "The Effectiveness of Early Head Start for 3-Year-Old Children and Their Parents: Lessons for Policy and Programs," *Developmental Psychology* 41, no. 6 (2005): 885–901.

52. Darcy I. Lowell, et al., "A Randomized Controlled Trial of Child FIRST: A Comprehensive Home-Based Intervention Translating Research Into Early Childhood Practice," *Child Development* 82, no. 1 (2011): 193–208.

53. Robert W. Glover, et al., *CareerAdvance: A Dual-Generation Antipoverty Strategy: An Implementation Study of the Initial Pilot Cohort, July 2009 through June 2010* (Austin, TX: Lyndon B. Johnson School of Public Affairs, 2010); *Two Generations, One Future: Moving Parents and Children Beyond Poverty Together*, An ASCEND at the Aspen Institute Report (Washington, DC: Aspen Institute, 2012), http://www.aspeninstitute.org/sites/default/files/content/docs/ascend/Ascend-Report-022012.pdf (accessed September 3, 2014).

54. Nena Cunningham, interview by Jelene Britten, October 2014, over the telephone, Chicago, IL.

55. Heather Weiss and Lisa Klein, *Changing the Conversation about Home Visiting: Scaling Up with Quality* (Cambridge, MA: Harvard Family Research Project, Harvard Graduate School Education, 2006); Council on Community Pediatrics, "The Role of Preschool Home-Visiting Programs in Improving Children's Developmental and Health Outcomes," *Pediatrics* 123, no. 2 (2009): 598–603, doi: 10.1542/peds.2008-3607.

56. Lenette Azzi-Lessing, "Serving Highly Vulnerable Families in Home-Visitation Programs," *Infant Mental Health Journal* 34, no. 5 (2013): 376–90; *The Home Visit Experience* (Denver, CO: Nurse-Family Partnership, 2013), http://www.nursefamilypartnership.org/assets/PDF/Nurse-documents/home_visit_experience (accessed September 3, 2014).

57. Andrew Burwick, et al., *Costs of Early Childhood Home Visiting: An Analysis of Programs Implemented in the Supporting Evidence-Based Home Visiting to Prevent Child Maltreatment Initiative* (Princeton, NJ: Mathematica Policy Research, 2014). Home-visiting programs have different staff qualifications and levels of intensities. Implementation costs for home-visiting programs vary, and cost differences can be observed within models, as well. The Healthy Families America framework has an average cost of $5,615 per family, with a range of $2,848–$10,502; the Nurse

Family Partnership model has an average cost of $8,003 per family, with a range of $4,228–$13,692; and the Parents as Teachers model has an average cost of $2,372 per family, with a range of $2,122–$2,622. Agency characteristics and the scope of the services provided influence the ultimate cost per family. Factors that tend to increase costs include offering intensive wraparound services (including professional mental health treatment); a focus on particularly high-risk populations, such as parents with a history of substance abuse or mental health issues; and focusing on suburban or urban populations.

58. Mary Wagner, et al., *Parental Engagement in Home Visiting Programs: Findings from the Parents as Teachers Multisite Evaluation* (Menlo Park, CA: SRI International, 2000); Lenette Azzi-Lessing. "Home Visitation Programs: Critical Issues and Future Directions," *Early Childhood Research Quarterly* 26, no. 4 (2011): 387–98; Ruth A. O'Brien, et al., "Mixed Methods Analysis of Participant Attrition in the Nurse-Family Partnership," *Prevention Science* 13, no. 3 (2012): 219–28.

59. *Nurse Story: Vickie* (Denver, CO: Nurse-Family Partnership), http://www.nursefamilypartnership.org/assets/PDF/Nurse-stories/NFP_Nurse_Vickie (accessed September 5, 2014).

60. *Preliminary Findings from the Early Head Start Prekindergarten Followup* (Washington, DC: US Department of Health and Human Services, 2006), http://www.acf.hhs.gov/sites/default/files/opre/prekindergarten_followup.pdf (accessed September 14, 2014).

61. Christina Walker and Stephanie Schmit, "Head Start Children, Families, Staff, and Programs in 2013," *Strengthening Children, Youth & Families: Child Care & Early Education* (blog), CLASP, August 14, 2014, http://www.clasp.org/issues/child-care-and-early-education/in-focus/head-start-children-families-staff-and-programs-in-2013 (accessed September 14, 2014).

62. *Head Start Program Facts: Fiscal Year 2013* (Washington, DC: Office of Head Start, Administration for Children and Families), https://eclkc.ohs.acf.hhs.gov/hslc/data/factsheets/docs/hs-program-fact-sheet-2013.pdf (accessed September 5, 2014).

63. Ibid.

64. W. Steven Barnett, et al., *The State of Preschool 2013: State Preschool Yearbook* (New Brunswick, NJ: National Institute for Early Education Research, 2013), 13.

65. Ibid., 16.

66. Julia B. Isaacs, *Impacts of Early Childhood Programs* (Washington, DC: First Focus and Brookings Institution, 2008), http://www.brookings.edu/~/media/research/files/papers/2008/9/early%20programs%20isaacs/09_early_programs_isaacs.pdf (accessed September 14, 2014).

67. Elliot Regenstein and Rio Romero-Jurado, *A Framework for Rethinking State Education Accountability and Support from Birth through High School*, Policy Conversation no. 3 (Chicago: The Ounce of Prevention Fund, 2014), 26, http://www.theounce.org/what-we-do/policy/policy-conversations (accessed December 21, 2014); Elliot Regenstein, et al., *Changing the Metrics of Turnaround to Encourage Early Learning Strategies,* Policy Conversation no. 4 (Chicago: The Ounce of Pre-

vention Fund and Mass Insight Education, 2014), 13, http://www.theounce.org/what-we-do/policy/policy-conversations (accessed December 21, 2014).

68. Regenstein, et al., *Changing the Metrics of Turnaround to Encourage Early Learning Strategies.*

69. Council of the Great City Schools, Research Department, *Urban School Superintendents: Characteristics, Tenure, and Salary. Seventh Survey and Report,* (Washington, DC: Council of the Great City Schools, 2010), http://www.cgcs.org/cms/lib/DC00001581/Centricity/Domain/4/Supt_Survey2010.pdf (accessed January 7, 2015).

70. Regenstein, et al., *Changing the Metrics of Turnaround to Encourage Early Learning Strategies,* 15–16; Elliot Regenstein and Rio Romero-Jurado, "Early Learning Needs Accountability, Too. Systems Should Focus on Birth Through High School," *Education Week,* November 25, 2014, http://www.edweek.org/ew/articles/2014/11/25/13regenstein.h34.html.

71. Regenstein, et al., *Changing the Metrics of Turnaround to Encourage Early Learning Strategies,* 16; David T. Burkham, Valerie E. Lee, and Julie Dwyer, *School Mobility in the Early Elementary Grades* (Ann Arbor: University of Michigan, 2009), http://fcd-us.org/sites/default/files/BurkamSchoolMobilityInThe%20EarlyElementaryGrades.pdf (accessed January 7, 2015).

72. Maria V. Mayoral, *Fact Sheet: Building Partnerships between Early Head Start Grantees and Child Care Providers* (Washington, DC: ZERO TO THREE, 2013), http://www.zerotothree.org/policy/docs/ehs-child-care-partnerships-fact-sheet-ztt-04-04-2014.pdf (accessed September 14, 2014).

73. Hannah Matthews and Rhiannon Reeves, *Child Care and Development Block Grant Participation in 2012* (Washington, DC: CLASP, 2014), http://www.clasp.org/resources-and-publications/publication-1/CCDBG-Participation-in-2012-Final.pdf (accessed September 14, 2014).

74. Karen Schulman and Helen Blank, *Pivot Point: State Child Care Assistance Policies 2013,* (Washington, DC: National Women's Law Center, 2013). Child care subsidies are limited to the lowest-income working parents, with the income cutoff set by states—ranging from a high of 278 percent of poverty in Alaska to a low of 117 percent of poverty in Nebraska.

75. Stephen Wood, Lynette Fraga, and Michelle McCready, *Parents and the High Cost of Child Care. 2014 Report.* (Arlington, VA: Child Care Aware of America and Hanover Research, 2014), 22–23, http://www.usa.childcareaware.org/costofcare (accessed December 21, 2014).

76. Regenstein and Romero-Jurado, *A Framework for Rethinking State Education Accountability and Support from Birth through High School.*

77. Marcy Whitebook and Laura M. Sakai, *Turnover Begets Turnover: An Examination of Occupational Instability among Child Care Center Staff* (Berkeley, CA: Center for the Study of Child Care Employment, 2003).

78. James J. Heckman, *Policies to Foster Human Capital,* NBER Working Paper No. 7288 (Cambridge, MA: National Bureau of Economic Research, 1999).

79. Frank Porter Graham Child Development Institute, *Educare Implementation Study Findings—August 2012* (Chapel Hill, NC: Frank Porter Graham Child De-

velopment Institute, 2012); see also *It's Possible: Closing the Achievement Gap in Academic Performance.*

80. *Preliminary Findings from the Early Head Start Prekindergarten Followup*; see also Isaacs, *Impacts of Early Childhood Programs.*

81. Michael Puma, et al., *Third Grade Follow-Up to the Head Start Impact Study: Final Report*, OPRE Report 2012-45 (Washington, DC: US Department of Health and Human Services, Administration for Children and Families, 2012); James Heckman, Rodrigo Pinto, and Peter Savelyev, "Understanding the Mechanisms through which an Influential Early Childhood Program Boosted Adult Outcomes," *American Economic Review* 103, no. 6 (2013): 2052–86.

82. Ibid., 151.

83. Ibid., 143; Grover J. "Russ" Whitehurst and David J. Armor, *Obama's Preschool Proposal is Not Based on Sound Research*, The Brown Center Chalkboard (Washington, DC: Brookings Institution, 2013), http://www.brookings.edu/blogs/brown-center-chalkboard/posts/2013/07/24-preschool-proposal-whitehurst (accessed September 14, 2014).

84. Aphra R. Katzev, Clara C. Pratt, and William McGuigan, *Oregon Healthy Start 1999–2000 Status Report: July 1, 1999–June 30, 2000* (Corvallis, OR: Oregon State Family Policy Program, 2001); see also *Learning Begins at Birth* (Chicago, IL: Ounce of Prevention Fund), http://www.ounceofprevention.org/news/pdfs/LearningBeginsAtBirth.pdf (accessed September 14, 2014).

85. *A Strategic Road-Map: Committed to Bringing the Voice of Pediatricians to the Most Important Problem Facing Children in the US Today*, APA Task Force on Childhood Poverty (McLean, VA: Academic Pediatric Association, April 2013); Paula Braveman and Susan Egerter, *Overcoming Obstacles to Health in 2013 and Beyond* (Princeton, NJ: Robert Wood Johnson Foundation, 2013).

86. Brooke Fisher, Ann Hanson, and Tony Raden, *Start Early To Build A Healthy Future: The Research Linking Early Learning and Health* (Chicago: Ounce of Prevention Fund, 2014).

87. Donald A. Rock and Judith M. Pollack, *Early Childhood Longitudinal Study—Kindergarten Class 1998–99 (ECLS-K), Psychometric Report for Kindergarten through First Grade*, NCES 2002-05 (Washington, DC: US Department of Education, National Center for Education Statistics, 2002); see also Isaacs, *Impacts of Early Childhood Programs.*

88. Barnett et al., *Abbott Preschool Longitudinal Effects Study: Fifth Grade Follow Up* (New Brunswick, NJ: National Institute for Early Education Research, 2013), http://nieer.org/sites/nieer/files/APPLES%205th%20Grade.pdf (accessed July 14, 2014).

89. Cynthia Lamy, W. Steven Barnett, and Kwanghee Jung, *The Effects of Oklahoma's Early Childhood Four-Year-Old Program on Young Children's School Readiness* (New Brunswick, NJ: National Institute for Early Education Research, 2005).

90. Whitehurst and Armor, *Obama's Preschool Proposal is Not Based on Sound Research*; David J. Armor, "The Evidence on Universal Preschool," *Policy Analysis: Cato Institute*, no. 760 (2014).

91. Hilary M. Shager, et al., "Can Research Design Explain Variation in Head Start Research Results? A Meta-Analysis of Cognitive and Achievement Outcomes," *Educational Evaluation and Policy Analysis* 35, no. 1 (2012): 76–95; *Understanding the Head Start Impact Study* (Washington, DC: US Department of Health and Human Services, Administration for Children and Families, Office of Planning, Research and Evaluation, 2010), http://www.nhsa.org/files/static_page_files/0BF4EB6E-1D09-3519-ADBFF989BFF11535/2-10ForumEvalScienceBrief_HeadStart.pdf (accessed September 15, 2014).

92. *It's Possible: Closing the Achievement Gap in Academic Performance*; Grover J. "Russ" Whitehurst, "Can We Be Hard-Headed about Preschool? A Look at Head Start," The Brown Center Chalkboard (Washington, DC: Brookings Institute, 2013), www.brookings.edu/blogs/brown-center-chalkboard/posts/2013/01/16-preschool-whitehurst (accessed September 14, 2014).

93. James Heckman, Rodrigo Pinto, and Peter Savelyev, *Perry Preschool & Character: Character Skills Are More Important than IQ in Driving Better Life Outcomes* (Chicago: The Heckman Equation); *Why Business Should Support Early Childhood Education* (Washington, DC: Institute for a Competitive Workforce, US Chamber of Commerce, 2010), http://www.uschamberfoundation.org/sites/default/files/publication/edu/ICW_EarlyChildhoodReport_2010.pdf (accessed September 4, 2014); *Debunking the Myths: The Benefits of Preschool* (New Brunswick, NJ: National Institute for Early Education Research), http://nieer.org/resources/factsheets/13.pdf (accessed September 14, 2014).

94. Regenstein, et al., *Changing the Metrics of Turnaround to Encourage Early Learning Strategies*.

95. Armor, "The Evidence on Universal Preschool"; Whitehurst, "Can We Be Hard-Headed about Preschool? A Look at Head Start."

96. Barnett et al., *The State of Preschool 2013: State Preschool Yearbook*, 10–12.

97. Julie Greenberg, Arthur McKee, and Kate Walsh, *Teacher Prep Review* (Washington, DC: National Council on Teacher Quality, 2013); Donald Heller, Avner Segall, and Corey Drake, "An Open Letter to NCTQ on Teacher Prep," *Education Week*, December 10, 2013, http://www.edweek.org/ew/articles/2013/12/11/14heller.h33.html; Kate Walsh, "NCTQ Responds to Critics of Its Teacher-Prep Ratings," *Education Week*, December 12, 2013, http://www.edweek.org/ew/articles/2013/12/12/15walsh.h33.html.

98. Barnett et al., *The State of Preschool 2013: State Preschool Yearbook* 16; *Early Child Care and Education: HHS and Education Are Taking Steps to Improve Workforce Data and Enhance Worker Quality* (Washington, DC: Government Accountability Office, 2012), http://www.gao.gov/assets/590/588577.pdf (accessed September 2, 2014).

99. *Head Start Program Facts: Fiscal Year 2013*.

100. Marcy Whitebook, *Building a Skilled Teacher Workforce: Shared and Divergent Challenges in Early Care and Education and in Grades K–12*, (Washington, DC: Bill & Melinda Gates Foundation, 2014).

101. Armor, "The Evidence on Universal Preschool"; Chester E. Finn, Jr., "The Preschool Picture," *Education Next* 9, no. 4 (2009), http://educationnext.org/the-preschool-picture/.

102. Timothy J. Bartik, "The Effectiveness of Many State and Local Pre-K Programs Has Been Backed by Sound Research," *Investing in Kids* (blog), July 24, 2013, http://investinginkids.net/2013/07/24/the-effectiveness-of-many-state-and-local-pre-k-programs-has-been-backed-by-sound-research/.

103. Lally, *The Science and Psychology of Infant–Toddler Care: How an Understanding of Early Learning Has Transformed Child Care*; Jennifer L. Bernhardt, "A Primary Caregiving System for Infants and Toddlers: Best for Everyone Involved," *Young Children* 55, no. 2 (2000): 74–80.

104. Ibid.

105. Alexandra Beatty, rapporteur, *Student Mobility: Exploring the Impact of Frequent Moves on Achievement: Summary of a Workshop* (Washington, DC: National Academies Press, 2010), http://www.nap.edu/catalog.php?record_id=12853.

106. Gina Adams and Hannah Matthews, *Confronting the Child Care Eligibility Maze: Simplifying and Aligning with Other Work Supports* (Washington, DC: Urban Institute, 2013), http://www.urban.org/publications/412971.html.

107. Zaslow, et al., *Quality Dosage, Thresholds, and Features in Early Childhood Settings: A Review of the Literature.*

108. Barnett, et al., *The State of Preschool 2013: State Preschool Yearbook*, 13.

109. Elizabeth Morgan Russell, Sue W. Williams, and Cheryl Gleason-Gomez, "Teachers' Perceptions of Administrative Support and Antecedents of Turnover," *Journal of Research in Childhood Education* 24, no. 3 (2010): 195–208.

110. Marcy Whitebook, et al., *Preparing Teachers of Young Children: The Current State of Knowledge and a Blueprint for the Future* (Berkeley, CA: Center for the Study of Child Care Employment, 2009), http://www.irle.berkeley.edu/cscce/2009/preparing-teachers-of-young-children/ (accessed September 4, 2014).

111. Shonkoff and Phillips, eds., *From Neurons to Neighborhoods: The Science of Early Child Development.*

112. "Leading Pre-K-3 Learning Communities: Competencies for Effective Principal Practice," National Association of Elementary School Principals, http://www.naesp.org/llc (accessed September 15, 2014). The National Association of Elementary School Principals has published a guide for principals that addresses not only transition issues but also a range of issues relating to the connection between early learning and K–12.

113. Marielle Bohan-Baker and Priscilla M.D. Little, *The Transition to Kindergarten: A Review of Current Research and Promising Practices to Involve Families* (Cambridge, MA: Harvard Family Research Project, 2002); Sharon L. Kagan and Michelle J. Neuman, "Lessons from Three Decades of Transition Research," *Elementary School Journal* 98, no. 4 (1998): 365–79; see also Tout, et al., *The Research Base for a Birth through Age Eight State Policy Framework.*

114. Amy B. Schulting, Patrick S. Malone, and Kenneth A. Dodge, "The Effect of School-Based Kindergarten Transition Policies and Practices on Child Academic Outcomes," *Developmental Psychology* 41, no. 6 (2005): 860–71; see also Tout, et al., *The Research Base for a Birth through Age Eight State Policy Framework.*

115. Alan Fogel, "Theoretical and Applied Dynamic Systems Research in Developmental Science," *Child Development Perspectives* 5, no. 4 (2011): 262–72.

116. "Early Kindergarten Transition Program," Multnomah County, https://multco.us/sun/early-kindergarten-transition-program (accessed September 3, 2014).

117. Schulting, Malone, and Dodge, "The Effect of School-Based Kindergarten Transition Policies and Practices on Child Academic Outcomes."

118. *Family Engagement in Transitions: The Transition to Kindergarten*, Understanding Family Engagement Outcomes: Research to Practice Series (Washington, DC: National Center on Parent, Family, and Community Engagement, 2013), http://eclkc.ohs.acf.hhs.gov/hslc/tta-system/family/docs/transitions-kindergarten.pdf (accessed September 3, 2014).

119. "Table 216.90. Public Elementary and Secondary Charter Schools and Enrollment, by State: Selected Years, 1999–2000 through 2011–12," *Digest of Education Statistics,* http://nces.ed.gov/programs/digest/d13/tables/dt13_216.90.asp.

120. Barnett et al., *The State of Preschool 2013: State Preschool Yearbook,* 8.

121. Sarah Garland, "D.C. Charters Tackle Preschool," *Washington Post,* April 3, 2011, http://www.washingtonpost.com/local/education/dc-charters-tackle-preschool/2011/03/29/AFHzRHXC_story.html.

122. AppleTree Institute for Education Innovation, 2014, http://www.appletreeinstitute.org/; Cara Stillings Candal, *Seeds of Achievement: AppleTree's Early Childhood D.C. Charter Schools* (Boston: Pioneer Institute, 2014), http://pioneerinstitute.org/download/seeds-of-achievement-appletrees-early-childhood-d-c-charter-schools/.

123. Kara Christenson, "Kindergarten Transition Programs Find Growing Success," *Children's Institute* (blog), http://www.childinst.org/news/blog/590-kindergarten-transition-programs-find-growing-success (accessed September 4, 2014).

124. "Early Kindergarten Transition Program."

125. Christenson, "Kindergarten Transition Programs Find Growing Success."

126. Kirsty Clarke Brown et al., *What Do We Know About Principal Preparation, Licensure Requirements, and Professional Development for School Leaders?* CEELO Policy Report (New Brunswick, NJ: Center on Enhancing Early Learning Outcomes, 2014), http://ceelo.org/wp-content/uploads/2014/07/ceelo_policy_report_ece_principal_prep.pdf. Illinois recently required early childhood content to be included in its principal-preparation programs. In addition to receiving a generalized certification that must include early childhood content, candidates can pursue a B-3 endorsement that prepares them to be instructional leaders in early childhood and early elementary settings. Starting in 2013, Connecticut's Office of Early Childhood, in partnership with the University of Connecticut, began offering a pre-K–3 Executive Leaders certificate through its 3 to 3 Institute. After a competitive selection process, participants in the program attend a full-day symposium on pre-K–3 issues and received continued support from a trained facilitator as they adopted lessons learned from the training session.

127. Katia Riddle and Marina Merrill, *Leading the Way: Why Four Oregon Superintendents Embraced Early Learning* (Portland, OR: The Children's Institute, 2014), http://www.childinst.org/images/stories/ci_publications/leading-the-way2014.pdf. For example, leaders in school districts across Oregon have made notable efforts in prioritizing early learning. Although the superintendent of the Galdston School

District chose to direct school district funds to an early learning center, the superintendent of the David Douglas School district has aligned early learning with early elementary schooling for some district schools. The former superintendent of Maryland's Montgomery Public Schools aligned early learning with the K–12 system.

128. Bette Hyde and Linda Sullivan-Dudzic, *Starting Early for Success: Early Childhood Care and Education: A Community Working Together* (Bremerton, WA: Bremerton School District), http://bremertonschools.schoolwires.net/cms/lib/WA01001541/Centricity/Domain/75/ThriveByFive9-4-07rev.pdf; "Creating the Future Through Collaboration," All Our Kids Early Childhood Networks, accessed September 3, 2014, http://www.aoknetworks.org. An Oregon school district superintendent facilitated collaboration between community-based and school-based early childhood programs by inviting all early learning staff in the district to professional development sessions for elementary school teachers. This helped childhood teachers gain an understanding of approaches and standards for children in later grades. The superintendent connected early and elementary learning in an even more intentional manner by facilitating the process by which the community selected an aligned pre-K–3 curriculum. Once the community made the joint decision, the school district bought the curriculum and loaned it to preschools in order to encourage vertical alignment and establish consistent standards. In Illinois, state agencies and local communities have worked to create local networks of connected early childhood systems in which partners work together to provide comprehensive and high-quality services for children and families in the community.

129. Julie Cohen, et al., *Inspiring Innovation: Creative State Financing Structures for Infant-Toddler Services* (Chicago: ZERO TO THREE and Ounce of Prevention Fund, 2009), http://main.zerotothree.org/site/DocServer/Ounce_brief_Oct6B.pdf?docID=9642; "About Thrive by Five Washington," Thrive by Five Washington, http://thrivebyfivewa.org/about (accessed September 3, 2014). For example, Nebraska created an Early Childhood Education Endowment Fund that is composed of public and private funding, with $40 million from state sources and $20 million in private funding. Interest accrued from the fund is used to provide grants to schools and community-based organizations offering early childhood services and supports. By passing a constitutional amendment, which included early childhood providers in the definition of a common school, the state ensured that endowment fund can continue to be used to support early childhood programs. In Washington, Thrive By Five Washington and the Foundation for Early Learning joined together in January of 2014; by pooling their resources, this public-private partnership will be able to fund early childhood programming at an annual budget of $16 million dollars per year.

Chapter Nine

Poverty-Fighting Elementary Schools: Knowledge Acquisition Is Job One

Robert Pondiscio

For whosoever hath, to him shall be given, and he shall have more abundance: but whosoever hath not, from him shall be taken away even that he hath.

—Matthew 13:12

Upward mobility dies young in Mott Haven.

Located in the heart of New York City's South Bronx, the neighborhood has long claimed the dubious distinction of being America's poorest congressional district and a national symbol of urban decay. During the 1977 World Series, an ABC Sports aerial camera caught sight of a fire at PS 3, an abandoned elementary school a few blocks from Yankee Stadium. "There it is, ladies and gentlemen," Howard Cosell famously intoned. "The Bronx is burning." By the end of the decade, nearly half the neighborhood's buildings had been lost to fire, primarily arson. President Carter walked the streets of Mott Haven to view the devastation as residents shouted, "Give us money!" and "We want jobs!"[1]

Much of what the fires didn't destroy, the crack epidemic claimed in the 1980s. Crime soared to historic levels. The phrase "South Bronx" became synonymous with urban squalor, a reputation it struggles with to this day, even as neat rows of one- and two-family homes have filled in the gaps between the towering housing projects that loom over the neighborhood. The area is now largely Hispanic, heavily populated with immigrants, and still deeply impoverished. According to US Census data, 38 percent of residents and 49 percent of children live below the poverty line. Not even in Detroit is poverty deeper or more widespread.

Today, hard by the front door of the Mott Haven Community Center and across the street from a large public housing project, a blue and orange banner greets visitors. "Opportunity Starts Now," it reads in enormous letters. Smaller white type designates the site as an "Official NYC Department of Education Community-Based Early Childhood Center Pre-K Program." This is one of nearly two thousand sites that comprise New York City Mayor Bill de Blasio's signature education effort: a $445 million expansion of the City's universal pre-K program serving an estimated 65,000 four-year-olds as of September 2015.[2]

On a crisp Monday morning in November, parents file past the optimistic Department of Education banner and bring their four-year-old children upstairs to a classroom run by Julie Selby, a sixteen-year veteran preschool teacher.

"Come here, Elizabeth," Selby calls to a little girl in a princess dress and a pink birthday crown. "Let me see your tiara. What color is that? It's gorgeous!" Selby maintains a constant patter, engaging her students with conversation and questions filled with words like "tiara" and "gorgeous"—words that her children, largely Hispanic and all low-income, are unlikely to hear from their parents at home.

The classroom bursts with bright colors, attractive displays and language, and play areas—window displays representing the five senses near a sand and water table, laminated alphabet cards with upper- and lowercase letters, play sets and plastic carpentry tools, numerous books, and blocks. Around the room, every possible object is labeled in English and Spanish: closet, easel, clock ("El reloj"). Selby gathers her twenty little ones around her, pointing out which children are sitting in the "middle" of the rug and wondering who is sitting "next to" whom, all before asking each of them about their weekend. One little girl tells how she "helped my mommy cook, then visited my grandma, and then I went shopping and bought a new dress."

Selby seizes the teachable moment to present her children with yet another new word. "I like how you put those things in a *sequence,* Viviana," she observes, explaining that "sequence" means an ordered set. "Nice sequence!" she exults, then asks, "What color is your new dress?"

At times, the happy chatter stalls; many of the children offer only cursory answers. One little boy says only, "I slept." Others report watching television or playing video games. Selby is undaunted and nonjudgmental. When a boy named Abdulah says he watched a Curious George cartoon, Selby responds effusively, "I like how that little monkey is always looking for interesting things to do!" She points out that there are lots of Curious George books in the classroom. It's never too soon to spark a child's interest in books and reading.

By the time they leave her pre-K class, the twenty four-year-olds in Ms. Selby's care will know their numbers, letters, and colors. They will be able to spell and write their names. They will be ready for kindergarten. But look an unpleasant truth in the eye: They will graduate from this bright and cheerful room to attend some of New York City's lowest-performing elementary schools. The average Bronx elementary school has 15.5 percent of its students reading on grade level, compared to a citywide average of 28.4 percent.[3] The advocacy group Families for Excellent Schools identified 112 elementary and middle schools in which 90 percent of children read or do math below grade level.[4] Twenty-four of them—more than one in five—are in New York City's District 7, the South Bronx.

THE RICH VERBAL LIFE OF THE AFFLUENT CHILD

Three subway stops and the East River separate Mott Haven from Manhattan's Upper East Side, where parents eagerly spend north of $15,000 tuition—more than the cost of many colleges—for a coveted slot at an elite preschool. The right preschool can be a feeder to some of the nation's best private schools, and from there to elite colleges and universities. The grim competition and sense of purpose that attends admissions to schools like Dalton, Brearley, and Collegiate led to a cover story in *New York* magazine entitled "Give Me Harvard or Give Me Death."

Opportunity for children on the Upper East Side does not begin in preschool. It's largely a function of the lucky wombs from which they sprang. Language acquisition and kindergarten readiness isn't the first thing on these parents' minds. Nor should it be; to grow up as the child of well-educated parents in an affluent American home is to hit the verbal lottery.

From their earliest days, children of the wealthy and educated reap the benefits of parents who speak in complete sentences, engage them in rich dinner table conversation, and read them to sleep at bedtime. Verbal parents chatter incessantly, offering a running commentary on vegetable options in the produce aisle and pointing out letters and words in storefronts and street signs. Parents proceed, as Ginia Bellafante of the *New York Times* has described, "in a near constant mode of annotation. Reflexively, the affluent, ambitious parent is always talking, pointing out, explaining: Mommy is looking for her laptop; let's put on your rain boots; that's a pigeon, a sand dune, skyscraper, a pomegranate."[5]

Such children exist, Bellafante writes, "in continuous receipt of dictation." The rich cognitive input seldom rests. Weekends are filled with enrichment opportunities—playgroups, outings, museum visits, or birthday parties at pottery studios and the science center. When Mom and Dad need a break, they plunk the kids down in front of PBS Kids.

These are the indelible thumbprints of what sociologist Annette Lareau, in her 2003 book *Unequal Childhoods,* described as "concerted cultivation," a continuing state of engagement, development and stimulation.[6] This style of parenting is marked not merely by extensive organized activity, but also a verbal relationship among family members that encourages discussion, negotiation, and the questioning of authority.

She contrasts this style of parenting with another she calls "natural growth," much more common among working-class and economically disadvantaged families like those in Mott Haven. The children in "natural growth" homes hear much more directive language; negotiation is infrequent. Respect and trust for authority is expected and encouraged, and children are much more likely to direct their own play away from the constant oversight and monitoring of parents or caregivers.

To be clear, no value judgment is intended or implied in these contrasting parenting styles. In many significant ways, the "natural growth" families Lareau observed in her landmark work enjoyed greater independence, more intimate contact with their extended families, and enviable self-confidence. But they were also, as David Brooks noted in a 2006 column on Lareau's work, "not as well prepared for the world of organizations and adulthood":

Children, like their parents, were easily intimidated by and pushed around by verbally dexterous teachers and doctors. Middle-class kids felt entitled to individual treatment when entering the wider world, but working-class kids felt constrained and tongue-tied. . . . The perhaps overprogrammed middle-class kids got into good colleges and are heading for careers as doctors and other professionals. The working-class kids are not doing well.

The working-class parents were not bad parents, Brooks astutely observed, "but they did not prepare their kids for a world in which verbal skills and the ability to thrive in organizations are so important."[7]

This, then, is where any discussion of preparing low-income children for upward mobility must begin: by attending to their verbal skills and ability to thrive in the world we have—not the world we might wish for them.

Much has been made of the Niagara of words that the children of educated, affluent parents hear before day one of school. One of the most cited data points in educational research is the so-called "30 million word gap" between the children of professional and working class families. In 1995, University of Kansas child psychologists Betty Hart and Todd R. Risley found that the way parents and caregivers talk to their children from ages zero to three has a significant effect on the child's literacy and academic success later in life.[8] Their study of the words spoken in the homes of one- and two-year-olds demonstrated that the frequency and quality of words a child hears during her or his first three years of life are critically important in shaping language development. Hart and Risley estimated that children of affluent, professional families hear eleven million words per year, while those in working class families hear approximately six million words. Most tellingly, children of families on public assistance hear a relative pittance—only three million words annually. Accrued over the first four years of life, this adds up to a verbal advantage of thirty million words for the children of educated, professional class children before they enter kindergarten.

It is no exaggeration to say that for low-income American children, early disadvantages in language—both the volume of words and the way in which they are employed—establishes a kind of educational inertia that is immensely difficult to address. Schools will spend every moment trying to make up for the verbal gaps kids bring with them to school, which tend to grow wider year after year.

New York City's answer is to bet heavily on preschool. But the investment in preschool—even high-quality, language-rich preschool—will come to no good end if it is not the first step in an unbroken chain of superior schools from kindergarten to high school, and then on to college or a strong career and technical education program following graduation. Nothing else—and nothing less—will suffice if we wish to restore the promise of upward mobility for the next generation of low-income American children.

IT PAYS TO INCREASE YOUR WORD POWER

Setting America's poorest children on the path of upward mobility is far harder to accomplish than we generally care to admit. Effective schools can have a considerable impact, but it requires a clear-eyed view of the enormity of the task. The job, already daunting, is made more difficult still because educating for upward mobility and economic self-sufficiency also challenges some of our most revered educational traditions (particularly local control of curriculum), as well as pedagogical fashions like "child-centered" or "culturally relevant" education.

There is no best way or magic bullet. But if you were to strive for one positive outcome—and one only—that would set a low-income child on a path for upward mobility, you would almost certainly wish for that child to have a big vocabulary.

Vocabulary size, as E. D. Hirsch Jr. observed, "is a convenient proxy for a whole range of educational attainments and abilities."[9] A wealth of words signals competence in reading and writing. A substantial working vocabulary also correlates with SAT success, which in turn predicts the likelihood of college attendance, graduation, and the associated wage premium that has been fetishized by education reformers and has driven their agenda for decades. Hirsch noted that:

[s]tudies have solidly established the correlation between vocabulary and real-world ability. Many of these studies examine the Armed Forces Qualification Test (AFQT), which the military devised in 1950 as an entrance requirement and a job-allocating device. . . . The military has determined that the test predicts real-world job performance most accurately when you *double* the verbal score and add it to the math score. Once you perform that adjustment, according to a 1999 study by Christopher Winship and Sanders Korenman, a gain of one standard deviation on the AFQT raises one's annual income by nearly $10,000 (in 2012 dollars). Other studies show that much of the disparity in the black–white wage gap disappears when you take AFQT scores—again, weighted toward the verbal side—into account.[10]

Those old *Reader's Digest* vocabulary quizzes had it exactly right. It really *does* pay to increase your word power. College or no college, AFQT data tells an important story: Verbal proficiency is an essential precondition to upward mobility, even for enlisted members of the military. Raising it is as sure a bet as schools can make if their aim is to lift children from poverty.

For much of the past twenty years, most education debate has centered on the question of whether poverty matters—whether demographics are destiny or if schooling is enough to elevate the children of the poor into the world of work and opportunity. As in most tendentious education debates, both sides have a strong claim. *Of course* poverty matters. And with equal certainty, schools can make a difference—if not for all, then certainly for many more of our poorest children and families. But doing so will require a clear focus on the instructional approaches most likely to bear fruit.

"If we want to reduce economic inequality in America," Hirsch concluded succinctly, "a good place to start is the language-arts classroom."[11]

THE MATTHEW EFFECT

If you went to college, chances are good that at some point during your junior or senior year of high school you devoted many tedious hours to rote memorization of SAT words. Perhaps some of them—*assiduous, enervating, perfidious*—worked their way into your working vocabulary, and you use them to this day. A college freshman has command, on average, of sixty thousand to one hundred thousand words.[12] If you have a vocabulary of that size or larger, you owe no more than a tiny fraction of it to memorization. Learning that many words would require memorizing between ten and twenty new words every day from birth until freshman year in college.

Under no circumstances should we be tempted to convert early childhood education into extended vocabulary enhancement exercises with word lists to be memorized. Rather, it's essential to understand how big vocabularies are created. We don't learn words through memorization, but by repeated exposure to unfamiliar words in context.

Language growth is perhaps the clearest manifestation in K–8 education of the "Matthew effect," a term coined by University of Toronto cognitive scientist Keith Stanovich after this chapter's opening passage from the Gospel of Matthew: "For unto every one that hath shall be given, and he shall have abundance: but from him that hath not shall be taken away even that which he hath." Simply put, the rich get richer while the poor get poorer. This pattern can be particularly true of vocabulary: Early language advantages create the ideal conditions for the verbally rich to grow richer in knowledge and language, while the verbally poor fall further behind. When schools fail to address gaps in knowledge and language, the deficits widen.

Among educators, vocabulary is often described as "tiered." Tier-one words include basic words that most native speakers come to school with, regardless of upbringing: "baby," "dog," "run," "chair," "happy." Tier three represents specialized vocabulary associated with particular domains of knowledge and rarely heard elsewhere, such as "isotope" or "exposition." The sweet spot for vocabulary growth and language proficiency are tier-two words, which occur in a variety of domains. Words like "verify," "superior," "negligent"—or "gorgeous" and "sequence"—are common to sophisticated adult speech and reading; we perceive them as ordinary, not specialized, language. Tier-two words are essential to reading comprehension and undergird more subtle and precise use of language, both receptive (reading, hearing) and expressive (writing, speaking).

We directly learn and memorize only a tiny fraction of the words in our working vocabulary. The only reliable way to acquire new, sophisticated words is through repeated exposure—either through reading or hearing them. With each new encounter with the word, possible definitions are narrowed and refined until eventually the child has command of it and incorporates the world into his or her vocabulary.

Consider now how a child might come to encounter, and hopefully add to her or his vocabulary, the tier-two word "durable." The child would need multiple exposures to the word. More importantly, she or he would need enough background knowledge to properly contextualize the unfamiliar word in each encounter. Only by repeated exposure with the meaning, correctly inferred, will the child become familiar enough with it to understand it, use it correctly, and attain familiarity with the useful new word "durable."

Here are some potential uses of the word he or she might encounter:

• "The Egyptians learned how to make durable sheets of parchment from the papyrus plant."

- "With this lightweight and durable telescope, young scientists can explore the natural wonders of the earth or the craters of the moon and beyond."
- "The Qing Empire/China is easily among the ranks of the most successful and durable empires of the modern period."
- "Many durable ancient Roman concrete buildings are still in use after more than two thousand years."
- "Instead of having to find caves or create makeshift shelters for protection from the weather, man started to look for more durable materials with which to build long-lasting dwellings."

In order for the vocabulary-building process to work, the child must be able to understand the gist of what she or he hears or reads to contextualize the unfamiliar new word. In the previous examples, terms like *Egyptians, parchment, papyrus, makeshift shelters,* and *concrete* lend sense and meaning to the word "durable." Without the enabling context, language growth stalls.

This is the Matthew effect in action: Those who have the broadest general knowledge, whether acquired at home, school, or elsewhere in their lives, are most likely to possess the "schema" necessary to acquire more knowledge and language; those who do not fall further behind. Opportunities for vocabulary acquisition are strictly limited when children lack the background knowledge to optimize language growth.

Seen through this lens, it is immediately and abundantly clear that the key to language growth is the broadest possible knowledge base. The more background knowledge a child possesses, the greater the likelihood that she will have the ability to correctly contextualize what she reads and hears, which in turn increases the odds that new and useful words will enter her working vocabulary. And it proceeds from this that the best way to ensure language growth is a primary education that is as rich and varied as possible.

The impulse to focus on the "skill" of reading rather than the act of reading as a means of building literacy is paradoxically wrong. Once basic skills of decoding—translating written symbols into words and sentences—are mastered, you build strong readers by increasing a child's store of knowledge of the world.

The soul of language growth is the ability to contextualize and make correct inferences. Imagine how unlikely it would be for the word "durable" to enter the child's vocabulary if, in the previous examples, he or she didn't know who the Egyptians were or what papyrus was; if she or he was unfamiliar with the Qing dynasty; or if he or she could not accurately infer from context what it means for a two-thousand-year-old building to be *durable.* The background knowledge of these things makes the unique word stand out, its meaning inferable. In the absence of background knowledge, the word "durable" is one among many unfamiliar terms—"parchment," "craters," "makeshift," "Roman," "papyrus"—and unlikely to stick.

Once again, we see the advantage of growing up in a rich verbal stew with educated parents and a home full of books—and the challenge for those who do not. Unless schools address knowledge and language deficits directly and aggressively, there is no reason to expect anything other than for kids who grow up in a state of language poverty to remain there. Left unaddressed, this can be harshly determinative for low-income children and devastating to their educational opportunities and earning potential.

K–8'S UNFORGIVABLE BLUNDER

If it seems obvious that drenching students in context-giving knowledge and language throughout the foundational elementary years of school—and ideally sooner—is the surest way to boost language proficiency, the message has been largely lost on the American education system. The gravest mistake made in our schools is teaching and testing reading as if it is a skill, like riding a bike or throwing a ball, which can be applied to any random piece of text regardless of subject matter or context. The annual reading tests that we use to measure student proficiency—and, increasingly, teacher effectiveness—could be more accurately described as tests of background knowledge than of reading comprehension. It is not an exaggeration to say that there's no such thing as a reading test.[13]

Reading is best understood as a two-part process. First, children learn to "decode" the words on a printed page, ideally through rich and comprehensive phonics instruction. But when low-income children struggle with reading, the issue more often than not tends not to be decoding, but rather the second part of the process: comprehension.

Unlike decoding, reading comprehension is not a skill, or even a suite of skills that can be practiced or mastered in the abstract and applied to any passage or piece of text. Comprehension is chiefly "domain specific," or grounded in context. In order to fully comprehend a reading passage about architecture or football, you need to know at least a little about those topics—and sometimes quite a lot. In sum, there is much wisdom in the idea that "first you learn to read, then you read to learn."

However, the dominant methods of teaching reading comprehension in American elementary schools over the last few decades tend to assume that reading comprehension is a transferable skill. Reading instruction often involves teaching and practicing "reading strategies" such as visualizing, predicting, and finding the main idea, which students typically learn and practice on texts of their own choosing and at their "just-right" reading level.

When reading failure occurs, or when children remain stubbornly stuck at low reading levels, it is very often a failure of reading with comprehension, rather than one of decoding. This has little to do with the "skill" of reading, which is really not a skill at all, but a lack of background knowledge about the topic at hand.

The connection between background knowledge and reading comprehension is firmly established and readily demonstrated. A 1988 study by Donna Recht and Lauren Leslie looked at the importance of background knowledge on reading comprehension of a baseball-related text. The authors arranged a clever experiment in which students were divided into four groups according to reading ability (high or low) and domain knowledge concerning baseball (high or low). They found that students with high domain knowledge performed better on all assessment tasks.

In the study, students with low reading skills easily outperformed "strong" readers when they had high domain knowledge of baseball that more capable readers lacked. The authors wrote, "It appears that knowledge of a content domain is a powerful determinant of the amount and quality of the information recalled, powerful enough for poor readers to compensate for their generally low reading ability."[14]

In short, knowing a lot about the subject turned the poor readers into good readers—a powerful argument for reorienting elementary and middle school education around broad knowledge development across subject areas, thus increasing the number of subjects about which children can read with comprehension and mitigating the worst of the Matthew effect.

What this means for schools hoping to educate for upward mobility is that they should do everything in their power to make children richer in knowledge and language. The ability to read for understanding, write with clarity, and communicate with ease and fluency is essential not just for the college-bound.

Language proficiency is an essential component of a productive work life in nearly all careers and jobs, and it is highly predictive of future earnings, as the data from the Armed Forces Qualification Test demonstrate.

Any discussion of educating for upward mobility will almost inevitably focus on paths to prosperity that do not include college—including vocational education, military service, or professional certifications. But there is no reason to believe that the need for basic literacy will be any less urgent regardless of the academic or vocational path students ultimately choose. Indeed, the absence of a baseline level of literacy is nearly certain in itself to impede any path to upward mobility. Early and urgent attention to literacy and language growth is particularly important given evidence that nearly three out of four struggling third grade readers are still struggling in ninth grade.[15] Other

studies have demonstrated that high school graduation can be predicted by
knowing third-grade reading scores:

> A person who is not at least a modestly skilled reader by the end of third grade
> is quite unlikely to graduate from high school. Only a generation ago, this did
> not matter so much, because the long-term economic effects of not becoming a
> good reader and not graduating high school were less severe.[16]

The correlation of general knowledge and language proficiency—and of language proficiency and earning power—implies that schools should avoid at
all costs any impulse to narrow curricula to an ill-conceived regimen of reading skills and strategies at the expense of a well-defined program constructed
around coherent, sequential, and domain-based content.

Low-income children especially need more science, social studies, art, and
music—the better to build enabling "schema" to assist in comprehension and
language growth.

Robust, substantial, and coherent content, not skills and strategies, should
be at the very heart of literacy instruction from the first days of school. They
lay the foundation for language growth, which is critical for further college
and career opportunities.

The foundational role of knowledge acquisition across subject areas has
been neglected for too long by American elementary and middle schools. A
skills-focused orientation has led most schools to focus almost exclusively on
"leveled reading"—establishing a child's reading level and encouraging him
or her to read "high-interest" books at that level.

The dominant approach to building reading comprehension ability is to
teach and practice metacognitive "reading strategies" as students read independently or in small groups. Students are encouraged as they read, to "vi-
sualize," to "activate prior knowledge," and to "make connections" between
what they know and what they are reading about, among other strategies.
Broadly speaking, the idea is to encourage children to read with maximum
engagement in the hope of developing in each child a "lifelong love of reading."

To be clear, there is much wisdom to the idea that the best way to ensure
reading competence is simply to spur children to read a lot. Schools need to
encourage an enormous amount of reading, both at "instructional" (a stretch
for kids to read) and "independent" (kids can read it on their own) levels. The
language of children's books, in fact, has been found to be more linguistically
rich and complex than the conversation of even college graduates.[17]

More is better, therefore, when it comes to reading. But schools can optimize vocabulary growth by organizing curriculum and instruction coherently
across a wide variety of subjects. Studies have demonstrated that vocabulary

growth is accelerated when children read within familiar knowledge domains (remember, as in the "durable" example, that correct inferences enable developing readers to intuit and learn unfamiliar words in context).[18] This suggests that schools would be wise to stay on topics for extended periods (perhaps two weeks), creating optimal conditions for language growth.

Since broadening a child's knowledge base makes her more likely to be able to contextualize and understand new words, the principle can be summarized this way: Reading comprehension is not a skill you teach; it's a condition you create.

The most egregious error made by too many schools, however, is to worship nearly exclusively at the altar of student engagement. Too often we condescend to children by assuming that if a book or subject is not directly relevant to their own interests or experience, they will become bored and disengaged. Equally damaging is the idea that children will not or cannot engage if what they read is not pleasurable and makes too many demands of them. The clear connection between background knowledge, language growth, and reading comprehension makes it quite clear that these are self-limiting assumptions, however well-intentioned.

If school does not submerge a child in knowledge of the world—if the child is encouraged, for reasons that are deeply humane, to explore personal interests and read exclusively about topics of personal interest or entertainment—the child will remain in a state of language poverty and will likely be cemented in economic poverty for life.

HOW COMMON CORE MIGHT HELP

If schools understood the connection between knowledge and literacy, and between vocabulary and upward mobility, much of American education might look very different. Elementary education in particular would change from a "student-centered," skills-driven approach to one that sees its role as foundational, even determinative, of educational and economic success. Knowledge and language acquisition (which really cannot be separated from each other) would be at the core.

The long, skills-driven "literacy block" that chews up as much as two hours of the typical elementary school student's day would be reordered around coherent content across content areas like science, history, fiction and literature, geography, art, and music. Elementary school teachers, especially those who work with our poorest children, would be restored, in David Coleman's lovely and apt phrase, "to their rightful place as guides to the universe."[19]

At present, we know surprisingly little about what children do all day in school, as well as the degree to which teachers understand and act upon the imperative to help children—particularly the disadvantaged—build background knowledge. But what we do know is not encouraging. Studies by the National Institute of Child Health and Human Development have revealed that only 4 percent of first-grade class time in American elementary schools is spent on science, and just 2 percent on social studies.[20] In third grade, about 5 percent of class time goes to each of these subjects. Meanwhile a whopping 62 percent in first grade and 47 percent in third grade is spent on language arts.[21]

In most schools, the hours spent on literacy are something of a black hole. There is no way to know with any certainty whether there is any caloric value in the reading children do during the long hours of the literacy block— whether they are reading challenging texts aimed at building background knowledge and vocabulary or simply reading "leveled texts" pitched at each student's ostensible reading level.[22] In the absence of established curricula, it is impossible to know whether a second grader, for example, is spending those many hours with a basal reading program, tackling a nonfiction unit on the solar system, or idling away time reading *Captain Underpants* on the theory that all reading is good reading.

A shift in reading instruction from a skills-based approach to a content-based one is a signature feature of the Common Core State Standards in English language arts, which make it clear that all reading instruction should take place within the context of a knowledge-rich curriculum. In their "Anchor Standards for Reading," the Common Core's authors specify their purpose:

> By reading texts in history/social studies, science, and other disciplines, students build a foundation of knowledge in these fields that will also give them the background to be better readers in all content areas. Students can only gain this foundation when the curriculum is intentionally and coherently structured to develop rich content knowledge within and across grades.[23]

Because standards are not curriculum, the Common Core cannot prescribe, let alone dictate, the scope and sequence of a well-rounded K–8 education. Yet the architects of the Common Core have done all in their power to establish the standards' intent:

> Building knowledge systematically in English language arts is like giving children various pieces of a puzzle in each grade that, over time, will form one big picture. At a curricular or instructional level, texts—within and across grade levels—need to be selected around topics or themes that systematically develop the knowledge base of students.[24]

There has been in recent decades—and especially in the era of No Child Left Behind and its annual reading tests for grades 3 through 8—a tendency to see a rich curriculum in science, history, art, and music as something to be done either after or in addition to teaching reading. It is more accurate to view this knowledge-building function of education as the indispensable wellspring of reading proficiency.

"The mistaken idea that reading is a skill—learn to crack the code, practice comprehension strategies, and you can read anything—may be the single biggest factor holding back reading achievement in the country," University of Virginia cognitive scientist Daniel T. Willingham has observed. "Students will not meet standards that way. The knowledge base problem must be solved."[25]

By placing a premium on a coherent, sequential, knowledge-rich curriculum, the Common Core State Standards make it clear that all language arts instruction should take place against a curricular backdrop that (correctly) conceives of verbal proficiency as a function of background knowledge. While this is an essential conceptual pushback against the dominant skills-and-strategies approach prevalent in most US elementary schools, it also places a considerable burden on districts and schools to embrace the spirit of the standards and not merely the letter, pushing back against a general anti-curriculum ethos of American education that has dominated schools for the last half-century or more.[26]

If we retain the same random, incoherent, skills-based approach that dominates reading instruction and merely increase the amount of nonfiction kids read, there is no reason to suspect it will enhance reading ability—or drive the vocabulary gains one would expect from a coherent, sequential curriculum.

RESISTANCE TO A COHERENT CURRICULUM

To readers of a certain age—say, forty or older—one suspects that nothing of what has been suggested previously will seem even mildly controversial. Of course elementary and middle schools should offer children a rich blend of geography, science, history, art, and music, they might think. Of course schools should introduce them to the best of what has been thought, written, and said. "Why," they might be thinking, "that's what school is for!"

For the children of low-income parents, a foundational education rich in knowledge and language is an essential key to upward mobility. The long odds of upward mobility are made longer by a set of incorrect assumptions we make about schools and a general hostility toward an established curriculum.

Indeed, perhaps the stiffest challenge parents of low-income children face—even under Common Core—is the distinctly old-fashioned flavor of an education with knowledge and vocabulary acquisition at its heart. Districts, schools, and even (or especially) teachers generally eschew a fixed curriculum. They are far likelier to want to tailor instruction to subjects they or their students enjoy, or default to what they have taught for years. Likewise, education in the elementary and middle school levels broadly favors privileging skills such as critical thinking, problem solving, collaboration, and communication over any particular body of knowledge.

The popular homilies that guide teachers reinforce the general disregard shown to a content-rich education. "Be the guide on the side, not the sage on the stage," teachers are advised. "Teach the child, not the lesson." We unthinkingly repeat these clichés not because they are correct, but because they are inspiring and ennobling. Of all the maxims in education, though, none rankles more than this one: "Education is not the filling of a pail, but the lighting of a fire." The quote is typically (and mistakenly) attributed to the poet William Butler Yeats.

Writing at the *Washington Post*'s *Answer Sheet* blog, Carol Corbett Burris, a high school principal and an outspoken Common Core detractor, uses the aphorism to formulate her criticism of the standards:

> [T]he pail fillers are determining the fate of our schools. The "filling of the pail" is the philosophy of those who see students as vessels into which facts and knowledge are poured. The better the teacher, the more stuff in the pail. How do we measure what is in the pail? With a standardized test, of course. Not enough in the pail? No excuses. We must identify the teachers who best fill the pail, and dismiss the rest.[27]

The damage done by those who denigrate the importance of a knowledge-rich classroom—especially for our most disadvantaged learners—can scarcely be overstated. Education is neither the filling of a bucket nor the lighting of a fire. It's both. You can't light a fire in an empty bucket. When leading practitioners fail to grasp this notion at even a rudimentary level, it underscores the difficulty of any endeavor to raise the achievement level of our most disadvantaged children.

The most recent version of the skills delusion is the "twenty-first-century skills" movement. The appeal of such schemes is intuitive, seductive, and almost invariably wrong. Like reading comprehension, the ability to solve problems and think critically or creatively are not transferable skills that can be developed in the abstract and applied to novel areas of expertise. It is easy to be gulled into believing we can teach children to "think like a scientist" or "read like a historian." But they must first know what the scientist or historian knows.

Further resistance to a well-defined foundational curriculum comes from those who favor mass, technology-driven customization of curricula. There's a surface plausibility to allowing a student to chart his or her own academic path; it stands to reason that all students will be more engaged and persistent in their studies if they are intrinsically motivated and interested in subject matter they choose themselves.

But it is critical to recognize the degree to which, like it or not, language proficiency rests on a foundation of common knowledge. Individualization that begins too early is likely to do more harm than good, leaving low-income students in particular at a serious disadvantage when it comes to competing for educational and vocational opportunities. In the critical foundational years of K–8, the onus is on educators to ensure that every child has sufficient common knowledge and vocabulary to communicate clearly and with understanding with all other members of the speech community. Hyper-individualization of content risks leaving children with glaring gaps in their background knowledge that will interfere with mature language proficiency, hamper academic achievement *and* engagement, and stop upward mobility in its tracks.

Schools that would educate for upward mobility must resist the siren song of content-free skills. All of the goals we have for education, and thus for upward mobility, are grounded in broad general knowledge. In sum, a school without a well-defined scope and sequence describing a broad body of content across subject areas—at least from kindergarten to the fifth grade, and ideally to the eighth grade—can scarcely be described as having a curriculum at all. The absence of a coherent curriculum undergirding reading instruction can be fatal to mature language acquisition and proficiency.

The idea that there should be a firmly established core curriculum in the foundational years of schooling goes against the grain of much contemporary education thought and practice, both among those who favor strong local control of curriculum and among progressive educators.

Progressives who resist the notion that a coherently sequenced, knowledge-rich core curriculum is necessary to address income inequality might heed the words of one of their intellectual polestars, Diane Ravitch, who has argued for a voluntary national curriculum. "Many educators and parents worry that a national curriculum might be captured by 'the wrong people,' that is, someone whose views they do not share," she has written. But despite these concerns, Ravitch was persuaded of the need for common content as a means to "release us from the shackles of test-based accountability."[28]

Ravitch has famously repudiated nearly all of her previously held positions on testing and accountability. It is important to note, therefore, that the following provocative passage comes not from her early work, but from her 2010 book *The Death and Life of the Great American School System,* published after she had "switched sides":

> If it is impossible to reach a consensus about a national curriculum, then every state should make sure that every child receives an education that includes

history, geography, literature, the arts, the sciences, civics, foreign languages, health, and physical education. The subjects should not be discretionary or left to chance. Every state should have a curriculum that is rich in knowledge, issues, and ideas, while leaving teachers free to use their own methods, with enough time to introduce topics and activities of their own choosing.

Ravitch continues,

To have no curriculum, as is so often the case in American schools, leaves schools at the mercy of those who demand a regime of basic skills and no content at all. To have no curriculum is to leave the decision about what matters to the ubiquitous textbooks, which function as our de facto national curriculum. To have no curriculum on which assessments may be based is to tighten the grip of test-based accountability, testing only generic skills, not knowledge or comprehension.[29]

CULTURE AND LANGUAGE

An additional impediment to education for language proficiency and upward mobility—and one that is particularly sensitive—is cultural. To a degree that can be awkward to acknowledge, language is a cultural artifact, filled with assumed knowledge, allusion, and idioms that are a reflection of the culture that created it. Not for nothing did E. D. Hirsch Jr. title his 1987 bestseller on reading and language *Cultural Literacy.*

That book, and Hirsch's subsequent work, have tended to ignite firestorms of controversy, but critics have largely misunderstood Hirsch's thrust. His object has not been to establish a canon. Rather, his is a curatorial effort aimed at cataloging the knowledge that literate speakers and writers know—and take for granted that their audiences know as well.

The idea that American schools should explicitly familiarize children—especially those from other countries, cultures, or traditions—with a uniform body of knowledge in elementary and middle school falls upon contemporary ears as awkward, anachronistic, even inappropriate. We are far more likely to honor or even revere home language, culture, and dialect. But we must seriously consider the possibility that this impulse is wrong for all the right reasons.

Lisa Delpit, an African American literacy researcher and a 1990 MacArthur grantee, has written persuasively for many years about the "culture of power" in American schools and classrooms and the "schism between liberal educational movements and that of non-White, non-middle-class teachers and communities." In her seminal essay, "The Silenced Dialogue," she explains the implications of the culture of power:

This means that success in institutions—schools, workplaces, and so on—is predicated upon acquisition of the culture of those who are in power. Children from middle-class homes tend to do better in school than those from non-middle-class homes because the culture of the school is based on the culture of the upper and middle classes—of those in power. The upper and middle classes send their children to school with all the accouterments of the culture of power; children from other kinds of families operate within perfectly wonderful and viable cultures but not cultures that carry the codes or rules of power.[30]

To say this is an uncomfortable topic among educators is to vastly understate things, especially among those who are equally and earnestly committed to progressive ideals and progressive pedagogy. "The Silenced Dialogue" and the book it spawned, *Other People's Children,* are staples on the syllabus of teacher-education programs and often spark heated debate and wounded egos. "Those with power are frequently least aware of—or least willing to acknowledge—its existence," Delpit insists. She argues:

> To provide schooling for everyone's children that reflects liberal, middle-class values and aspirations is to ensure the maintenance of the status quo, to ensure that power, the culture of power, remains in the hands of those who already have it. Some children come to school with more accouterments of the culture of power already in place—"cultural capital," as some critical theorists refer to it (for example, Apple, 1979)—some with less. Many liberal educators hold that the primary goal for education is for children to become autonomous, to develop fully who they are in the classroom setting without having arbitrary, outside standards forced upon them. This is a very reasonable goal for people whose children are already participants in the culture of power and who have already internalized its codes.
>   But parents who don't function within that culture often want something else. It's not that they disagree with the former aim, it's just that they want something more. They want to ensure that the school provides their children with discourse patterns, interactional styles, and spoken and written language codes that will allow them success in the larger society.[31]

To be highly proficient in English requires mastery over not just an alphabet and rules of grammar, but also an enormous range of assumed knowledge, historical references, and cultural allusions commonly held by members of a speech community. "My kids know how to be Black," one parent tells Delpit. "You all teach them how to be successful in the White man's world."[32]

American education remains deeply reluctant to do this, since it requires overthrowing any number of traditions and practices: from child-centered pedagogies, assumptions about student engagement, and other progressive education ideals to local control of curriculum, the privileging of skills over content, and the movement toward mass customization of education. Each of these in ways great or small work against the cause of language proficiency; in doing so, they make the task of educating for upward mobility more difficult.

CONCLUSION

In 1994, Ron Suskind published *A Hope in the Unseen,* the story of a bright, ambitious young man from one of the worst high schools in Washington, DC, who defies the odds to win acceptance at Brown University. The book became one of the touchstones of the education reform movement because it appeared to demonstrate that demographics need not be destiny. You *can* grow up as dirt poor as its protagonist, Cedric Jennings, and still achieve at the highest levels academically—all the way to the Ivy League.

There is a brief but telling moment in the book when a Brown professor asks his class how many of them have ever been to Ellis Island. Jennings has never heard of it. "Ellis Island is not a core concept in Southeast Washington," Suskind wrote. Rather it is "the sort of white people's history passed over in favor of Afrocentric studies."[33]

Because of his lack of background knowledge, Jennings is at a decided disadvantage. He struggles through a lecture in which some students barely take notes and others literally sleep in class. "So many class discussions are full of references he doesn't understand," Suskind reports. "Maura knows what to write on her pad and the sleepers will be able to skim the required readings, all of them guided by some mysterious encoded knowledge of history, economics, and education, of culture and social events, that they picked up in school or at home or God knows where."[34]

The author does not dwell on the anecdote, but it is a critical insight. Jennings is a smart, driven young man who wants badly to succeed. He may be the grittiest in class and have first-rate work habits, but he has to work much harder, and his simple lack of background knowledge nearly derails his chance of succeeding in college. In the end, he succeeds not because of the formative years of his education, but in spite of them. His journey from poor urban schools, through the Ivy League, and onward to a life of economic mobility is made far more difficult than it needed to be. This remains the case in too many schools that serve almost exclusively low-income children.

It cuts against the received wisdom of pedagogical fashion and political tradition, but regardless of where one attends school—for reasons of language development, skills acquisition, and civic engagement—there should be far more similarities than differences in K–8 education in the United States. The promise of preparing children for academic achievement and upward mobility depends upon a base level of language proficiency. Elementary and middle school education should prepare students for independent exploration—it should not *be* independent exploration.

Insisting on hyper-local choice and encouraging wild experimentation in content is tantamount to promoting the use of different alphabets. Foundational knowledge across the curriculum not only sets the stage for further independent exploration, it provides the basis for language proficiency—for communication, collaboration, and cooperation between and among disparate people.

In short, language cares little about education trends toward child-centered schools and culturally relevant pedagogy. Language cares even less about local control of curriculum. There is a language of upward mobility in America. It has an expansive and nuanced vocabulary that it employs to nimbly navigate the world of organizations, institutions, and opportunities.

The most influential figure in the history of American education was, without question, the philosopher John Dewey. "What the best and wisest parent wants for his child," he famously observed, "that must we want for all the children of the community. Anything less is unlovely, and left unchecked, destroys our democracy."[35]

Perhaps Dewey was wrong. Rather that want what the best and wisest parents want for their child, we should want what those parents give to their child without even realizing it: a childhood rich in both words and knowledge. Anything else is inequitable and destroys any chance of upward mobility. At the very least, Dewey may have simply assumed that a sound basic education would endow every child with the knowledge and language that would propel her or him through a successful education and a lifetime of productive citizenship. We can no longer afford to take this for granted.

It is not an overstatement to suggest that without a common body of knowledge and its associated gains in vocabulary and language proficiency as a first purpose of American education, the achievement gap will remain a permanent fixture of American society, and that the challenge of upward mobility, always difficult, will be insurmountable.

NOTES

1. Lee Dembart, "Carter Takes 'Sobering' Trip to South Bronx," *New York Times,* October 6, 1997, http://query.nytimes.com/mem/archive-free/pdf?res=9C07E3D9153 DE034BC4E53DFB667838C669EDE.

2. "De Blasio Calls Universal Pre-K Deal 'Historic,' 'Incredible,'," CBS New York, March 31, 2014, http://newyork.cbslocal.com/2014/03/31/de-blasio-calls-universal-pre-k-deal-historic-incredible/; NYC Office of the Mayor, "New York City Launches Historic Expansion of Pre-K to More Than 51,000 Children," 2015. http://

www1.nyc.gov/office-of-the-mayor/news/425-14/new-york-city-launches-historic-expansion-pre-k-more-51-000-children#/0.

3. NYC Department of Education, "New York State Common Core English Language Arts (ELA) & Mathematics Tests Grades 3–8 New York City Results," 2014, http://schools.nyc.gov/Accountability/data/TestResults/ELAandMathTestResults.

4. Families for Excellent Schools. "The Forgotten Fourth," http://39sf0512acpc3iz0941zlzn5.wpengine.netdna-cdn.com/wp-content/uploads/2014/10/TheForgottenFourth_V4.pdf.

5. Ginia Bellafante, "Before a Test, a Poverty of Words," *New York Times,* October 5, 2012, http://www.nytimes.com/2012/10/07/nyregion/for-poor-schoolchildren-a-poverty-of-words.html.

6. Annette Lareau, *Unequal Childhoods: Class, Race, and Family Life* (Berkeley and Los Angeles: University of California Press, 2003).

7. David Brooks, "Both Sides of Inequality," *New York Times,* March 9, 2006. http://query.nytimes.com/gst/fullpage.html?res=9A0CEFDB1231F93AA35750C0A9609C8B63&module=Search&mabReward=relbias%3Ar%2C%7B%221%22%3A%22RI%3A8%22%7D.

8. Betty Hart and Todd R. Risley, "The Early Catastrophe," *American Educator,* 2003, https://www.aft.org/sites/default/files/periodicals/TheEarlyCatastrophe.pdf.

9. E. D. Hirsch Jr., "A Wealth of Words," *City Journal,* 2013, http://www.city-journal.org/2013/23_1_vocabulary.html.

10. Ibid.

11. Ibid.

12. Robert Pondiscio, "How to Get a Big Vocabulary," *Core Knowledge,* December 20, 2012, http://blog.coreknowledge.org/2012/12/20/vocabulary-is-the-new-black/.

13. E. D. Hirsch and Robert Pondiscio, "There's No Such Thing as a Reading Test," *The American Prospect,* June 13, 2010, http://prospect.org/article/theres-no-such-thing-reading-test.

14. Donna Recht and Lauren Leslie, "Effects of Prior Knowledge on Good and Poor Readers' Memory of Text," *Journal of Educational Psychology* 80, no. 1 (1988): 16–20.

15. J. M. Fletcher and G. R. Lyon, "Reading: A Research-based Approach," in W. Evers, ed., *What's Wrong in America's Classrooms* (Stanford, CA: Hoover Institute Press, 1998), 49–90.

16. C. E. Snow, M. S. Burns, and P. Griffin, *Preventing Reading Difficulties in Young Children,* (Washington, DC: National Academy Press, 1998), ERIC Document No. ED416465.

17. Anne E. Cunningham and Keith E. Stanovich, "What Reading Does for the Mind," *Journal of Direct Instruction* 1, no. 2 (2001), http://www.csun.edu/~krowlands/Content/Academic_Resources/Reading/Useful%20Articles/Cunningham-What%20Reading%20Does%20for%20the%20Mind.pdf.

18. E. D. Hirsch Jr., "Reading Comprehension Requires Knowledge—of Words and the World," *American Educator,* 2003, https://www.aft.org/sites/default/files/periodicals/AE_SPRNG.pdf.

19. Robert Pondiscio, "Nobody Loves Standards (and That's O.K.)," *Common Core Watch* (blog), June 13, 2012, http://edexcellence.net/commentary/education-gadfly-daily/common-core-watch/2012/nobody-loves-standards-and-thats-ok.html.

20. NICHD Early Child Care Research Network, "The Relation of Global First-Grade Classroom Environment to Structural Classroom Features and Teacher and Student Behaviors," *The Elementary School Journal* 102, no. 5 (2002).

21. NICHD Early Child Care Research Network, "A Day in Third Grade: A Large-Scale Study of Classroom Quality and Teacher and Student Behavior," *The Elementary School Journal* 105, no. 3 (2005), http://eric.ed.gov/?id=EJ696848.

22. Robert Pondiscio and Kevin Mahnken, "Leveled Reading: The Making of a Literacy Myth," *Common Core Watch* (blog), September 24, 2014, http://edexcellence.net/articles/leveled-reading-the-making-of-a-literacy-myth.

23. Common Core State Standards Initiative, "College and Career Readiness Anchor Standards for Reading," http://www.corestandards.org/ELA-Literacy/CCRA/R/.

24. Common Core State Standards Initiative, "Standard 10: Range, Quality, and Complexity," http://www.corestandards.org/ELA-Literacy/standard-10-range-quality-complexity/staying-on-topic-within-a-grade-across-grades/.

25. Daniel Willingham, "Willingham: Reading Is Not a Skill—And Why This Is a Problem for the Draft National Standards," *The Answer Sheet* (blog), *The Washington Post*, September 28, 2009, http://voices.washingtonpost.com/answer-sheet/daniel-willingham/willingham-reading-is-not-a-sk.html.

26. E. D. Hirsch Jr., "Sixty Years without a Curriculum," in *The Making of Americans: Democracy and our Schools* (New Haven, CT: Yale University Press, 2010).

27. Carol Corbett Burris, "Is 'Filling the Pail' Any Way to Train Teachers?," *The Answer Sheet* (blog), *The Washington Post,* July 5, 2012, http://www.washingtonpost.com/blogs/answer-sheet/post/is-filling-the-pail-any-way-to-train-teachers/2012/07/04/gJQADViVOW_blog.html.

28. Diane Ravitch, "In Need of a Renaissance: Real Reform Will Renew, Not Abandon, Our Neighborhood Schools," *American Educator* 34, no. 2 (Summer 2010).

29 Diane Ravitch, *The Death and Life of the Great American School System: How Testing and Choice Are Undermining Education* (New York: Basic Books, 2011).

30. Lisa Delpit, "The Silenced Dialogue: Power and Pedagogy in Educating Other People's Children," *Harvard Educational Review* 58, no. 3 (Fall 1988).

31. Ibid.

32. Ibid.

33. Ron Suskind, *A Hope in the Unseen: An American Odyssey from the Inner City to the Ivy League* (New York: Broadway Books, 1999).

34. Ibid.

35. John Dewey, *The School and Society* (Chicago: University of Chicago Press, 1907).

Chapter Ten

Tracking in Middle School

Tom Loveless

Education can always use an upbeat story. The past decade's expansion of the Advanced Placement (AP) program is surely one of those. The graduating class of 2013 included, for the first time ever, more than one million AP examinees. Participation doubled in only ten years. Among low-income kids, the expansion has been amazing. In 2003, 58,489 low-income students sat for AP tests. In 2013, the number was 275,864—a 370 percent increase. AP started as an elite high school curricular option, designed to serve the nation's top students, and it was democratizing. Students from privileged backgrounds had always been well represented in AP classes. Now academically talented students from poor families were joining them.[1]

But concerns about the success of the expansion have emerged. It's one thing to take an AP class; it's quite another to learn the material and to do well on AP exams. A 2013 story in the *Baltimore Sun* described the plight of thousands of low-income students who take AP classes, receive As and Bs in the courses—and then fail AP exams.

They don't fail by just a little bit. They fail by a lot, receiving a score of 1 or 2 when at least a 3 is required by some colleges to receive credit. Not only are these low-income kids denied college credit for their AP courses, but they also show up at college, the *Sun* reports, "with skills so low that they must take remedial classes." The *Sun's* summary of the local situation in Baltimore is stunning: "In at least 19 high schools throughout the Baltimore region, more than half of the students earning an A or B in an AP class failed the exam." The nineteen schools all serve low-income neighborhoods.[2]

Experts and AP officials pinpointed the same culprit: students' lack of preparation for AP classes. Too many low-income students arrive in high school with sterling academic records from middle school, but in reality are

216

light years away from knowing what they need to know to be successful in an AP class.

This chapter argues something unthinkable to a large number of analysts who consider themselves equity-minded: that tracking—the assignment of students to different classes on the basis of ability or achievement—may be a means of better preparing disadvantaged students for AP classes. This will require a mind-shift from policies emphasizing equal access to advanced courses for all or most youngsters to policies emphasizing talent development for high-achieving students. Middle schools prepare students for high school. By adequately preparing more impoverished middle school students for the academic demands of AP, tracking can serve as a tool for greater fairness.

This chapter's objective is to convince readers that this is a plausible hypothesis—and to do so empirically. It will not produce causal evidence that will prove or disprove the assertion. Such evidence does not currently exist. Evidence does exist, however, that supports three propositions. When logically connected, the three propositions bolster the likelihood of the hypothesis being true.

1. Poor, Hispanic, and black middle school students are less likely to be enrolled in tracked classes than students who are socioeconomically better off, white, and Asian.
2. Middle schools serving predominantly disadvantaged students are less likely to offer tracked classes than schools serving advantaged populations.
3. Research on tracking is mixed, but studies focusing on its distributional properties—that is, how tracking differentially affects different kinds of students—generally show a positive effect for high-achieving students. That is particularly true for classes that group academically talented students together and offer an enriched or accelerated curriculum.

The upshot of these propositions is that high-achieving eighth graders in socioeconomically disadvantaged communities are denied an opportunity that high-achieving peers in advantaged communities enjoy. Kids from middle- or upper-middle-class families are more likely to attend schools with tracked, high-achieving classes that prepare them for AP courses in high schools. They are more likely to have access to middle school classes that challenge them and allow them to excel. That's not fair.

Following this introduction, the second section of this chapter describes the academic achievement of students in poverty. A promising program that boosts the scores of high-achieving, disadvantaged youngsters through tracking also receives attention. The term *tracking* refers to assigning students to different curricula, classrooms, and teachers based on ability or prior achievement. Why isn't tracking used by more schools serving disadvantaged students? Section three answers that question by briefly describing the recent history of tracking reform, offering clues as to how we got to where we are now.

The fourth section digs into the latest National Assessment of Educational Progress (NAEP) data to describe the demographic characteristics of students and schools who are tracked or untracked. The fifth section looks at the research on tracking, concluding that although mixed in determining tracking's overall effect, the preponderance of evidence indicates that tracked classes are beneficial to high achievers. The sixth section concludes by offering several design characteristics that a tracking-for-equity program in mathematics should feature, operating in concert with the Common Core State Standards (CCSS) in math.

ACADEMIC ACHIEVEMENT AND STUDENTS IN POVERTY

As Sean Reardon has documented, in 1965 the test score gap between whites and blacks was much larger than the gap between rich and poor.[3] Today that situation has reversed. Children who were born into poor families in the 1950s, 1960s, and 1970s scored about 0.9 standard deviations (SDs) lower on achievement tests than children from wealthy families. The gap has expanded to 1.4 SDs among children born in the 1990s. Poverty has a depressing saliency to achievement that race had prior to the civil rights movement in the mid-twentieth century.

We know much more about race gaps in achievement than about gaps related to income. In a series of fascinating studies, Eric A. Hanushek and Steven G. Rivkin analyzed Texas data that documented students' achievement trajectories as they progressed through school. The black–white test score gap ballooned among higher-achieving students, growing much more than among students who were of average or below-average achievement. Although the pattern is evident in test-score changes from third to fifth grade, it is even more pronounced in fifth to eighth grade changes.

The researchers divided students into sixteen groups based on the students' scores as kindergartners. As the students moved through school grades, the black–white achievement gap changed. From fifth to eighth grade, the gap actually contracted in all but one of the seven bottom-achievement groups, expanded by at least 0.05 SDs in all but one of the next six groups, and expanded by at least 0.09 in the top three groups. For the entire third-to-eighth-grade span, the achievement gap increased two and a half times more in the top three achievement groups than in the bottom seven (0.25 vs. 0.10 SDs).[4]

Hanushek and Rivkin's analysis applied to high-achieving black students, not to high-achieving, low-income students. Nevertheless, it is not a stretch to believe that some of the reasons put forth for race gaps—negative peer influences, attending segregated and under-resourced schools, exposure to inexperienced or ineffective teachers, parents who aren't savvy about getting the most out of schools—also apply to the achievement gap between wealthy and poor students.

David Card and Laura Giuliano analyzed data from special classes serving gifted elementary youngsters in a large eastern US school district. In 2004 the district mandated that its elementary schools set up separate classrooms for gifted students in fourth and fifth grades. Pursuant to state law, the district used an IQ test score of 130 as criterion for being identified as gifted, with retesting allowed (including by a psychologist hired by the parents) if students scored at least 127.

The following year, concerns about underrepresentation in the program by low-income and minority students, particularly English language learners, led to universal screening using a nonverbal ability test and more flexible IQ cutoff (these were called "Plan B" gifted students).[5] The district also adopted an innovative policy to promote gifted classes in schools with large under-represented populations. Every school in the district was required to provide a special gifted class if it had even a single gifted student. Classes were to be filled out with high achievers—students who, although not certified "gifted," had scored the highest in the school on the previous year's state assessment.

Because classes are staffed at twenty to twenty-four pupils, that requirement forced schools serving predominantly low-income students to place their highest-achieving poor kids into gifted classes. The policy had its intended effect. Disadvantaged high achievers represent about 40 percent of students in the district's gifted classes. In very poor schools, they make up the vast majority of participants.[6]

Card and Giuliano exploited this unique policy to evaluate whether separate gifted tracks benefit gifted students as traditionally identified, Plan B students, or high achievers. They found no effect on the reading or math achievement of gifted students, regardless of how giftedness is identified. But they uncovered "positive and relatively large effects on the achievement of the non-gifted high achievers who fill the remaining seats in the class, concentrated among free/reduced price lunch participants and black and Hispanic students."

The authors conclude, "Our findings suggest that a comprehensive tracking program that establishes a separate classroom in every school for the top performing students could significantly boost the performance of the most talented students in even the poorest neighborhoods, at little or no cost to other students or the District's budget."[7] Despite these positive findings, tracking is more likely to be found in upper-middle-class, suburban schools than in schools serving low-income students. Why is that?

THE RECENT HISTORY OF TRACKING REFORM

Tracking is one of education's most controversial practices. Jeannie Oakes's 1985 book, *Keeping Track,* charged that schools inflict great harm on poor and minority students through tracking. Measures of achievement, which are the basis of most track placements, are highly correlated with students' socioeconomic characteristics. So the book's finding that high tracks were disproportionately populated by white, Asian, and wealthier students and low tracks by black, Hispanic, and poorer students was not surprising.[8]

But Oakes's book went a step further. Tracking's defenders had always argued that the practice is educationally sound, providing students with a curriculum better matched to individual needs compared to randomly grouping students into classes and then giving them all the same curriculum to study. Oakes repudiated the claim, asserting that when students are separated into classes matched to a hierarchy of course topics in mathematics (algebra, geometry, etc.) or assigned to honors, regular, and remedial courses in English language arts, students placed in the top classes are challenged and thrive academically; those in the bottom classes languish.

Moreover, Oakes's indictment embraced a political dimension. She charged that schools were catering to the interests of social elites by using tracking to perpetuate the past racial and economic inequities of American society. Tracking was racist and profoundly unfair to disadvantaged students. And it was not that way by accident.

The detracking movement had an impact on policy. By the mid-1990s, many schools—in particular, middle schools—were reducing or eliminating tracking.

A distinct pattern soon emerged as to where detracking was, and was not, implemented.[9] Schools responding positively to tracking reform tended to serve students who were allegedly harmed by the practice—urban or inner-city schools serving predominantly black, Hispanic, or poor populations. These schools began to detrack, abolishing both honors and remedial classes. The schools that resisted tended to be suburban, with predominantly white, Asian, middle- or upper-middle-class students.

By the end of the decade, the distribution of reformed tracking policies—how they mapped over schools with different demographic profiles—mirrored the political appeal of the antitracking crusade. An intriguing twist arose. The elites who were supposedly perpetrating tracking for the purpose of maintaining their privileged status—in particular, suburban whites—were imposing that unfair regime on their own children's schools. Disadvantaged and minority children, on the other hand, now were more likely to attend detracked schools with heterogeneously grouped classes.

THE DEMOGRAPHICS OF TRACKING AND DETRACKING

Let's examine the latest and most reliable data on the demographics of tracking and detracking. Tables 10.1 through 10.4 present demographic data from the NAEP on students who are in detracked classes.

Frequency of Detracking: Student Characteristics

The first table reports on eighth graders who are eligible for free and reduced-price lunch (FRL). In 2013, 25 percent of students eligible for FRL were in detracked math classes compared to 20 percent of students not eligible (from wealthier families). Disadvantaged students are more likely to attend detracked classes than students from more advantaged families.

Note that the difference narrowed from 2000 to 2013. Most of it was due to a decline in the frequency of detracked FRL students. In 2000, 34 percent of FRL students attended heterogeneously grouped classes, compared to 21 percent of students not eligible for FRL. Although stigmatized as harming disadvantaged children throughout the 1990s, tracking has staged a partial comeback since 2000. Poor kids were more likely to be tracked in 2013 than in 2000, but were still less likely to attend tracked classes than their peers from wealthier families.

Table 10.1. Percentage of Detracked Eighth Graders by Eligibility for Free and Reduced Lunch

Year	ELIG-FRL	Not ELIG-FRL
2013	25	20
2011	28	21
2009	28	20
2007	31	20
2005	33	23
2003	34	21
2000	34	21

Source: Compiled by author from NAEP Data Explorer (http://nces.ed.gov/nationsreportcard/naepdata/).

Most of the narrowing occurred after 2007. It is possible that recent changes in eligibility for FRL (there have been several) are skewing the data. Policy innovations, such as allowing schools to offer free and reduced-price meals to all students if 50 percent or more qualify for the program, might draw students into the FRL program whose families have higher incomes than the FRL threshold.[10] Free and reduced-priced lunch data are losing their cachet as an indicator of poverty. Tables 10.2 and 10.3 provide a check on FRL's weakening validity, and by examining other student characteristics, also allow a more complete picture to emerge of the demographics of tracking.

Table 10.2 looks at tracking and parent education. The columns are arranged left to right by increasing levels of education, meaning that, given the strong relationship between education and income, the columns also correlate with family socioeconomic status (SES).

In 2013, 24 percent of students whose parents lacked a high school diploma were in detracked classes compared with only 20 percent of students whose parents were college graduates. Consistent with the FRL data in the previous table, table 10.2 shows that disadvantaged students are more likely to be detracked than advantaged students. There is also a hint of narrowing from 2000–2013 as the four percentage-point difference between "No HS Diploma" and "College Grad" in 2013 is the smallest of the period. The ten-point difference in 2003 is the largest.

Table 10.3 examines detracking by students' race and ethnicity. Black students are consistently more likely to attend detracked classes than white and Asian/Pacific Island students. In 2013, 29 percent of blacks were in detracked classes versus 22 percent of Hispanics, 19 percent of Asian/Pacific Islanders, and 21 percent of whites. But also note that by 2013, Hispanic students had closed what was a huge gap in 2000 (fourteen percentage points compared to whites). In 2013, the frequency of Hispanic students studying math in detracked classes was statistically indistinguishable from whites.

Table 10.2. Percentage of Detracked Eighth Graders by Parent Education

	No HS Diploma	HS-Grad	Some Post-HS Ed	Coll Grad
2013	24	26	24	20
2011	30	27	25	22
2009	28	27	24	20
2007	30	28	26	22
2005	32	30	28	24
2003	32	29	27	22
2000	28	27	25	22

Source: Compiled by author from NAEP Data Explorer (http://nces.ed.gov/nationsreportcard/naepdata/).

Table 10.3. Percentage of Detracked Eighth Graders by Race/Ethnicity

	Hsp	Blk	Asian/PI	White
2013	22	29	19	21
2011	29	30	22	21
2009	25	32	15	21
2007	29	33	21	21
2005	30	35	20	25
2003	32	35	20	22
2000	34	33	24	20

Source: Compiled by author from NAEP Data Explorer (http://nces.ed.gov/nationsreportcard/naepdata/).

Frequency of Detracking: School Characteristics

Tables 10.1 through 10.3 reveal how student characteristics are related to attending detracked classes. Students from impoverished backgrounds are less likely to be tracked, and the data on both parent education and race/ethnicity confirm the tendency. Looking at student characteristics only goes so far, however, in explaining why some students are more likely to be tracked than others. School characteristics are also important. It's reasonable to assume that some students are tracked or detracked because of the schools they attend, not necessarily because of their own individual characteristics.

Table 10.4 shows the percentage of detracked students by schoolwide statistics on FRL. This is a measure of concentration of poverty, and the columns are arranged left to right with the level of school poverty descending.

Table 10.4. Percentage of Students Detracked By School's Percentage of Students Eligible for Free and Reduced Lunch

Year	99–76%	75–51%	50–26%	25–1%
	High Poverty <------------ — — — — — — ——> Low Poverty			
2013	30	23	22	16
2011	35	27	22	16
2009	38	27	20	15
2007	42	27	23	16
2005	43	32	26	17

Note: Author's calculations (narrower categories of NAEP data have been aggregated). Schools with 100% and 0% FRL omitted.

Source: Compiled by author from NAEP Data Explorer (http://nces.ed.gov/nationsreportcard/naepdata/)

Schools in the farthest left-hand column (99–76 percent eligible for free lunch) are high-poverty schools; schools in the farthest right-hand column (25–1 percent eligible) are low-poverty (serving students from wealthier families). Schools with 100 percent of students eligible for FRL have been omitted. They only compose 3 percent of schools, and omitting them helps dampen any skewing caused by recent FRL policy changes that artificially boosted their numbers. Schools with 0 percent FRL have also been omitted. They do not represent enough schools in the NAEP sample to generate reliable data.

The two extreme categories offer a telling comparison.[11] In 2013, high-poverty schools were about twice as likely to have detracked math classes as low-poverty schools (30 percent vs. 16 percent). But again, there is a clear trend toward increased tracking over the past decade, especially in high-poverty schools. In 2005, 43 percent of high-poverty schools and only 17 percent of low-poverty schools were detracked. The percentage of detracked schools has remained stable in schools serving advantaged communities but is clearly falling in schools serving children in poverty.

RESEARCH ON THE EFFECTS OF TRACKING

The literature on tracking goes back to the early twentieth century. Most tracking studies unfortunately are vulnerable to selection effects; that is, they cannot untangle the effects of different tracks from the characteristics of students populating those tracks. When high-track students outgain low-track students on achievement tests, is it because of advantages produced by enrollment in a high track? Or would they have outscored low-track students under any conditions, considering that some students are assigned to high tracks because of their strong academic abilities and other students to low tracks because of their academic weaknesses?

Even studies that attempt to control for initial achievement (e.g., use test scores prior to track placement as covariates) can overlook bias introduced by omitted variables. Schools may place two students with the same initial test scores into different tracks because one student has better attendance, consistently puts forth greater effort, or has a highly involved parent who aggressively lobbies the school for assignment to the high track. If such variables are unmeasured or unaccounted for in estimating track effects—and if they are correlated with the outcome variable of interest (student achievement)—the results of statistical models may be biased.

Experimental studies featuring random assignment and quasiexperimental studies with strong designs try to mitigate both of these shortcomings and offer the best evidence on tracking's effects. Metaanalyses of experimental and quasiexperimental studies have been conducted by Kulik and Kulik (1982), Slavin (1990), and Mosteller, Light, and Sachs (1996).[12] These metaanalyses reach remarkably similar conclusions about tracking's effect on mean student achievement—that it's statistically insignificant.[13] Schools can choose to track or to group students heterogeneously and the decision will have no impact on average achievement.

Does Tracking Benefit High Achievers?

Where the metaanalysts disagree is on the distribution of effects—whether some students benefit or are harmed by either practice. Slavin's review of twenty-nine studies of tracking found tiny, insignificant effect sizes for high achievers (+0.01), students near average achievement (−0.08), and low achievers (−0.02). Mosteller, Light, and Sachs identified only ten experiments that evaluated the distribution of effects from tracking (which they call "skill grouping").

Noting that the small number of studies left the analysis underpowered (i.e., a larger number of studies may have detected an effect), Mosteller, Light, and Sachs found statistically insignificant effects but described "a slight tilt toward skill grouping being more favorable for high-skill than for medium- and low-skill students. The estimates of average effect sizes were 0.08 for high, −0.04 for medium, and −0.06 for low-skill groups."

These reviews focused on XYZ-style tracking, named for a program that began in Detroit in 1919. The school system administered IQ tests to all incoming first graders and then divided students into three separate classes: X for the top 20 percent, Y for the middle 60 percent, and Z for the bottom 20 percent. The three classes all received the same curriculum.

Kulik and Kulik's review of XYZ studies found a small positive effect for high achievers, but not large enough to represent a substantive, real-world benefit. But Kulik and Kulik went a step further by separately analyzing programs in which curricular differentiation occurred. They argued that modern tracking, at least since the 1950s, exists to match students with an appropriate curriculum, not just to reduce the heterogeneity of ability within classes.

Here they discovered a huge benefit. They found that talented students who were tracked into classes with an enriched curriculum made significant gains (mean effect size 0.41) compared with students of equal ability who were untracked. High-ability students who were placed in tracks featuring an accelerated curriculum, meaning the curriculum covered topics from later grades, benefitted the most, gaining a whopping 0.87 SDs (nearly a year of learning) compared to untracked peers.

The last experimental study in the Mosteller, Light, and Sachs metaanalysis was conducted in 1974. The next experiment to evaluate tracking was conducted in Kenya in 2005. Like most experiments in education, a propitious set of circumstances allowed for the random assignment of students to treatment groups. Schools in western Kenya received extra funds to hire first-grade teachers. At the time, 121 of these schools had only one teacher teaching first grade, meaning that they would now go from one to two first-grade classes. The schools were randomly assigned to either: (1) a tracked condition, in which students above the mean were assigned to one class and students below the mean to the other; or (2) an untracked condition, in which students were randomly assigned to the two classes.

The experiment ran for eighteen months. All students in the tracked classes benefitted, with a mean advantage of 0.18 SDs after controlling for baseline scores. Students in the top half of the preassignment distribution (i.e., higher achievers) gained 0.19 SDs, and those in the bottom half (i.e., lower achievers) gained 0.16 SDs. Students in the middle of the preassignment distribution—near the cut point for assignment to either the top or bottom class—gained as much as either the top or bottom students.

Students were tested again one year after the experiment ended. The positive effect persisted, with students in the tracked condition continuing to score 0.18 SDs higher than students in the heterogeneously grouped classes. The authors speculated that teachers were better able to tailor instruction to students' academic needs in the tracked classes, regardless of whether a student attends a high- or low-ability class. Data on instruction were not collected in the study.

Argys, Reese, and Brewer analyzed data from the National Education Longitudinal Study of 1988. They looked at tenth-grade math scores and measured the effect of students being placed in a heterogeneously grouped class as opposed to an above-average, average, or below-average tracked class. From this analysis, they were able to predict the advantage or disadvantage that tracking provides to students in different tracks.

The main finding of the study is that tracking creates winners and losers. High- and average-track students are both winners under tracking. Being placed in an above-average track produces a 6 percent gain in achievement compared to being placed in a heterogeneously grouped class. Being placed in an average track yields a 2 percent gain. Low-track students, on the other hand, pay a price under tracking, with a loss of about 5 percent in math achievement. The gains and losses average out to a 1.7 percent gain, the magnitude of achievement benefit expected if a detracked school switched to tracking.

Elaine Allensworth and other researchers from the University of Chicago Consortium on Chicago School Research investigated a detracking policy in Chicago.[14] In 1997, the school system adopted an "Algebra for All" policy for ninth graders. Remedial math was abolished and mixed-ability algebra classes were created. Using a discontinuity design, the researchers found that the detracking effort increased the number of students receiving algebra credits but had no effect on the test scores of average and below-average students who were intended to benefit from the policy. Failure rates in math classes increased for average students.

Takako Nomi examined the effect of the policy on high-achieving students.[15] Although these students were not the targets of the policy—they would have taken algebra anyway regardless of the policy change—they were affected by the change in classroom composition of Algebra I classes. Their classes now held low-achieving peers. Detracking had the unintended effect of driving down the scores of high achievers.

In 2009, I conducted a survey of tracking practices in Massachusetts middle schools. In addition to finding the same demographic pattern as reported above in NAEP data—high-poverty, urban schools were less likely to offer tracked classes than suburban schools serving mostly advantaged students—regression analysis controlling for SES characteristics found that detracked schools lagged in achievement, especially when it came to high achievers. Schools featuring three eighth-grade math tracks were associated with a 6 percentage point gain in the number of students scoring at the "advanced" level in mathematics, compared to detracked schools offering heterogeneously grouped math classes. Considering that only 18 percent of eighth graders scored "advanced" at the average middle school in the state, a 6 percentage point gain would represent a significant, real-world impact on school achievement.

These data did not allow for causal conclusions. Were tracked schools creating more advanced students with their high tracks—or were families with advanced students simply more likely to attend tracked schools? David N. Figlio and Marianne E. Page (2002) were able to tease out causal effects by investigating tracking and its relationship to school choice. They found that tracked schools attract and retain families with greater wealth. And after controlling for confounding factors with an instrumental variable strategy, Figlio and Page also discovered that disadvantaged students make larger test-score gains in tracked rather than detracked schools.

They concluded, "We can find no evidence that detracking America's schools, as is currently in vogue, will improve outcomes among disadvantaged students. This trend may instead harm the very students that detracking is intended to help."[16]

CONCLUSION

Teachers find teaching classrooms with vast heterogeneity in ability a hindrance to effective instruction. A 2007 survey by the National Math Advisory

Panel reported that a majority of algebra teachers viewed mixed-ability grouping as a moderate (28 percent) or serious (23 percent) problem. And the problem seems to be getting worse. The Met Life Survey of the American Teacher asked about the impact of class heterogeneity in 1998 and 2008.

The percentage of teachers either agreeing somewhat or agreeing strongly to the statement "My classes have become so mixed in terms of students' learning abilities that I can't teach them effectively" grew from 39 percent in 1998 to 43 percent in 2008. Considering the stark wording of the prompt— the consequence of instructing students of mixed abilities being "that I can't teach them effectively"—the fact that the statement resonates with more than 40 percent of teachers is indeed troubling.

The CCSS in mathematics offer an excellent opportunity to experiment with tracking for equity. Implementing CCSS is itself an experiment. The CCSS math standards recognize that differentiation may have to take place as schools implement curriculum. The CCSS math standards are only written through Algebra II in the junior year of high school. Some advanced math students will be able to move faster than that.

Appendix A of the CCSS math standards suggests "compacting" in middle school as an acceleration strategy, defining it as:

> A "compacted" version of the Traditional pathway where no content is omitted, in which students would complete the content of 7th grade, 8th grade, and the High School Algebra I course in grades 7 (Compacted 7th Grade) and 8 (8th Grade Algebra I), which will enable them to reach Calculus or other college level courses by their senior year.

Appendix A goes on to state the rationale for compacting:

> Based on a variety of inputs and factors, some students may decide at an early age that they want to take Calculus or other college level courses in high school. These students would need to begin the study of high school content in the middle school, which would lead to Precalculus or Advanced Statistics as a junior and Calculus, Advanced Statistics or other college level options as a senior.[17]

Design Features of Tracking for Equity in Mathematics

As the previous literature review suggests, tracking entails risks. Opponents of tracking are justifiably concerned about the effects of tracking on students in low tracks. Adam Gamoran warns,

> "[I]t is important to acknowledge that most studies of ability grouping and curriculum tracking have found that high-achieving students tend to perform better when assigned to high-level groups than when taught in mixed-ability settings.

Proponents of tracking tend to emphasize the benefits of high-level classes for high-achieving students with little attention to implications for inequality, while critics tend to focus on the inequality without acknowledging the effects for high achievers. As a result, proponents and critics are apt to talk past one another with little chance for resolution."[18]

With that warning in mind, I propose design features of a tracking-for-equity program in middle school mathematics, a program that would offer an accelerated math track. These features are intended to maximize the benefits of tracking for high achievers while minimizing any potential negative impact on low-achieving students. The program offers an accelerated option for states following the Common Core. It costs next to nothing. A tracking-for-equity program could be adopted by most low-income schools tomorrow.

1. Create an accelerated track for seventh and eighth graders that would complete three years of mathematics—meeting the standards for seventh grade, eighth grade, and Algebra I—in two years.
2. Implement the program in low-income schools first. An analysis of students scoring at the highest levels on the NAEP math test discovered a huge pool of untapped talent among disadvantaged eighth graders. In 2005, approximately one-quarter of black, Hispanic, and low-income eighth graders were enrolled in a course lower than Algebra I (pre-algebra or regular eighth-grade math) despite scoring at the 90th percentile on the NAEP.[19]
3. Track by performance on subject-specific assessments. Research on omnibus tracking programs in secondary schools is mixed. By "omnibus" tracking, I am referring to programs that identify students with an IQ test or comprehensive test of academic abilities and then track students into all or most subjects. Indeed, this is how most US high schools tracked until the early 1970s, as students were placed into honors, regular, or vocational tracks that dictated how they were grouped for all subjects. Omnibus systems may not adequately match students to curriculum. Students who are great at math but struggle with reading will not receive a mathematics curriculum appropriate to their talents if the placement assessment is heavily weighted toward verbal skills. English language learners who are talented at math may also be overlooked.

   Omnibus tracking between schools describes the tracking programs of most European and Asian nations. Students typically take a high-stakes test at the end of junior secondary school (i.e., middle school in the United States) and the test score on that exam decides whether they attend an academic, technical, or vocational high school. Omnibus tracking also describes American exam schools. Research on their effectiveness is rare, but a couple of recent, high-quality studies found that exam schools have no effect.

4. Alter the curriculum to match the track. Tracking appears to produce its greatest benefits when curriculum is altered to correspond to the levels of students. Compacting three years of CCSS into a two-year program would provide the necessary acceleration for talented math students.

5. Attend to the lowest track. Offering an accelerated track in low-income schools means that some students will not be accelerated, with the risk that students in nonaccelerated classes will encounter low expectations or that the classes will deteriorate into curricular dead ends. In addition, teachers of low tracks in middle schools must be skilled in classroom management, because low-achieving students often exhibit a constellation of antilearning behaviors by the time they reach middle school. Chicago addressed this problem by providing a double-dose of algebra—two periods daily—to students who scored below the national median on incoming math assessments.

The results from the double-dose intervention are encouraging. Kalena Cortes and Joshua Goodman find that the increased class time devoted to studying algebra led to significant positive effects on both short-term math achievement and longer-term outcomes (e.g., course-taking in high school). In this program, as in the many evaluated in the research summarized previously, tracking had been effectively enlisted in the cause of equity.[20]

This analysis supports the hypothesis that tracking may be deployed in the pursuit of equity. Identifying academically talented students in high-poverty middle schools and offering them a curriculum tailored to their needs could create a pipeline of academic excellence running from middle school to high school AP classes. It promises better preparation of disadvantaged students for high school AP courses than that provided by current policies and practices.

Low-income middle school students do not have access to high tracks because, in contrast to schools serving predominantly advantaged students, schools in low-income communities are more likely to be untracked. They have adopted an ethos of equal access to all courses; thus, their toughest, most academically challenging classes may be populated with students so heterogeneous in ability that students two or more years above grade level sit alongside students two or more years below grade level—all students studying the same curriculum and receiving the same instruction. Teachers have difficulty teaching such classes.

What middle schools in poor communities need is an ethos of identifying and developing academic talent. This already happens in sports, often to an extreme.[21] It's time to destigmatize the word "tracking." A middle school curricular program that offers high-achieving, disadvantaged students the opportunity to excel would advance the cause of educational equity.

NOTES

1. College Board, *The 10th Annual AP Report to the Nation,* 2014, page 6.

2. Liz Bowie, "Maryland Schools Have Been Leader in Advanced Placement, but Results Are Mixed," *Baltimore Sun,* August 21, 2013.

3. Sean Reardon, "The Widening Achievement Gap between the Rich and the Poor," in *Whither Opportunity? Rising Inequality, Schools, and Children's Life Chances* (New York: Russell Sage Foundation: 2011).

4. Eric A. Hanushek and Steven G. Rivkin, "School Quality and the Black–White Achievement Gap," NBER Working Paper Series, Working Paper 12651 (Cambridge, MA: National Bureau of Educational Research, October 2006).

5. David Card and Laura Giuliano, "Does Gifted Education Work? For Which Students?" NBER Working Paper Series, Working Paper 20453 (Cambridge, MA: National Bureau of Educational Research, September 2014).

6. Card and Giuliano, "Does Gifted Education Work?" 5–6.

7. Card and Giuliano, "Does Gifted Education Work?" 33–34.

8. Jeannie Oakes, *Keeping Track: How Schools Structure Inequality* (New Haven, CT: Yale University Press, 1985).

9. Tom Loveless, *The Tracking Wars: State Reform Meets School Policy* (Washington, DC: Brookings Institution Press, 1999).

10. Sarah D. Sparks, "Popular Child-Poverty Measure Gets Another Look," *Education Week,* August 19, 2014.

11. Schools with 99-76 percent of students eligible for FRL were about 19 percent of schools in the 2013 NAEP. Schools with 25–1 percent FRL were about 23 percent of the sample.

12. A more recent metaanalysis is Hattie (2009), which is essentially a metaanalysis of metaanalyses. I did not include Hattie's estimates in the narrative because he did not limit the metaanalysis to studies meeting criteria for methodological quality. Nonetheless, the effect sizes he reports for ability grouping (0.12) and ability grouping for gifted students (0.30) do not contradict the findings of the other metaanalyses discussed. Hattie uses the term *ability grouping* for tracking.

13. The earliest study in Slavin's metaanalysis is from 1927.

14. E. Allensworth, T. Nomi, N. Montgomery, and V. E. Lee, "College-preparatory Curriculum for All: The Consequences of Raising Mathematics Graduation Requirements on Students' Course Taking and Outcomes in Chicago." *Educational Evaluation and Policy Analysis,* 31 (2009): 367–91.

15. Takako Nomi, "The Unintended Consequences of an Algebra for All Policy on High-Skill Students: Effects on Instructional, Organization and Students' Academic Outcomes," *Educational Evaluation and Policy Analysis,* 34, no. 4, (December 2012): 489–505.

16. David N. Figlio and Marianne E. Page, "School Choice and the Distributional Effects of Ability Tracking: Does Separation Increase Inequality?" *Journal of Urban Economics,* 51, no. 3, (May 2002): 497–514.

17. Common Core State Standards for Mathematics, appendix A, page 3.

18. Adam Gamoran, "Tracking and Inequality: New Directions for Research and Practice," Working Paper No. 2009-6, Wisconsin Center for Education Research, 2009, 8–9.

19. Tom Loveless, *High Achieving Students in the Era of NCLB* (Washington, DC: Thomas B. Fordham Institute, 2008). (This refers to part 1. Part 2 is by Steve Farkas and Anne Duffett.)

20. Kalena E. Cortes and Joshua S. Goodman, "Ability Tracking, Instructional Time, and Better Pedagogy: The Effect of Double-Dose Algebra on Student Achievement," *American Economic Review: Papers & Proceedings 2014* 104, no. 5, 400–405.

21. Adam Himmelsbach and Pete Thamel, "Middle School is Basketball's Fiercest Recruiting Battleground," *New York Times,* June 25, 2012. The University of Washington and Louisiana State University have promised scholarships in exchange for signed letters of commitment from eighth-grade football players. In 2010, David Sills, a thirteen-year-old quarterback in Elkton, Maryland, committed to USC when he was in seventh grade.

Conclusion

Michael J. Petrilli

In the introduction to this book, I asked whether education reform is on the right track to assist poor children in achieving a full measure of the American Dream. In particular, I asked whether our focus on college as *the* springboard to the middle class might be misguided or too narrow.

Lest readers doubt that throngs of education reformers are obsessed with four-year college degrees, consider that, as of 2012–2013, just a *few dozen* of the more than five thousand charter schools in the country were "vocational," according to the National Center for Education Statistics. Or take a closer look at the major charter school networks. Of the thirty-five such organizations supported by the New Schools Venture Fund, not one is oriented around career and technical education (CTE). Or read the subtitle of Doug Lemov's *Teach Like a Champion 2.0*, now akin to a bible for reform-minded teachers: *62 Techniques that Put Students on the Path to College.*

Ten chapters later, it's clear that completing college is, in fact, a very effective on-ramp to upward mobility. As Ron Haskins and Andrew Kelly demonstrate in chapters 1 and 2, a four-year degree brings a strong payoff, particularly for young people growing up in poverty. According to Pew's *Pursuing the American Dream* study, such individuals are almost *five times* likelier to escape the lowest income quintile as adults if they obtain a bachelor's degree.[1]

And that's not just because of the selection effect—the fact that colleges attract relatively able and motivated young people who may have done well regardless of their path. There's strong evidence that college adds real value in terms of students' skills, knowledge, and career preparation, value that translates into higher earnings.[2] Nor is money the only payoff; we're all familiar with the "scissors charts," popularized by Robert Putnam, showing the relationship between college attainment, the formation of two-parent families, and other positive life outcomes, including health and even happiness.[3]

What's sobering, though, and should serve as a warning bell for single-minded education reformers, is that so few low-income students actually obtain four-year college degrees. The Census Bureau estimates that just 9 percent of young people who grow up in families in the lowest quartile of the income distribution do so; Andrew Kelly puts it at 14 percent for those in the bottom third.[4] Either way, these are dismaying figures. Can anyone claim with a straight face that we have any reasonable prospect of helping every single low-income youngster complete college with a bachelor's degree? Doubling or tripling today's numbers would be an incredible accomplishment, but it would take decades and still leave many poor students needing another path to the middle class.

There's good news, however: Four-year degrees are not the only postsecondary credentials that add value. As Tamar Jacoby demonstrates in chapter 3, industry certifications can also be powerful enablers of opportunity. They generally cost less and are arguably better suited to today's workplace than many bachelor's degrees, especially those from marginal universities or in esoteric majors. Certificates and two-year degrees can also be wise steps on the way to further education, enabling students to get work experience, enter the labor market with less debt, and decide about continuing when they are better able to finance more college and surer of their career paths. Some evidence even indicates that these other credentials are as valuable as bachelor's degrees in terms of earnings.[5]

But what about poor students who don't earn a postsecondary credential? Are they destined to a life of poverty? There's some good news here, too. Ron Haskins's "success sequence" analysis shows that even young people with just a high school diploma can make it into the middle class—*if* they work full time and delay parenthood until marriage. *Ninety-eight percent* of the people who followed those norms aren't poor; the vast majority are solidly middle-class.

Put all these insights together and the outline of a promising "Education for Upward Mobility" agenda starts to come into focus:

1. Prepare many more low-income students for success by completing bachelor's degrees.
2. Prepare many more low-income students for success by earning associate's degrees and industry credentials.
3. Prepare many more low-income students for success by following the success sequence.

The rest of this chapter amplifies this outline. It argues that the education reform movement does indeed need to make some midcourse corrections to balance its fixation on the first strategy with suitable attention to the second and third strategies as well.

PREPARING MORE LOW-INCOME STUDENTS TO OBTAIN FOUR-YEAR COLLEGE DEGREES

This is where the education reform movement is mostly on the mark. It's a full-fledged national outrage that so few low-income students earn bachelor's degrees. National foundations, charter school networks, civil rights groups, and others are correct to focus on fixing the pipeline to college completion, which, as Kelly writes, is leaky at every stage along the way.

Much of today's school reform agenda, then, is on target when it comes to "college for more":

- Start with high-quality preschool programs, targeted at the kids who need them most, that impart preliteracy and prenumeracy skills as well as essential character and behavioral strengths—programs like those described by Elliot Regenstein, Bryce Marable, and Jelene Britten, in chapter 8.
- Raise the quality of K–12 teaching and learning by aligning expectations with rigorous academic standards such as the Common Core.
- Ramp up entrance standards for teachers and provide them with ongoing support to improve instruction and help students make rapid gains.
- Expand learning time, and make efficient use of it by implementing technology thoughtfully. Use that time to also build students' "noncognitive" skills, including through sports and the arts.
- Hold schools and educators to account for helping students make strong progress over time.
- Set cut scores on state tests at appropriately high levels in order to report honestly to students and families whether they are on track for college success.
- Build true college-prep high schools like those profiled by Joanne Jacobs in chapter 6, replete with opportunities for poor teenagers to take rigorous, college-level courses, including Advanced Placement and International Baccalaureate.
- Provide college counseling and related opportunities to help low-income students picture themselves on campus and understand how to get there.
- Embrace charter schools and other structural and governance innovations as ways to make all of these changes more quickly and effectively, and without the barriers posed by many district bureaucracies and teachers' union contracts.

That's a long, ambitious list, yet it omits other important items—blind spots for many of today's reformers:

1. Put in place a content-rich curriculum, especially in the early grades
2. Prioritze the needs of the low-income students with the best shot at making it to and through four-year college degrees

Let's give both of those a look.

A Content-Rich Curriculum: A Must-Have, Not an Afterthought

As Robert Pondiscio argues in chapter 9, curriculum is the neglected stepchild of the education reform movement, the low-hanging fruit that, in most places, remains to be plucked. Common Core's admonition that schools adopt a "content-rich curriculum" in order to help students learn to read is not being widely heeded, but it is finally garnering attention in some quarters. High-profile charter networks like the Knowledge Is Power Program (KIPP) and Achievement First, for example, have recognized the need for more instruction in history, science, art, and music in the early grades; educators nationwide are downloading the free, content-rich Engage New York curriculum enthusiastically.

This is all to be celebrated because, as Pondiscio explains, nothing better predicts college success than a student's verbal prowess. But as he also explains, the usual school strategies for teaching literacy—repeated, content-agnostic instruction in "reading comprehension"—isn't getting the job done. Beyond learning to decode English words, what students need more than anything is to learn about the world so that they can understand whatever piece of text they might encounter. Affluent students receive much of this instruction from their parents at home, or via enrichment opportunities. Poor children almost certainly must get it at school, or they won't get much of it at all.

For those policymakers and education leaders who want many more of their low-income students to make it to and through college, here's a simple question: What's your elementary school curriculum like? Is it fanatical about teaching a broad base of knowledge? Does it assume that teaching content is teaching literacy? If not, fixing that situation should jump to the top of your priority list.

Prioritizing the Needs of the "Strivers"

The last few years have brought long-overdue attention to the needs of high-achieving, low-income students. Organizations including the College

Board, the Jack Kent Cooke Foundation, and Bloomberg Philanthropies have launched initiatives to ensure that such students have opportunities to take rigorous coursework in high school and are encouraged to apply to selective colleges upon graduation. A recent analysis by Susan Dynarski at the University of Michigan illustrates why this is so important: Even when poor students boast high test scores, they are less likely to graduate from college than their affluent peers.[6]

But as welcome and important as these initiatives are, they must be complemented by efforts to help high-potential, low-income students much earlier in their academic careers.

As Tom Loveless argues in chapter 10, affluent high-achievers who come into school with so many advantages also typically enjoy opportunities that prepare them well for college: gifted-and-talented programs, accelerated courses, and classes with high-achieving peers. That's because their places of learning—typically public schools in the leafy suburbs, or else private or magnet schools that practice selective admissions—never embraced the "detracking" movement entirely, and their politically powerful parents ensure that their schools meet their needs.

Low-income high-achievers, on the other hand, are typically denied these opportunities. Their urban school systems don't offer (or greatly restrict) gifted-and-talented programs; they mandate "heterogeneous" groupings of students and tell teachers to do their best meeting a panoply of diverse needs with "differentiated instruction." Out of fealty to the principle of equity, they avoid "tracking" at all costs—even if an advanced academic track would help to *reduce* inequalities in opportunity between rich and poor (and suburban and urban) students with great academic promise.

Partly as a result of federal pressure, many large urban districts have also embraced the idea that they should slash student suspensions and expulsions on the grounds that doing so will interrupt the "school-to-prison pipeline." The impulse is understandable, but if it results in more disruption in urban schools (an all-too-likely consequence), well-behaved and academically striving low-income students will lose out yet again. Who is looking out for *their* interests?

As Loveless argues, these issues tend to come to a head in middle school. If traditional public schools refuse to provide a safe, orderly, academically enriching environment for young adolescents to prepare for college-prep high schools or high-quality career and technical options, then we should encourage the development of charter schools, magnet schools, and other choice strategies that do. By focusing so much energy on the toughest cases—the poorest kids, in the most difficult circumstances—we overlook the needs of their low-income peers with the best shot at making it. That needs to change.

PREPARING MORE LOW-INCOME STUDENTS TO EARN ASSOCIATE'S DEGREES AND INDUSTRY CREDENTIALS

The second pillar of a robust Education for Upward Mobility agenda involves preparing students to successfully obtain technical degrees at the postsecondary level, which instantly raises the question: Does the K–12 system need to do anything differently to prepare students for such technical credentials versus traditional four-year degrees? Why not offer a robust college-prep program for all and then let eighteen-year-olds decide which path they want to pursue once on campus?

Yet that's only partly correct. It's true that much of the "uniform" approach makes sense for everybody, particularly through the eighth grade. High expectations, great teaching, rigorous coursework, content-rich curricula, a disciplined environment, and a balance of academic and "noncognitive" skills: Those are the hallmarks of an excellent foundational education, and they should be universal.

Our approach to high school, however, needs a major rethinking. Mostly, we shuffle kids through large, bureaucratized schools where the focus is increasingly on academic college-prep courses. According to the most recent data, 81 percent of high school students were taking an academic route; only 19 percent were "concentrating" in CTE (meaning earning at least three credits in a single CTE program area).[7]

How is this working? About 20 percent of students still don't graduate from high school at all, including 28 percent of economically disadvantaged students.[8] Of those who do graduate, about two-thirds matriculate to some form of college, including about half of low-income students.[9] But a majority of students entering community colleges—and 20 percent of those going into four-year colleges—land in remedial ("development") education because they are not academically prepared for college. Two-thirds of low-income students at community colleges start in remedial classes that earn them no degree credit.[10] As figure C.1 below[11] shows, lots more young people matriculate to college than are ready for college—and this is even truer today than in 1995.

Here's where things really fall apart: Just *10 percent* of community college students who start in remedial courses complete a degree within three years; 40 percent don't ever get beyond the remedial stage.[12] It's not hard to understand why. Our K–12 system, especially the high school level, is simply not getting most such students ready for success. It's not working.

Some reformers look at this situation and propose "corequisite coursetaking"—encouraging students to start college in credit-bearing courses and providing them the support necessary to succeed there. That way, the theory

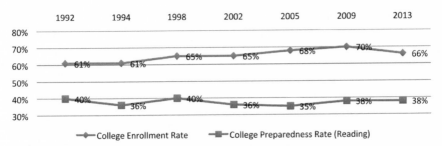

Figure C.1.   Note: The college enrollment numbers come from Census Bureau Table 276—College Enrollment of Recent High School Completers, defined as "persons 16 to 24 years old who graduated from high school in the preceding 12 months. Includes persons receiving GEDs." The college readiness numbers come from the National Assessment of Educational Progress.

goes, they won't get trapped in the quicksand that is credit-free remediation. And it's worth trying; it will surely work for some young people. Just as surely, though, it won't work for students who are *far* below the college-ready level. Meanwhile, that approach risks diluting the quality of those credit bearing courses for the students who do enter them prepared.

All too often, then, the outcome of our current strategy is that a young person drops out of college at age twenty with no postsecondary credential, no work skills, and no work experience, but a fair amount of debt. That's a terrible way to begin adult life, and even worse so if the young adult aims to escape poverty.

As argued in by Robert Lerman in chapter 4 and Robert Schwartz and Nancy Hoffman in chapter 7, a better approach for many young people would be to develop coherent pathways, from high school onward, into authentic technical education options at the postsecondary level. This can start with CTE or apprenticeships in high school. (We must bear in mind, though, that students must enter *those* programs with high levels of academic and other skills by the end of middle school; these pathways are just as intellectually and personally demanding as traditional college prep.)

Such efforts show great promise in better engaging students, helping them succeed academically, boosting their college-going and college completion rates, and brightening their career prospects. The best programs tend to span grades 9 through 14: They start after middle school and have formal agreements with local community colleges or technical colleges that enable dual enrollment for older high school students. These arrangements not only provide access to workplaces where students can apply their skills, but also offer seamless transitions into postsecondary education, apprenticeships, and employer-provided learning opportunities. These initiatives ensure that nobody falls through the cracks in the pipeline, because those cracks do not exist or have been minimized. By age twenty, graduates of such programs have academic credentials, technical credentials, and work experience—and usually good-paying jobs.

To make this option a reality, however, local communities and education leaders will have to overcome today's aversion to differentiating the high school experience. In other words, we have to move past the painful legacy of old-fashioned tracking. It simply doesn't work to wait until kids are eighteen for them to choose an academic path that leads to four-year college or a technical path that leads to an associate's degree, certification, or license. The handoff of graduates from comprehensive, vaguely college-prep high schools into the postsecondary universe is failing. And generic high school experiences are not preparing low-income students to thrive in either academic or technical routes after they receive their diplomas.

As long as the destination is postsecondary success, then school boards, charter authorizers, and educators should be agnostic about whether young people choose a purely academic or academic–technical focus. The choice should be the student's, not the system's. But being agnostic about students' choices does not mean neglecting the creation of solid options for them to choose among. In many places, that means bringing back high-quality CTE and youth apprenticeship programs, because there aren't nearly enough of these sorts of schools today. As Peter Meyers illustrates in chapter 5, New York's highly successful small schools movement proves that it's possible.

Tracking as practiced in the twentieth century was pernicious. It sent lots of kids—especially poor and minority kids—into dead-end tracks because of the color of their skin or the contents of their parents' bank accounts. What I am proposing is not that. It's about options. It's about success. And it's a strategy we need to embrace.

PREPARING MORE LOW-INCOME STUDENTS TO FOLLOW THE SUCCESS SEQUENCE

Let me say it again: Preparing students for success in college and other quality postsecondary options should remain the core mission of education reformers and of the US pre-K–12 education system. But what if college isn't the only springboard to the middle class? What about "the success sequence as a springboard to the middle class"? What can schools do to encourage young people to follow the success sequence, including delaying parenthood (ideally until after marriage)?

No good can come from shaming moms and dads who have already gone down the road to single parenthood, many of whom are doing their very best in difficult circumstances. Of course we should support them and their children in all the ways we can. My focus here, however, is on the young people whose family formation decisions still lie ahead of them—those who might, in Isabel Sawhill's telling phrase, "drift into parenthood."[13] I contend that educators and reformers should worry as much about the future parenting decisions of their charges as they do about their future educational choices. That's because the evidence is undeniable that single parenthood is generally related to diminished academic attainment.[14] It is both a cause of America's growing inequality and a result of it.

It should not be out of bounds, therefore, to encourage educators and education reformers to consider what we might do to encourage more young people to follow the "success sequence"—including working full time and waiting to have children—as a sure route to the middle class.

Our first challenge is to understand why so many young people—especially those who are poor—are having children before marriage. A related question is why most affluent, well-educated young adults wait until their late twenties or thirties, and for marriage, before having children. Assuming that we don't want to encourage teenage parents to marry, what can we do to encourage teens and those in their early twenties to wait until they are older, educated, employed, and married before becoming parents?

This has been the subject of vast debate—and increasingly sophisticated research—for decades. A foundational question is whether young adults are "choosing" to have children, or whether they are accidentally becoming parents by having sex without using birth control. Are they deciding to start a family, or are they "drifting" into parenthood?

The current consensus is that most young people who have babies before marriage aren't exactly doing so on purpose, but they also aren't trying very hard to prevent it. It's not that they don't understand how birth control works or they fail to use effective methods (though that's part of it). Rather, they make a somewhat conscious decision to stop using birth control once they have been with a partner for a while. Many pregnancies, then, are "planned but not planned."[15]

A key issue, therefore, is motivation.[16] In particular, how can we motivate more young women, and particularly young, low-income women, to wait until they are older, educated, employed, and married before they have children? The answer: First, help them develop strong prospects for interesting, decently paid careers. Second, give them access to "marriageable men"—young men who themselves have strong career prospects.

We've already discussed the role that well-designed CTE programs and youth apprenticeships can play in getting young people ready for postsecondary education and work. CTE also appears to have a positive impact on the success sequence itself. A sophisticated evaluation by the Manpower

Demonstration Research Corporation found that young men who had graduated from a career academy were 33 percent more likely to be married and living with their spouse than were their peers in a control group. They were also significantly likelier to have custody of their children.[17] Whether that was because the graduates developed skills that helped them form more stable relationships, or whether they became more "marriageable" because of their stronger career prospects, the lesson is clear: work works. So does CTE.

What else can schools do to encourage their students to follow the success sequence? They can also help their students develop "performance character"—particularly drive and prudence. Brookings scholar Richard Reeves explains why these attributes are so essential:

> People with drive are able to stick with a task, even when it gets boring or difficult; they work hard and don't leave a job unfinished. Drive includes not just the ability to work hard (industriousness) but also the ability to overcome setbacks and to keep going (resilience).
>
> Prudent people are able to defer gratification and plan for the future; they can make sacrifices today in order to ensure a better tomorrow. The better developed a person's character strength of prudence, the less they suffer from what economists call "present bias," the tendency to underweight future utility. They can both plan for the future and exert self-control in the moment to reach their long-term goals.

Reeves and others point to evidence regarding the importance of drive. For example, the fact that students' high school grade-point averages predict college completion better than SAT scores may be one indication that hard work and resilience pay off even more than talent. The evidence for "prudence" is even stronger, ranging from Walter Mischel's work on delayed gratification to Angela Duckworth's findings about the importance of grit and self-control for long-term success.[18]

How can schools teach these skills and habits? The time-honored way is with the help of religion. Catholic schools in particular have long been singled out by social scientists for their strong graduation and college-going rates. These solid long-term outcomes—which tend to be much larger than the short-term test score gains—likely reflect Catholic schools' focus on discipline and character as much as their excellent academics and overt religious instruction. In the early 1980s, James Coleman and his colleagues found that Catholic school students were significantly more likely to report that their schools' approach to discipline was "excellent or good" than were their public school peers.[19] Later research by Anthony Bryk confirmed this view with Catholic school administrators, who were much less likely to report student behavior problems than their public school colleagues.[20]

A 2012 study by David Figlio and Jens Ludwig found that Catholic high school students were less likely to participate in risky behaviors, including teen sexual activity, arrests, and cocaine use. They speculated that Catholic schools put the fear of God into their students. Religious instruction, they reported, "could affect students' 'tastes' for misbehavior, or increase the perceived costs of misbehavior by defining a number of activities as sins that have eternal consequences." And there was also the role of positive peer pressure—by "exposing them to more pro-social peer groups," particularly by selecting out or expelling students more likely to engage in risky behaviors.[21]

A newer and explicitly secular approach to teaching character is best illustrated by KIPP, which has placed character education at the heart of its "no-excuses" ethos. As made famous by Paul Tough's best-selling book *How Children Succeed,* many KIPP schools now use a "character growth card" to help teachers, students, and parents work together to develop specific character traits like optimism and curiosity.[22] Some KIPP schools are incorporating "mindfulness training" and even yoga to help their students build the self-control necessary to make better choices that build their long-term success.[23]

Not all such actions are easily implanted in our traditional public school system, which clearly cannot teach religion but which also struggles to enforce high expectations around student behavior. Parental choice, then, must be an important part of this strategy, because it allows parents and their children to opt into schools, including religious schools, that share their values.

There's one more way schools can help students develop important character strengths while keeping them off the streets: provide an excellent suite of extracurricular offerings. This might be one secret to Catholic schools' success; in the same paper mentioned previously, Figlio and Ludwig report that students in Catholic schools "spend more time on homework and extracurricular activities than those in public schools. . . . Private schools may thus reduce delinquency if only because of an 'incapacitation effect'—teens who are doing homework or running track are not out looking for trouble."

Extracurricular activities, including athletics, appear to be important for public school students, too; as June Kronholz reported in *Education Next,* studies have long found that disadvantaged students who participate in such activities are less likely to drop out, use tobacco or alcohol, or get pregnant, and are more likely to score well on tests, enroll in college, and complete college.[24]

It is therefore counterproductive, if not tragic, that schools serving high concentrations of poor students are less likely to offer extracurricular activities. In an innovative 2009 study, University of North Carolina researchers Elizabeth Stearns and Elizabeth J. Glennie scoured yearbooks and state administrative data to determine the number of activities offered (and the percentage of students participating) in every Tarheel high school. High-poverty schools offered fewer activities and showed lower participation rates than low-poverty schools.[25]

It seems self-evident, then, that schools that want their charges to follow the "success sequence" can build a sense of hope and purpose by offering a clear path to education and work; the development of suitable character attributes; and opportunities for high-quality extracurricular activities.

CONCLUSION

It's easy to become pessimistic when looking at data on upward mobility in today's America. There's little doubt that too many US children are born into dysfunctional families, bleak economic circumstances, and broken communities, and that our governmental institutions designed to provide support aren't up to the task.

Yet I hope readers will agree that this book is fundamentally optimistic. While our education system alone cannot solve the stubborn, tragic problem of persistent poverty, there's much it can do for the children entrusted to it. But first we have to change the way we think about the problem and its possible solutions.

Our first step is to protect the gains we've made via education reform over the past twenty years. And those gains are real—low-income students are achieving two or more grade levels ahead of where they were in the 1990s, at least in grades 4 through 8.[26] High school graduation rates are up. The quality of teachers coming into the classroom is also up.[27] These are all very positive trends.

Staying the course with rigorous standards, suitable assessments, and transparency around results; continuing to grow the number of high-quality charters and other school options; and raising the bar even higher for new teachers are doable steps, and likely ones in the years ahead. These should help immensely.

But we reformers also need to make some midcourse corrections. We have to add solid curricula to the structural reforms that dominate our attention. We have to prioritize the needs of "strivers" by allowing for more acceleration and ability grouping, as well as ensuring environments in which learning can truly occur. We have to build many more career and technical high schools and youth apprenticeship programs, including some inside the charter sector. If we want to give students the option of starting technical programs as freshmen and seamlessly continuing them into postsecondary education without remediation, we also have to make sure that our high school accountability systems—and teacher certification and evaluation rules—don't preclude the option.

We also have to worry as much about off-ramps to upward mobility as about on-ramps. That means getting serious and strategic about tough and touchy topics, especially family formation. Education reform will only take us so far if young people continue to re-create the types of fragile families many were born into. Character education programs, high-quality extracurricular activities, and faith-based schools are therefore critically important, too.

The next chapter of reform will be written by the educators, innovators, and policymakers willing to tackle these issues head-on, to experiment with bold solutions. Will you be one of them?

NOTES

1. The Pew Charitable Trusts, *Pursuing the American Dream: Economic Mobility Across Generations,* July 2012.

2. Dylan Matthews, "The Tuition Is Too Damn High, Part II: Why College Is Still Worth It," *Wonkblog,* August 27, 2013, http://www.washingtonpost.com/blogs/wonkblog/wp/2013/08/27/the-tuition-is-too-damn-high-part-ii-why-college-is-still-worth-it/.

3. Robert D. Putnam, *Our Kids: The American Dream in Crisis* (New York: Simon & Schuster, 2015).

4. The Pell Institute and University of Pennsylvania Alliance for Higher Education and Democracy, *Indicators of Higher Education Equity in the United States, 45 Year Trend Report, 2015 Revised Edition,* p. 30.

5. Mark Schneider, "A Bachelor's Degree Isn't the Only Path to Good Pay," *Wall Street Journal,* June 4, 2015.

6. Susan Dynarski, "For Poor, Getting to College is Only Half the Battle," *New York Times,* June 2, 2015.

7. "Career/Technical Education (CTE) Statistics," National Center for Education Statistics, http://nces.ed.gov/surveys/ctes/tables/h124.asp.

8. "Graduation Gaps: Disparities in H.S. Completion," *Education Week,* June 2, 2014, http://www.edweek.org/ew/dc/2014/graduation-gaps.html.

9. "The Condition of Education: Immediate College Enrollment Rate," National Center for Education Statistics, last updated March 2015, http://nces.ed.gov/programs/coe/indicator_cpa.asp.

10. Complete College America, *Remediation: Higher Education's Bridge to Nowhere,* April 2012, http://completecollege.org/docs/CCA-Remediation-final.pdf.

11. Michael J. Petrilli and Chester E. Finn, Jr., "College preparedness over the years, according to NAEP." *Flypaper,* April 8, 2015, http://edexcellence.net/articles/college-preparedness-over-the-years-according-to-naep.

12. Complete College America, *Remediation: Higher Education's Bridge to Nowhere,* April 2012, http://completecollege.org/docs/CCA-Remediation-final.pdf.

13. Isabel V. Sawhill, *Generation Unbound: Drifting into Sex and Parenthood Without Marriage* (Washington, DC: Brookings Institution Press, 2014).

14. Kathleen M. Ziol-Guest, Greg J. Duncan, and Ariel Kalil, "One-Parent Students Leave School Earlier," *Education Next,* Spring 2015.

15. Amber Lapp, "When Pregnancy Is 'Planned But Not Planned,'" *Family Studies,* April 20, 2015, http://family-studies.org/when-pregnancy-is-planned-but-not-planned/.

16. For an extended discussion of this issue, see Michael J. Petrilli, "How Can Schools Address America's Marriage Crisis?" *Education Next,* Spring 2015.

17. James J. Kemple, "Career Academies: Long-Term Impacts on Work, Education, and Transitions to Adulthood," MDRC, June 2008.

18. Richard V. Reeves, Joanna Venator, and Kimberly Howard, "The Character Factor: Measures and Impact of Drive and Prudence," October 22, 2014, http://www.brookings.edu/research/papers/2014/10/22-character-factor-opportunity-reeves.

19. James S. Coleman, Thomas Hoffer, and Sally Kilgore, *High School Achievement: Public, Catholic, and Private Schools Compared* (New York: Basic Books, 1982).

20. Anthony S. Bryk, Valerie E. Lee, and Peter B. Holland, *Catholic Schools and the Common Good* (Cambridge, MA: Harvard University Press, 1993).

21. David Figlio and Jens Ludwig, "Sex, Drugs, and Catholic Schools: Private Schooling and Non-Market Adolescent Behaviors," *German Economic Review* 13, no. 4: 385–414.

22. Paul Tough, *How Children Succeed: Grit, Curiosity, and the Hidden Power of Character* (New York: Mariner Books, 2013).

23. Marc Mannella, "Character Strengths Can Be Taught," *Flypaper,* October 2, 2014, http://edexcellence.net/articles/character-strengths-can-be-taught.

24. June Kronholz, "Academic Value of Non-Academics," *Education Next,* Winter 2012.

25. Elizabeth Stearns and Elizabeth J. Glennie, "Opportunities to Participate: Extracurricular Activities' Distribution Across and Academic Correlates in High Schools," *Social Science Research* 39, no. 2 (2010): 296–309.

26. "Trends in Academic Progress," National Center for Education Statistics, 2012, http://nces.ed.gov/nationsreportcard/subject/publications/main2012/pdf/2013456.pdf.

27. Dan Goldhaber and Joe Walch, "Gains in Teacher Quality," *Education Next,* Winter 2014.

About the Contributors

EDITOR

Michael J. Petrilli is an award-winning writer and president of the Thomas B. Fordham Institute, one of the country's leading education-policy think tanks. He is the author of *The Diverse Schools Dilemma: A Parent's Guide to Socioeconomically Mixed Public Schools,* and co-editor of *Knowledge at the Core: Don Hirsch, Core Knowledge, and the Future of the Common Core.* He is a research fellow at the Hoover Institution and executive editor of *Education Next.*

CONTRIBUTORS

Jelene Britten
Marketing and Media Manager, Educare Learning
Network at the Ounce of Prevention Fund

Britten develops external-marketing, media-relations, and internal-communications strategies for the Network. Britten previously served in communications roles at Chapin Hall at the University of Chicago and the Donors Forum of Chicago, where she created and implemented communications plans, managed media-relations campaigns, and coordinated events. She also served on the board of the Young Nonprofit Professionals Network of Chicago, where she led a rebranding initiative and created a social media marketing plan. She received her bachelor's degree in journalism at the Medill School of

Journalism at Northwestern University and a certificate in integrated marketing from the University of Chicago.

Ron Haskins
Co-director, Center on Children and Families,
Brookings Institution

Haskins is a senior fellow in the economic studies program and co-director of the Center on Children and Families at the Brookings Institution and senior consultant at the Annie E. Casey Foundation. He spent fourteen years on the staff of the Human Resources Subcommittee on the House Ways and Means Committee, first as welfare counsel to the Republican staff, then as the subcommittee's staff director. He was the senior advisor to the president for welfare policy at the White House. Haskins has been a senior researcher at the Frank Porter Graham Child Development Center at the University of North Carolina–Chapel Hill. He is a senior editor of *The Future of Children,* a journal on policy issues that affect children and families, and has co-edited and co-authored several books. In 1997, Haskins was selected by *National Journal* as one of the one hundred most influential people in the federal government. He received a Lifetime Achievement Award from the Federal Office of Child Support Enforcement; the President's Award for outstanding contributions to the field of human services from the American Public Human Services Association; and the Lion Award from the Grantmakers for Children, Youth, and Families.

Nancy Hoffman
Vice President and Senior Advisor, Jobs for the Future

Hoffman is the co-lead of the Pathways to Prosperity State Network with Robert Schwartz (Harvard Graduate School of Education). The Network seeks to ensure that many more youth complete high school, attain a post-secondary credential with currency in the labor market, and get launched on a career. Hoffman has held teaching and administrative posts at a number of US universities, and currently teaches a course on nongovernmental organizations, philanthropy, and education improvement at Harvard Graduate School of Education. She has served as a consultant for the education policy unit of the Organisation of Economic Cooperation and Development and is engaged in studying strong vocational education and training systems. Her most recent book is *Schooling in the Workplace: How Six of the World's Best Vocational Education Systems Prepare Young People for Jobs and Life.* Hoffman holds a BA and PhD in comparative literature from the University of California–Berkeley. She serves on the Massachusetts Board of Higher Education as well as on the board of North Bennet Street School, which offers intensive, hands-on training in traditional trades and fine craftsmanship.

Joanne Jacobs
Education Journalist

Jacobs, a media fellow at the Pacific Research Institute for Public Policy and at the Hoover Institution at Stanford, is the founder of joannejacobs.com, a prominent education policy blog. She also writes *Community College Spotlight* (ccspotlight.org) for the Hechinger Institute and writes on community-college issues for *U.S. News*. She was the editorial writer and twice-weekly op-ed columnist at the *Mercury News,* where she also served on the editorial board. She has also served on the board of the *Stanford Daily* and the Women's Freedom Network. Jacobs was a Michigan Journalism Fellow and a Casey Fellow. She served as a *Stanford Daily* trustee and wrote *Our School: The Inspiring Story of Two Teachers, One Big Idea and the Charter School that Beat the Odds*. With two colleagues, she won a Casey medal in 1999 for the series "Making Welfare Work," which followed six welfare families in their struggle for independence.

Tamar Jacoby
President and CEO, Opportunity America

Jacoby is president and CEO of Opportunity America, as well as Immigration Works USA, a national federation of small-business owners working to advance better immigration law. She is a nationally known journalist and author. Her articles have appeared in the *New York Times,* the *Wall Street Journal,* the *Washington Post,* the *Weekly Standard,* and *Foreign Affairs,* among other publications, and she is a regular guest on national television and radio. She is author of *Someone Else's House: America's Unfinished Struggle for Integration* and editor of *Reinventing the Melting Pot: The New Immigrants and What It Means To Be American,* a collection of essays about immigrant integration. From 1989 to 2007, she was a senior fellow at the Manhattan Institute. Before that, she was a senior writer and justice editor for *Newsweek*. From 1981 to 1987, she was the deputy editor of the *New York Times* op-ed page. Jacoby is a recipient of the 2010/2011 Berlin Prize Fellowship from the American Academy in Berlin. Jacoby also won an Alicia Patterson Journalism Fellowship in 1974 to research and write about "what happened to racial integration in the United States."

Andrew P. Kelly
Director, Center on Higher Education Reform,
American Enterprise Institute

Kelly is the director of the Center on Higher Education Reform and a resident scholar in education policy studies at the American Enterprise Institute (AEI). His research focuses on higher education policy, innovation, financial aid reform, and the politics of education policy. Previously, he was a research assistant at AEI, where his work focused on the preparation of school leaders, collective bargaining in public schools, and the politics of education. His research has appeared in the *American Journal of Education, Teachers College Record, Educational Policy, Policy Studies Journal,* and *Education Next,* as well as popular outlets such as *Education Week, Inside Higher Education, Forbes,* the *Atlantic, National Affairs,* the *Weekly Standard,* and Huffington Post. He is co-editor of *Stretching the Higher Education Dollar: How Innovation Can Improve Access, Equity, and Affordability; Getting to Graduation: The Completion Agenda in Higher Education; Carrots, Sticks, and the Bully Pulpit: Lessons from A Half-Century of Federal Efforts to Improve America's Schools;* and *Reinventing Higher Education: The Promise of Innovation.* In 2011, Kelly was named one of sixteen "Next Generation Leaders" in education policy by the *Policy Notebook* blog at *Education Week.*

Robert Lerman
Institute Fellow, Center on Labor, Human Services
and Population, Urban Institute

Lerman is the Urban Institute's first institute fellow in labor and social policy. He is a leading expert on how education, employment, and family structure work together to affect economic well-being. Lerman was director of the institute's Labor and Social Policy Center from 1995 to 2003. The author of more than 150 articles, monographs, reports, reviews, and conference papers, Lerman has held dual appointments with the Urban Institute and the economics department at American University since 1995. He chaired the American University economics department from 1989 to 1995 and continues to be a professor of economics there. Lerman has served on a variety of panels and commissions, including the board of the National Fatherhood Initiative and the National Academy of Sciences panel looking at the nation's postsecondary education and training system for the workplace. He has testified before congressional committees on such topics as youth apprenticeship, child-support policies, and the information-technology labor market. He taught at the University of Pittsburgh and Brandeis University, where he also served as research director in the Heller School of Social Welfare's Center for Human Resources. He conducted research on social security and housing policy as a research associate at the Brookdale Institute of Gerontology in Jerusalem. His public-policy experience includes positions as staff economist with the Congressional Joint Economic Committee and special assistant for youth and welfare policy at the US Department of Labor.

Tom Loveless
Senior Fellow, Brown Center on Education Policy,
Brookings Institution

Loveless is a nonresident senior fellow for the Brown Center on Education Policy at the Brookings Institution. While teaching sixth grade, he served on numerous state and local curriculum committees. After receiving his PhD, Loveless joined the faculty of Harvard University's John F. Kennedy School of Government, where he served as both assistant and associate professors of public policy. Loveless was selected as a National Academy of Education Spencer postdoctoral fellow. Loveless represented the United States at the General Assembly of the International Association for the Evaluation of Educational Attainment, a sixty-nation organization that governs international testing. He served on the President's National Mathematics Advisory Panel. He authors the *Brown Center Report on American Education,* an annual report explaining important trends in achievement test scores. His op-eds have been published in *the Christian Science Monitor,* the *Los Angeles Times,* the *Wall Street Journal, Newsday,* the *Washington Post, USA Weekend,* the *New York Times,* and *Education Week.* And his work has appeared in *Wilson Quarterly, Education Next, American Journal of Education, Educational Policy, Educational Leadership, Educational Administration Quarterly, and Educational Evaluation,* and *Policy Analysis.*

Bryce Marable
Health Policy Analyst, Health and Disability Advocates

Marable earned a master's degree in Social Work from the University of Illinois at Chicago, with a concentration in Community Health and Urban Development. Her research interests include early childhood education and early childhood health.

Peter Meyer
Adjunct Fellow, Thomas B. Fordham Institute

Meyer is an adjunct fellow with the Thomas B. Fordham Institute, former news editor of *Life* magazine, and author of numerous nonfiction books, including the critically acclaimed *The Yale Murder* and *Death of Innocence*. Over the course of his three-decade journalism career, Meyer has written hundreds of stories on subjects as varied as antiterrorist training for American ambassadors to the history of the 1040 income tax form. His work has appeared in such publications as *Harper's, Vanity Fair, National Geographic, New York, Life, Time,* and *People*. Since 1991, Meyer has focused his attention on education reform in the United States. He helped found a charter school, served on his local board of education (twice), and, for the last eight years, has been an editor at *Education Next*. His articles for the journal include "The Early Education of Our Next President," "New York City's Education Battles," "Learning Separately," and "Can Catholic Schools Be Saved?" Meyer also writes and edits, mostly on education, for the American Enterprise Institute and the Manhattan Institute.

Robert Pondiscio
Senior Fellow and Vice President for External Affairs, Fordham Institute

Pondiscio is senior fellow and vice president for external affairs at the Thomas B. Fordham Institute. He is also a senior advisor to Democracy Prep Public Schools, a network of high-performing charter schools based in Harlem, New York. He writes and speaks extensively on education and education-reform issues, with an emphasis on literacy, curriculum, teaching, and urban education. After twenty years in journalism, including senior positions at *TIME* and *BusinessWeek*, Pondiscio became a fifth-grade teacher at a struggling South Bronx public school in 2002. He subsequently served as vice president for the Core Knowledge Foundation. His articles and op-ed columns on education have appeared in the *Wall Street Journal*, the *Atlantic*, the *New York Daily News, Education Next,* and many other publications. A frequent speaker and expert guest on education issues, he has appeared on the Fox News Channel, CNN, and elsewhere.

Elliot M. Regenstein
Senior Vice President, Ounce of Prevention Fund

Regenstein is senior vice president of advocacy and policy at the Ounce of Prevention Fund, leading national policy consultation practice and coordinating overall state and national policy efforts. He has extensive experience in working directly with states on policy development and is a frequent speaker and author on topics including governance, data systems, and linkages between early learning and K–12. He also partners with the First Five Years Fund to support policy change at the federal level. Regenstein was one of the chief architects of Illinois's 2006 Preschool for All program, while serving in the governor's office as director of education reform. Regenstein co-chaired the Illinois Early Learning Council and currently serves as a member of the council's executive committee, co-chairing its data, research, and evaluation committee.

Robert Schwartz
Professor Emeritus, Harvard University

Schwartz is professor emeritus of practice in educational policy and administration at Harvard University. He held a wide variety of leadership positions in education and government before joining the Harvard faculty in 1996. Schwartz served as president of Achieve, Inc., and directed the education-grantmaking program of Pew Charitable Trusts. He has been a high school English teacher and principal; an education adviser to the mayor of Boston and the governor of Massachusetts; an assistant director of the National Institute of Education; a special assistant to the president of the University of Massachusetts; and executive director of the Boston Compact, a public–private partnership designed to improve access to higher education and employment for urban high school graduates. Schwartz has written and spoken widely on topics such as standards-based reform, public–private partnerships, and the transition from high school to adulthood. In recent years Schwartz has contributed to three volumes: *Teaching Talent, Surpassing Shanghai,* and *The Futures of School Reform.* He currently co-leads the Pathways to Prosperity Network, designed to ensure that many more young people graduate high school, attain an initial postsecondary degree or credential with value in the labor market, and get launched on a career while leaving open the possibility of further education.